CATECHIST GUIDE

ONE FAITH, ONE LORD

A STUDY OF BASIC CATHOLIC BELIEF

Kathy Hendricks
Gloria Hutchinson

Special Consultant
Rev. Msgr. John F. Barry, P.A.

FIFTH EDITION

Sadlier
A Division of William H. Sadlier, Inc.

The Subcommittee on the Catechism, United States Conference of Catholic Bishops, has found the doctrinal content of this manual, copyright 2009, to be in conformity with the *Catechism of the Catholic Church.*

Acknowledgments
Excerpts from the English translation of *The Roman Missal* © 2010, International Committee on English in the Liturgy, Inc. All rights reserved.

Scripture excerpts are taken from the *New American Bible with Revised New Testament and Psalms* Copyright © 1991, 1986, 1970 Confraternity of Christian Doctrine, Inc., Washington, DC. Used with permission. All rights reserved. No part of the *New American Bible* may be reproduced by any means without permission in writing from the copyright owner.

Excerpts from the English translation of the *Catechism of the Catholic Church* for use in the United States of America, Copyright © 1994, United States Catholic Conference, Inc.—Libreria Editrice Vaticana. Used with permission.

Excerpts from the *General Directory for Catechesis* © 1997, Libreria Editrice Vaticana—United States Catholic Conference, Inc. Used with permission. All rights reserved.

Excerpt from the English translation of *Order of Christian Funerals* © 1985, International Committee on English in the Liturgy, Inc.; excerpt from the English translation of *Rite of Christian Initiation of Adults* © 1985, International Committee on English in the Liturgy, Inc. All rights reserved.

Blessing adapted from the *Book of Blessings,* additional blessings for use in the United States © 1988 United States Catholic Conference, Inc.; Washington, DC. Used with permission. All rights reserved.

Excerpt from "To Be Black and Catholic", Sister Thea Bowman, FSPA (1937– 1990), address to US Catholic Bishops, Seton Hall University, South Orange, NJ, June 17, 1989.

Printed in the United States of America.

S is a registered trademark of William H. Sadlier, Inc.

William H. Sadlier, Inc.
9 Pine Street
New York, NY 10005-4700

ISBN: 978-0-8215-5561-3
9 10 11 12 13 WEBC 21 20 19 18 17

Official Theological Consultant
Most Rev. Edward K. Braxton, Ph.D., S.T.D.
Bishop of Belleville

Consultants
Vilma Angulo
Director of Religious Education
All Saints Catholic Church
Sunrise, Florida

John Benson
Catechist
All Saints Catholic Church
Sunrise, Florida

Carol Craven
Director of Religious Education
St. Paul the Apostle Catholic Church
New Middletown, Ohio

Deanna Ricciardi
Catechist
Immaculate Heart of Mary Catholic Church
Scarsdale, New York

Maruja Sedano
Director of the Office for Catechesis
Archdiocese of Chicago

Fr. Nicholas Shori
Pastor
St. Paul the Apostle Catholic Church
New Middletown, Ohio

Sadlier Consulting Team
Michaela Burke Barry
Ken Doran
Dulce M. Jiménez-Abreu
Saundra Kennedy, Ed.D.
William M. Ippolito
Ida Iris Miranda
Victor Valenzuela

Writing/Development Team
Rosemary K. Calicchio
Vice President of Publications

Carole M. Eipers, D.Min.
Vice President, Executive Director of Catechetics

Blake Bergen
Editorial Director

Melissa D. Gibbons
Director of Research and Development

Joanne McDonald
Senior Editor

Publishing Operations Team
Deborah J. Jones
Vice President of Publishing Operations

Vince Gallo
Creative Director

Francesca O'Malley
Associate Art Director

Jim Saylor
Photography Manager

Design Staff
Debrah Kaiser
Sasha Khorovsky

Production Staff
Diane Ali
Brent Burket
Cheryl Golding
Vincent McDonough
Maureen Morgan

CONTENTS

Before You Use ONE FAITH, ONE LORD

Unit 1
Created and Saved

Unit 2
Welcomed into the Church

Unit 3
Eucharist & Reconciliation

Unit 4
Our Catholic Life

Living Our Faith

PROGRAM OVERVIEW

ONE FAITH, ONE LORD is a single comprehensive volume that presents the fundamental beliefs and practices of the Catholic faith. This popular text has proven an ideal introduction for those who have minimal catechesis. It can be used effectively in developing and assessing readiness for the Sacraments of Penance and Eucharist, or as a review for Confirmation candidates.

Each chapter incorporates teachings from the CATECHISM OF THE CATHOLIC CHURCH:

Unit 1
Created and Saved
Our Catholic Roots
God the Creator
The Fall and the Promise
The Promise Fulfilled
Jesus, the Savior

Unit 2
Welcomed into the Church
Jesus Sends the Holy Spirit
The Catholic Church
The Seven Sacraments
Becoming Catholic

Unit 3
Eucharist & Reconciliation
The Eucharist
The Mass
The Sacrament of Penance and Reconciliation

Unit 4
Our Catholic Life
Living God's Law
Jesus' Way of Loving
In the Service of Others
Life Everlasting

Text Features

Each chapter introduction sets the tone and theme through an invitation to personal reflection set in a context of stunning artwork

CHAPTER 14

Jesus' Way of Loving

Love is a word that we hear all the time and in many different situations. Some people say that the word has become overused and that the true meaning of love is lost.

What do you think the word love means?

How do your actions show love for your family and friends?

90

1 Jesus asks us to love.

God's laws guided his people in the right way to live. At times, however, the people forgot or turned away from the way of God. In making the covenant and in giving the Ten Commandments, God wanted the people to observe the commandments out of love for him and for one another. The great prayer of the Old Testament summed up the commandments:

> Hear, O Israel! The LORD is our God, the LORD alone! Therefore, you shall love the LORD, your God, with all your heart, and with all your soul, and with all your strength.
> Deuteronomy 6:4–5

The people were also told, "You shall love your neighbor as yourself" (Leviticus 19:18). The Ten Commandments were concrete laws that showed them how to love God and neighbor.

Jesus observed and respected the laws of the covenant. He told his disciples, "Do not think that I have come to abolish the law or the prophets. I have come not to abolish but to fulfill" (Matthew 5:17).

Once a scholar asked Jesus which commandment in the law was the greatest. Jesus replied by bringing together the teachings of the Old Testament into the *Great Commandment*:

> You shall love the Lord, your God, with all your heart, with all your soul, and with all your mind. This is the greatest and the first commandment. The second is like it: You shall love your neighbor as yourself. The whole law and the prophets depend on these two commandments.
> Matthew 22:37–40

91

16 core chapters, each presenting three key doctrinal points; well-organized and designed to foster faith development through the following:

- Knowledge of basic Catholic beliefs, which are Trinitarian, Christocentric, and Ecclesial
- Identification with Jesus Christ and the Church
- Interaction with the Church community
- Personal reflection
- Prayer experiences

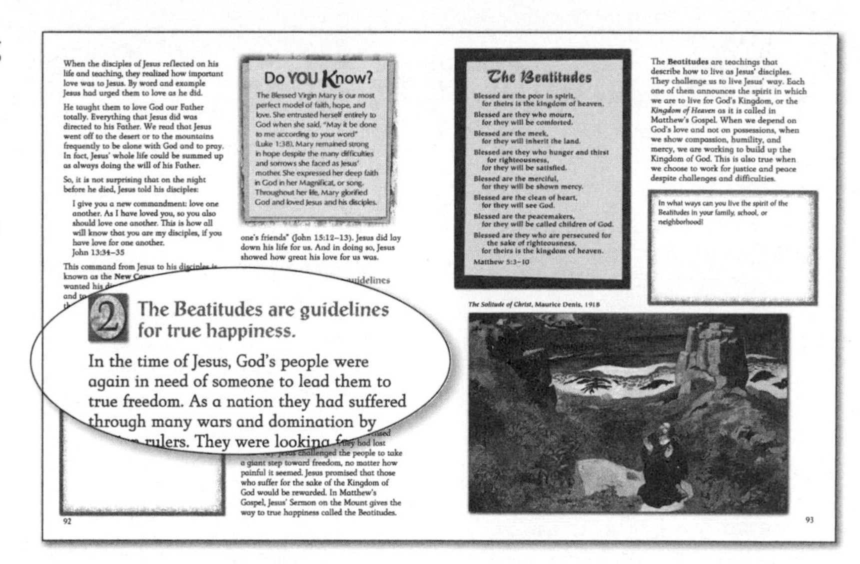

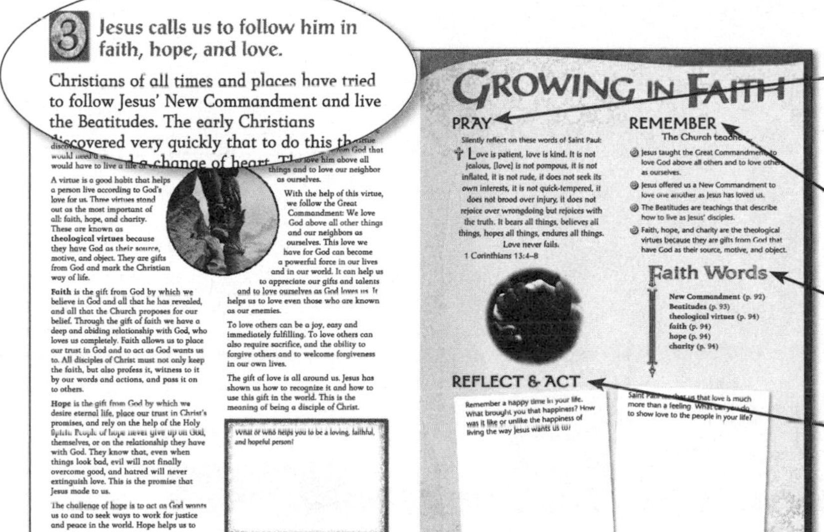

Chapters conclude with:

Pray
deepens faith through prayer related to the lesson's theme

Remember
recalls and synthesizes chapter content

Faith Words
recalls the faith-based vocabulary introduced in the chapter

Reflect & Act
poses two questions, one reflective and one call to living faith

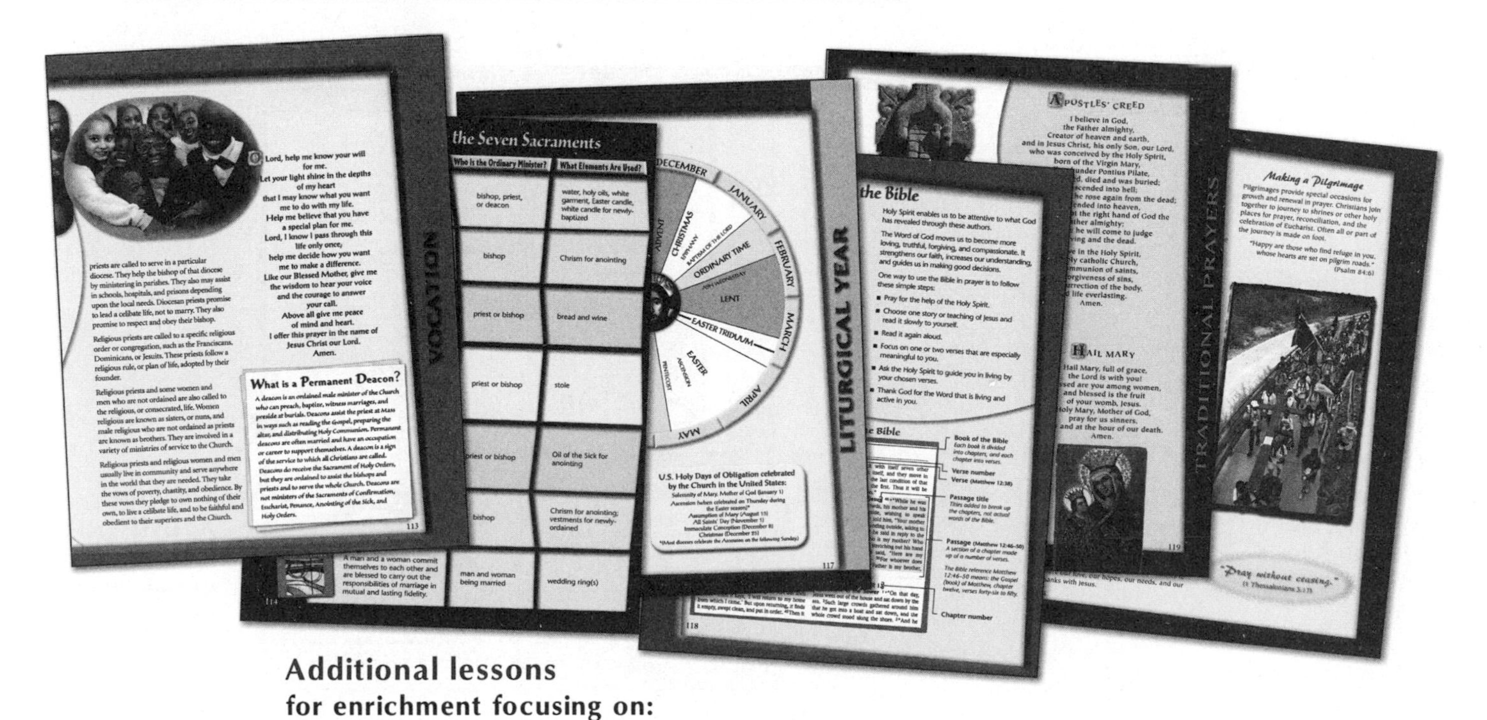

Additional lessons for enrichment focusing on:

- Vocations
- Seven Sacraments
- Liturgical Year
- Using the Bible
- Traditional Prayers
- Catholic Practices

Catechist Guide Features

The easy-to-use wrap around format provides preparation for the catechist as well as a three-step lesson plan—Introduction, Presentation, and Conclusion.

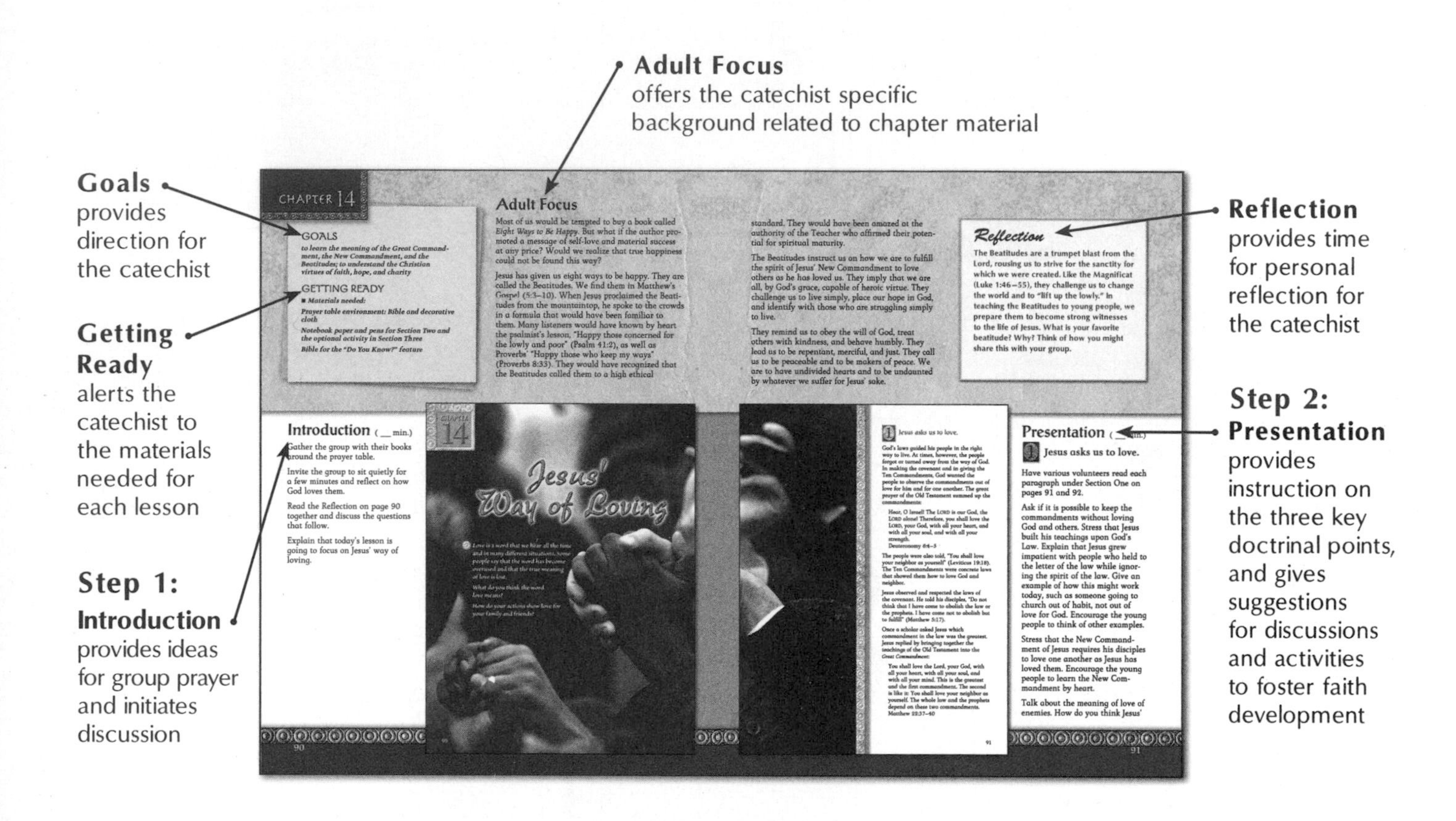

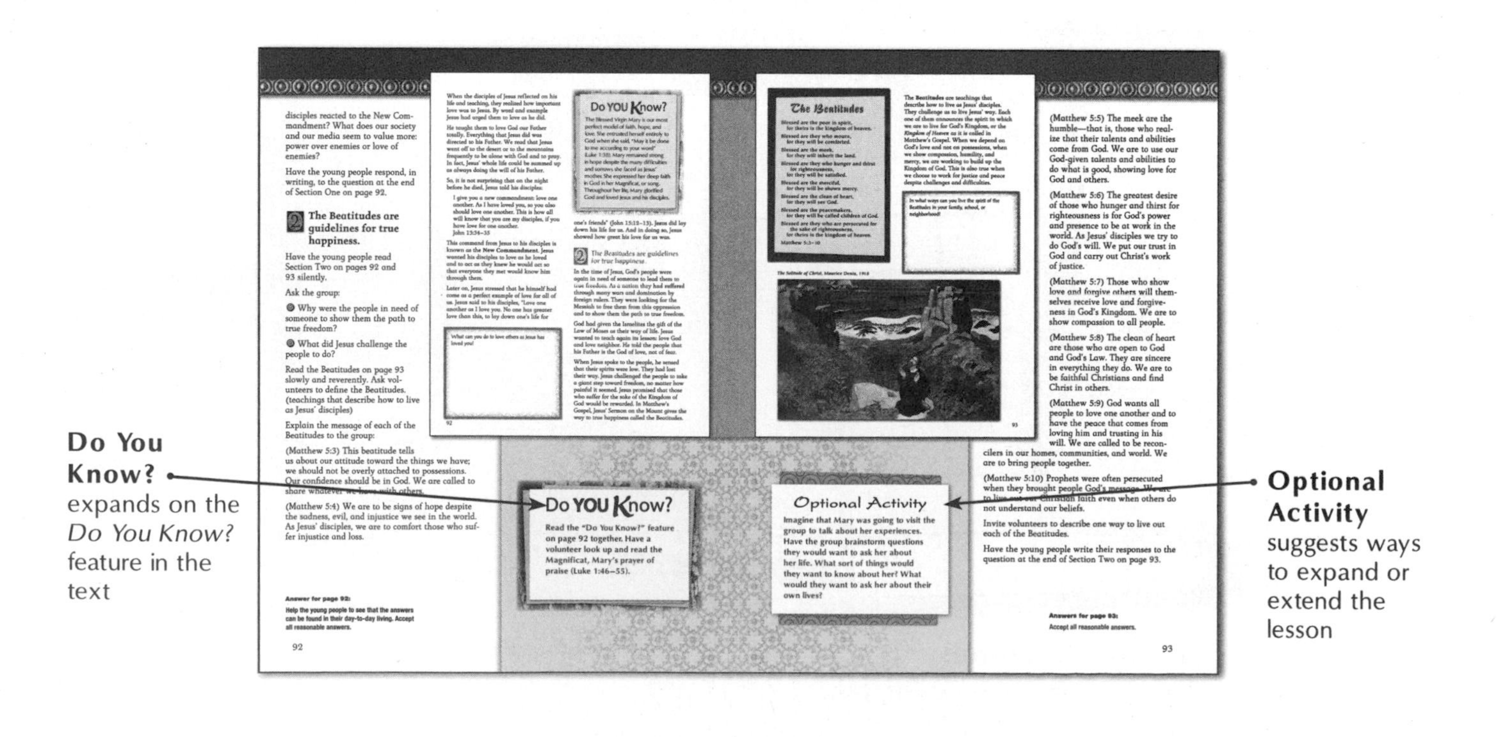

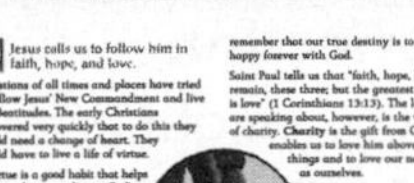

Jesus calls us to follow him in faith, hope, and love.

Have the group read Section Three on page 94 silently.

Discuss the theological virtues with these young people striving to grow in the spiritual life. Help them to see that a virtuous life, far from being a boring one, is a life filled with challenge and commitment. Ask the young people to explain in their own words the virtues of faith, hope, and charity. Stress that these three virtues are gifts from God.

Persons of faith, hope, and charity are people who are willing to take risks and sacrifice, and not to compromise Christian values. Have the young people complete these statements by describing persons who practice the theological virtues:

- A person of faith ______
- A person of hope ______
- A person of charity ______

How do we grow in a life of virtue? (We grow through reflecting on Scripture and participating in the sacraments, through prayer, through an active life in the Church community, and through works of justice and charity.)

Have the young people write their responses to the question at the end of Section Three on page 94. Invite volunteers to share their responses.

Answers for page 94:
Accept all reasonable answers. Allow each person to give a reason for his or her choice.

94

Growing in Faith

PRAY

REMEMBER

Faith Words

REFLECT & ACT

Conclusion

Growing in Faith

Have the group close their books. Ask them what they have learned in this lesson about the Great Commandment, the New Commandment, the Beatitudes, and the theological virtues. Reopen the books to page 95. Was everything from the **Remember** and **Faith Words** sections named? If not, point these out and help the group name the remaining concepts.

Invite the young people to read the **Reflect and Act** section. Encourage them to think of ways of showing love to the people in our lives. Then, have them write their responses in the spaces provided. If desired, play some soft instrumental music while they do this.

Point out the **Pray** section on page 95. Explain that Saint Paul wrote a beautiful description of love to the Christians in Corinth (1 Corinthians 13:4–7). Read and pray together the passage.

Answer page 95:
Left:
Accept all reasonable answers.
Right:
Have the young people reflect on the prayer from Saint Paul. Help them to see that being patient, kind, etc. are among the ways to show love.

95

Optional Activity

Invite the young people to write a story about someone who is faithful, hopeful, and/or loving. The story should include the following elements:

- what challenges that person faces
- how he or she shows faith, hope, or charity through that challenge
- how this life/action touches someone else.

Catechism Focus

"The Beatitudes depict the countenance of Jesus Christ and portray his charity. . . . they shed light on the actions and attitudes characteristic of the Christian life; they are the paradoxical promises that sustain hope in the midst of tribulations; they proclaim the blessings and rewards already secured, however dimly, for Christ's disciples." (CCC, 1717)

For additional reference and reflection, see CCC, 1716–1729.

Step 3: Conclusion
offers suggestions for review and reinforcement of chapter material, and engages the group in prayer

Catechism Focus
provides a content-related quote from the *Catechism of the Catholic Church* and additional reference for the catechist

Visit **www.onefaithonelord.com** for additional ideas and activities to use with the *One Faith, One Lord* program.

Teaching Strategies

"The Church, in transmitting the faith, does not have a particular method nor any single method." (*General Directory for Catechesis*, 148)

The use of varied teaching strategies better serves the different ways in which people learn. Here are some teaching strategies appropriate for use with this age group.

Peer Collaboration
The ability to get along with others and to work together for common purposes is important at any age. Provide opportunities for your young people to work together in small groups or with a partner whenever possible.

Group Discussion
Group discussion blends both spontaneity and structure. The catechist helps the group to focus on a topic, to respect the contributions of each member, to make sure that all participants have a chance to speak, and to conclude when the discussion has run its course.

Role-playing
Role-playing offers young people an opportunity to take on character roles and act out situations that may or may not be part of one's personal experience. It helps young people observe how they and others respond to different situations, and to develop skills that will assist them in living their faith in everyday life.

Brainstorming
Brainstorming is a way to elicit as many ideas and solutions as possible on a particular topic or problem. No idea or solution is subject to criticism or negative comment. After the ideas and suggestions have been listed on a chalkboard or poster board, everyone reflects on the list. This can be followed by a guided discussion or referred to later in the lesson for review and possible revision.

Scripture Reflection
One Faith, One Lord offers many appropriate passages from Scripture for reflection and discussion. The catechist can assist young people to benefit from such reflection by:

- explaining the context and meaning of a given passage
- creating an environment that is conducive to such reflection
- making sure that the passage is read with preparation and care
- initiating a discussion on the passage.

Guest Speakers
Some topics might be enhanced by input from an outside source. Young people can be helped to grow in their faith by meeting, hearing, and conversing with Catholics whose faith values are central to their personal and professional lives. Look for these speakers within your own parish or school, your diocese, or in the larger community.

Visuals
The pictures, graphics, and accompanying captions in the text can serve as visual statements of the content, as links to activities in the lesson, or as catalysts for exploring initial thoughts and emotions. Visuals provoke good discussion when paired with interesting and thoughtful questions.

Multimedia
Videos and music are effective tools for communicating religious truths. These resources can be found in your parish media center or in that of a neighboring parish, in a diocesan media center, in local video rental outlets, or online. Preview all materials in preparation for the lesson and check to make sure the equipment is available and in good working order.

Praying With Young People

"When catechesis is permeated by a climate of prayer, the assimilation of the entire Christian life reaches its summit." (*General Directory for Catechesis*, 85)

As a catechist, you are in a privileged situation to introduce and initiate formative experiences of prayer. One way to promote prayer with your young people is to create an environment for prayer in your classroom. Designate an easily accessible area of your classroom as the group's prayer space. The prayer space will be the focal point and a gathering place for prayer. In the space, set up a small table or bench as a prayer table. Cover the prayer table with a cloth of the color for the current liturgical season. Display an open Bible, a cross, and a candle on the prayer table. Modify the prayer space throughout the year using the suggestions found in each lesson of *One Faith, One Lord.*

Help your young people expand their understanding and practice of prayer by incorporating the following prayer forms in your catechetical sessions:

Blessing and Adoration

One of the most common experiences of communal prayer is participating in grace before meals. These simple prayers allow us to express our love for God and to embrace God's love for us. Make use of blessing prayers that are found in *One Faith, One Lord* lessons and other prayer resources.

Thanksgiving

Each day is filled with potential to help us become more aware of the goodness of God. Use symbols from the Bible, nature, and liturgy (water, wind, oil, fire, light, incense) and invite young people to use the symbols to inspire written or spoken prayers of thanksgiving for God's gifts.

Praise

When we praise God, we give him glory. Take time to praise God together in word, song, and prayerful gestures. Pray together psalms of praise, particularly Psalm 147 through 150.

Petition

Jesus invited us to take all of our needs to God in prayer. In prayers of petition we show that we are aware of our relationship with God. Through our prayer we ask forgiveness for our sins, turning our hearts and minds back to God. The Act of Contrition is prayer of petition.

Intercession

Intercession is a type of petition. When we pray a prayer of intercession, we are asking on behalf of another person or a group of people. Use current events or news headlines to help young people expand these prayers beyond their own immediate needs and to consider those who are poor, suffering, or in need of consolation.

Praying with Scripture

One of the oldest forms of prayer is called *lectio divina*—a way of praying with Scripture that is reflective and reverent. A passage of Scripture is read two or three times, with time for quiet reflection between each reading. In this way God's Word becomes more meaningful for us. It is an effective way to help young people discover the beauty and peace that comes with quiet prayer.

Praying with Music

The use of religious, classical, or contemporary music is a way to pray that goes beyond words. Play soft instrumental music to help move young people toward meditation, or invite them to share a favorite song that reminds them of God's presence in their lives.

Using the ONE FAITH, ONE LORD Program Survey

Preview Lesson

Before your group begins the *One Faith, One Lord* catechetical program, use the program survey on page XIII to evaluate their current knowledge of various topics that will be explored in the *One Faith, One Lord* text.

Provide a copy of the survey (see page XIII) for each young person in your group. Direct the young people to write their names and any other information (for example: parish name, contact information, sacraments received, etc.) at the top of the survey page. Read the survey questions aloud. Allow time for reflection. Encourage the young people to respond to each question.

Collect the completed surveys and place them in a large envelope/folder. (When today's session is over, read the completed surveys to determine the needs of your group. Refer to them during the program/year.) Then, have the young people turn to the Table of Contents of the *One Faith, One Lord* text. Point out the similarities between the survey topics and topics found in the Table of Contents. Encourage the young people to look through their texts and note any questions that they might have.

Postscript Lesson

As your group concludes the *One Faith, One Lord* catechetical program, use the program survey on page XIV to evaluate their current knowledge of the topics explored in the *One Faith, One Lord* text.

Provide a copy of the survey (see page XIV) for each young person in your group. Direct the young people to write their names at the top of the survey page. Read the survey questions aloud. Allow time for reflection. Encourage the young people to respond to each question.

Review the completed surveys to assess the progress the young people have made during the program/year in learning about the Catholic faith. (You may want to return the "pre" and "post" surveys to the young people at a later date.)

ONE FAITH, ONE LORD Program Survey

Before you begin the *One Faith, One Lord* catechetical program, please respond with your understanding of the Church's teaching on the following topics:

a) God the Father ______

b) God the Son (Jesus Christ) ______

c) God the Holy Spirit ______

d) the Blessed Trinity ______

e) the Creation of the universe ______

f) sin and evil ______

g) Mary ______

h) the Resurrection ______

i) the Church ______

j) the Ten Commandments ______

k) death ______

l) the Seven Sacraments ______

m) the Sacrament of Penance and Reconciliation ______

n) the Sacrament of the Eucharist ______

o) helping others ______

p) prayer ______

q) peace and justice ______

r) love ______

s) Heaven ______

t) saints ______

ONE FAITH, ONE LORD Program Survey

Now that you have completed the *One Faith, One Lord* catechetical program, please respond with your understanding of the Church's teaching on the following topics:

a) God the Father ____________________

b) God the Son (Jesus Christ) ____________________

c) God the Holy Spirit ____________________

d) the Blessed Trinity ____________________

e) the Creation of the universe ____________________

f) sin and evil ____________________

g) Mary ____________________

h) the Resurrection ____________________

i) the Church ____________________

j) the Ten Commandments ____________________

k) death ____________________

l) the Seven Sacraments ____________________

m) the Sacrament of Penance and Reconciliation ____________________

n) the Sacrament of the Eucharist ____________________

o) helping others ____________________

p) prayer ____________________

q) peace and justice ____________________

r) love ____________________

s) Heaven ____________________

t) saints ____________________

DETERMINING READINESS FOR THE SACRAMENTS OF PENANCE AND EUCHARIST

It is likely that some of the young people in your group may not have celebrated the Sacraments of Penance and/or Eucharist. *One Faith, One Lord* is not intended to be a sacramental preparation program. However, it does include an in-depth presentation of the meaning, purpose, and celebration of the Sacraments of Penance and Eucharist (Chapters 10–12). As such, *One Faith, One Lord* can be used as an integral part of sacramental preparation in your parish.

Sacramental readiness is discerned in a number of ways. It requires observance and attentiveness by parents, clergy, catechists, and others involved in the faith formation of the young person. As young people grow in faith and understanding, their readiness and receptivity for the sacraments will become more evident.

- Because of age differences, readiness needs, or time factors, it may not be feasible to involve the young people in regular sacramental programs and classes. Do include them, however, in prayers, blessings, and rituals for candidates who are preparing for First Penance and First Eucharist.
- Consider and consult with all those involved with the young person in the sacramental process, especially the parent or guardian and other family members, as well as the DRE or sacramental program director, the pastor, the pastoral associates, the RCIA director, and leaders of any other parish ministries.
- Pages XVII and XVIII can be used to help the catechist, parent, DRE, and pastor discern a young person's readiness to celebrate the sacraments. These pages are best used after the completion of the third unit. This will allow for the completion of the important chapters on the sacraments.

CATECHESIS FOR FIRST PENANCE

The following points are essential to a basic understanding of the Sacrament of Penance. These are based on the guidelines for catechesis for First Penance as outlined in the *National Directory for Catechesis* and developed throughout the *One Faith, One Lord* text.

1. God loves us unconditionally and Jesus shows us how to love God, others, and ourselves. The Sacrament of Penance restores us to loving relationships with God and the faith community. It celebrates God's mercy and forgiveness.

- Stress the unconditional love of God when teaching Chapters 2 and 8.
- Emphasize how Jesus is the model for love, compassion, and faith when teaching Chapters 8 and 12.
- Throughout the teaching of *One Faith, One Lord*, encourage the young people to consider the loving choices they can make within their daily lives.

2. There is both good and evil in the world. Sin is freely choosing to do what we know is wrong and against God's will. When we realize we have chosen to sin, we turn to Christ and the Church for sacramental forgiveness and reconciliation.

- Emphasize these points when teaching Chapters 3, 12, 13, and 14.
- Whenever talking about sin, make clear the distinction between sinful choices and mistakes.

3. Our conscience is the most basic awareness in us of what is right or wrong. It is very important that we form our conscience by the teachings of Christ and the Church. Examining our conscience each day helps us grow closer to God, to seek his forgiveness, and to make loving choices. The Holy Spirit is our guide in developing an informed conscience.

- Emphasize these points when teaching Chapters 6 and 12.
- Acknowledge how difficult it is to make good choices, especially when we are under peer pressure. Encourage your group to pray often to the Holy Spirit for guidance, grace, and courage.

4. Praying an Act of Contrition involves two parts: expressing sorrow for our sin and resolving not to sin again.

- Emphasize this point when teaching Chapter 12 and the Act of Contrition on page 121.
- Encourage the young people to pray often for forgiveness and for the ability to forgive others. Incorporate this type of prayer into the lessons throughout the year.

5. Two ways that the Church celebrates the Sacrament of Penance are presented in the text: celebrating individually or celebrating communally. Emphasize this point when teaching Chapter 12. See the charts on page 80 that detail both of these forms of the Rite.

■ Invite the group to visit a reconciliation room or confessional in your parish. If possible, have a priest accompany you in order to explain the sacramental action, symbols, and prayers, and to answer questions.

6. Peace means being in harmonious relationships with God, with those around us, and with ourselves. Sharing the peace of Christ with others is an important and ongoing part of the Sacrament of Penance.

■ Emphasize this point when teaching Chapters 12 and 15.

■ Invite young people to reflect on what type of peace they long for, what the world needs, and how it can be brought about.

These points are drawn out in a handout on page XVII. Copy the page, and give it to the young people in your group who are preparing for First Penance. Invite the young people to write their responses to questions 1–6. You can use the discussion questions as part of an interview, group discussion, or at-home sharing with parents and other family members.

CATECHESIS FOR FIRST EUCHARIST

The following points are essential to a basic understanding of the Eucharist. These are developed in *One Faith, One Lord.*

1. In the Eucharist the Catholic community comes together to celebrate its faith in Christ as the Son of God. This community lives out its faith in Christ through the way its members show love and compassion towards others.

■ Emphasize this point when teaching Chapters 7 and 8.

■ Use the liturgical year chart on page 117 to emphasize that the Catholic community expresses its faith in Jesus through the celebration of seasons and feasts.

2. As a community of believers we are nourished and guided by the Word of God. In the Mass Catholics hear God's Word through the readings from the Old and New Testaments.

■ Emphasize this point when teaching Chapters 8 and 11.

■ Help your class become familiar with the Lectionary, the cycle of readings used at Mass throughout the liturgical year.

■ Show the *Book of the Gospels* which a deacon or priest uses to proclaim the Gospel at Mass.

3. The Eucharist commemorates the life, Death, Resurrection, and Ascension of Jesus. When we celebrate the Eucharist we give thanks for the love given and the sacrifice offered for us by Jesus for the Salvation of all.

■ Emphasize this point when teaching Chapters 5, 10, and 11.

■ Cultivate a spirit of thanksgiving among the young people, emphasizing that this is what the word *Eucharist* means.

4. In the Eucharist, the sacrifice of Jesus on the cross is made present. Jesus' words and actions from the Last Supper are repeated: taking, blessing, breaking, and eating. When we share the Eucharist we do so in remembrance of Jesus Christ, who is really present in the form of bread and wine.

■ Emphasize this point when teaching Chapters 10 and 11.

■ Stress the Real Presence of Christ in the Eucharist and refer often to the actions mentioned above.

■ Explain the difference between the Eucharist and ordinary bread.

5. When we pray the Our Father we pray the prayer that Jesus taught us. Our *Amen*, uttered before receiving Holy Communion, affirms our belief in the Real Presence of Jesus in the Eucharist.

■ Emphasize this point when teaching Chapters 8, 10, and 11.

■ Pray the Our Father often with your group and encourage them to reflect upon it.

■ Demonstrate the two ways we can receive Holy Communion—in the hand or on the tongue. Encourage the young people to approach this ritual with reverence and awe.

6. When we receive Holy Communion, we are nourished by Jesus himself. Christ enters our lives. We are strengthened by the Holy Spirit so that we might share the life of Christ with others.

■ Emphasize this point when teaching Chapters 7 (the work of the Church), 11, and 15.

■ Throughout the *One Faith, One Lord* program, encourage the young people to name specific ways they can be witnesses to their faith—in their homes, schools, and neighborhoods.

These points are drawn out in a handout on page XVIII. Copy the page, and give it to the young people in your group who are preparing for First Eucharist. Invite the young people to write their responses to questions 1–6. You can use the discussion questions as part of an interview, group discussion, or at-home sharing with parents and other family members.

PREPARING FOR THE SACRAMENT OF PENANCE AND RECONCILIATION

Write your responses to the following questions.

1. Use your own words to tell about the Sacrament of Penance and Reconciliation. How does it restore us to loving relationships with God and other people?

 ____

 ____

2. What is sin? What is the difference between committing a sin and making a mistake?

 ____

 ____

3. Explain what it means to make an Examination of Conscience.

 ____

 ____

4. What prayer of forgiveness do we use in the Sacrament of Penance and Reconciliation? What does this prayer express?

 ____

 ____

5. Name two ways of celebrating the Sacrament of Penance and Reconciliation.

 ____

 ____

6. How does the Sacrament of Penance and Reconciliation restore peace in our lives?

 ____

 ____

Discuss.

- How does Jesus teach us to show love towards God and other people? What can draw us away from this love?
- Why is it sometimes hard to make choices that show love for God, for others, and for ourselves?
- Why is it important to think each day about the good and bad choices we make? When and how might we do this?
- When we pray to forgive others, what help might we ask of God? When we pray for others to forgive us, what might we ask God to help us do?
- What questions do you have about celebrating the Sacrament of Penance and Reconciliation for the first time?
- Name one way young people can bring the peace of Christ to others each day.

PREPARING FOR THE SACRAMENT OF EUCHARIST

Write your responses to the following questions.

1. Why does the parish community come together for Sunday Mass?

____

____

2. Where do the readings at Mass come from?

____

____

3. When we celebrate the Mass, what do we remember about the sacrifice that Jesus made for us?

____

____

4. What did Jesus share with his disciples at the Last Supper? What did he ask us to do "in remembrance" of him?

____

____

5. How is Jesus present to us in the Eucharist?

____

____

6. How does the Eucharist nourish us and help us to show the love of Christ to others?

____

____

Discuss.

- What are some ways for young people to participate in the life of the parish?
- Name one of your favorite stories about Jesus.
- What do we give thanks for when we celebrate the Mass? What gifts of God are you thankful for?
- What questions do you have about receiving Holy Communion for the first time?
- How is Jesus present to us each day?
- What are some ways that young people can share the love of Christ with others?

Time Allotment Charts

Three charts are offered to show how each chapter might be treated in alternative ways according to a five-day, a three-day, or a once-a-week program.

Five-Day Program				
Opener	**Section One**	**Section Two**	**Section Three**	**Review**
Introduction	Presentation	Presentation	Presentation	Conclusion

Three-Day Program		
Section One	**Section Two**	**Section Three**
Introduction Presentation	Presentation	Presentation Conclusion

Once-a-Week Program

Although there are time constraints in a once-a-week program, the catechist needs to emphasize key doctrinal points and, subsequently, use the results from the *One Faith, One Lord* program survey to determine what points still require clarification for the young people.

After doing so, the catechist would:

A. Use the Introduction to engage young people in examining their own questions about life and faith.

B. Discuss the content of the three doctrinal points found in the Presentation.

C. Use the Growing in Faith pages found in the Conclusion to pray and plan ways to live their faith.

CHAPTER 1

GOALS

to develop an understanding of the concept of faith; to appreciate the sources of our Catholic faith

GETTING READY

■ *Materials needed:*

A simple prayer environment: Bible, decorative cloth, etc., student books on or near prayer table

Bibles—preferably one for each young person

One Faith, One Lord *program survey (see pages XII and XIII) for each student*

poster board

Adult Focus

When you say that you know someone well, it means that you have had more than an occasional encounter with that person. You have done more than observe his or her activities and accomplishments. You have talked with the person on a deeper level. In other words, the person has "revealed" his or her inner self to you.

We can know something of God from Creation, for the world around us is a blueprint of the Creator. Our reason tells us that the Creator must be wise and intelligent to have made such a universe. However, just as people must reveal their inner selves to us in order for us to know them well, so God must reveal himself to us in a special encounter.

Divine Revelation—God's making himself known to us—takes place in the living experience of

Introduction (__ min.)

Designate an easily accessible area of your classroom as the group's prayer space. Use the prayer space to gather the group together before presenting each lesson.

Lead the group in prayer by praying the following:

Lord God,
your Spirit of wisdom fills the earth and teaches us your ways.

Look upon these young people.
Let them enjoy their learning and take delight in new discoveries.
Help them to persevere in their studies
and give them the desire to learn all things well.

Grant that young people and teachers alike may follow Jesus Christ,
the way, the truth, and the life,
for ever and ever.
Amen.

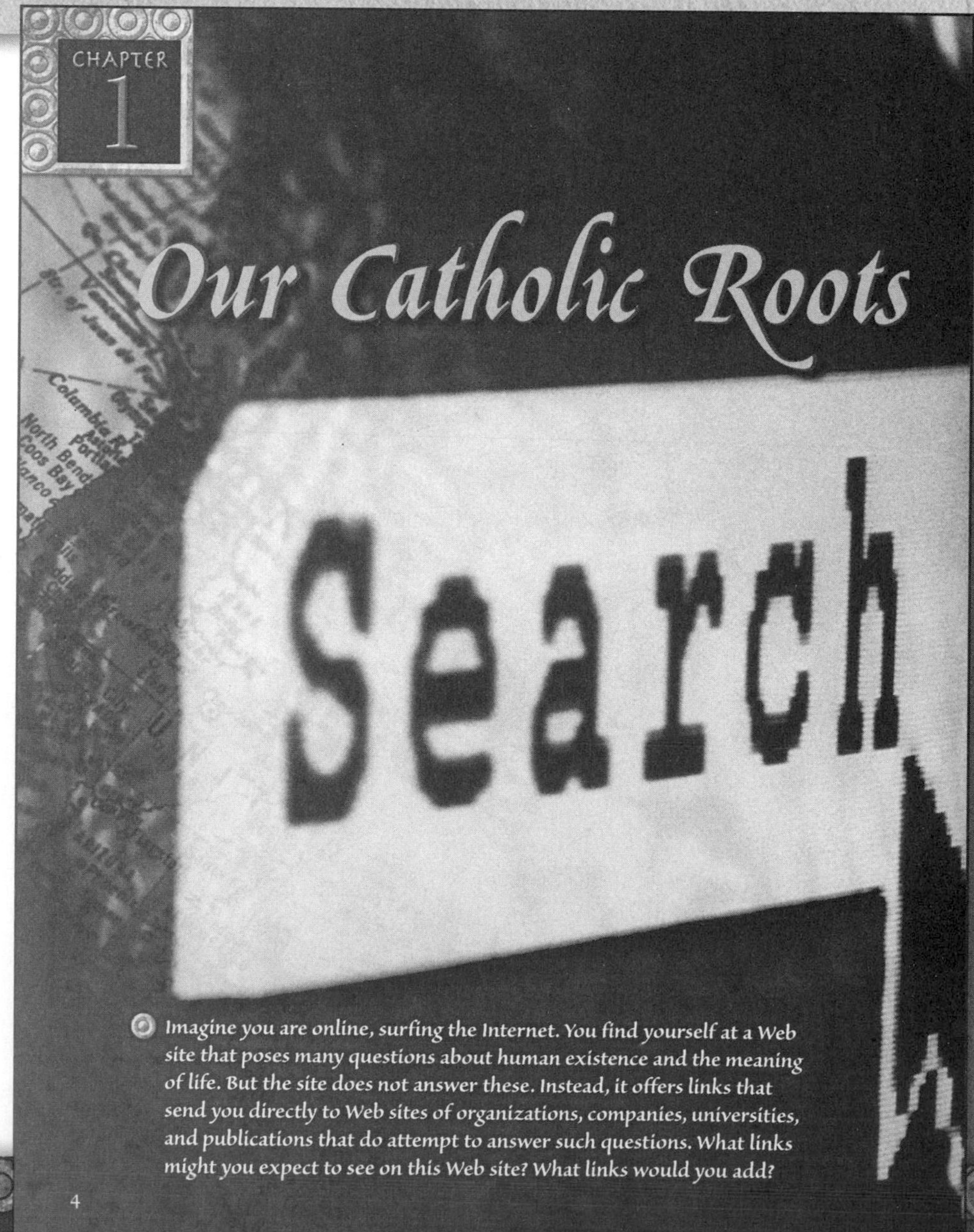
CHAPTER 1

Our Catholic Roots

Imagine you are online, surfing the Internet. You find yourself at a Web site that poses many questions about human existence and the meaning of life. But the site does not answer these. Instead, it offers links that send you directly to Web sites of organizations, companies, universities, and publications that do attempt to answer such questions. What links might you expect to see on this Web site? What links would you add?

4

people in a community of faith. He has made himself known to us through his saving actions in our history. God revealed himself in a unique way to the Israelites, and he offered his complete and full Revelation in Jesus Christ, his Son. We come to understand this full Revelation in Jesus through Scripture and Tradition. Scripture and Tradtion are the sources of God's Revelation to us. But despite all that God has made known to us, he still remains a mystery. This is why faith is so important. Faith helps us to believe what we will never completely understand.

As you begin this first chapter of *One Faith, One Lord*, consider the young people who will be in your care. Your task will be to help them better understand the Catholic faith and come to a deeper sense of their own relationship with God.

Reflection

Before you begin, take some time to pray for the young people with whom you will share the faith. Give thanks for the gift of being able to be with them during this part of their journey of faith. Ask God's guidance and grace as you prepare for this first lesson.

Our Catholic faith helps us to discover the meaning of life.

Human beings have always asked questions about the meaning of life and the origin of the world. No other creatures on earth can ask, "Where do things come from?" "Why are things the way they are?" or "What is the meaning of life?"

These are only some of the exciting questions that we can ask. For centuries, people have tried to answer such questions and to make sense out of life. They have tried to find satisfying answers in the following ways:

- reasoning, thinking, and generating ideas
- reflecting on their own experiences
- reaching out and exploring beyond everyday knowledge
- listening to those with whom they live and work.

All of these ways of discovery are wonderful—but they are limited. Reason and experience have never answered fully everything we need or want to know. They can only take us so far. We need something more. For Catholics, that something more is faith.

What is faith? Faith is not just another point of view. Faith is a gift from God. Faith helps us to begin to see our lives and the world as God sees them.

A person of faith knows that there is more to life than can be seen. Through the eyes of faith, we know that God is near, closer than we can imagine, and that God is the source of all life.

Take time for each young person to introduce himself or herself to the group. Encourage the young people to share something about themselves. For example: My name is _____.

Three adjectives that describe me are _____.

Distribute the *One Faith, One Lord* textbooks.

Turn to page 4, and read aloud the opening paragraph. Ask the group to brainstorm a list of links that might appear on a Web site that attempts to answer questions of human existence and the meaning of life.

Presentation (__ min.)

Our Catholic faith helps us to discover the meaning of life.

Have volunteers read aloud the paragraphs in Section One on pages 5 and 6. Follow with a discussion on the various ways people find answers to questions.

◉ Where do you turn for answers to questions?

◉ Which way have you found most helpful?

Stress that faith brings a whole new way of looking at life. Faith helps us to see things as God does. Our faith grows as we grow. "Faith is a gift destined to grow in the hearts of believers." (*General Directory for Catechesis*, 56)

Distribute a copy of the *One Faith, One Lord* program survey (see pages XII and XIII) for each member of the group to complete. Allow some time for reflection. Encourage the young people to answer the questions completely. Collect the completed surveys from each young person, and place them in a large envelope. You may want to refer to them throughout the year/program.

Then, have the young people write their responses to the question at the end of Section One on page 6.

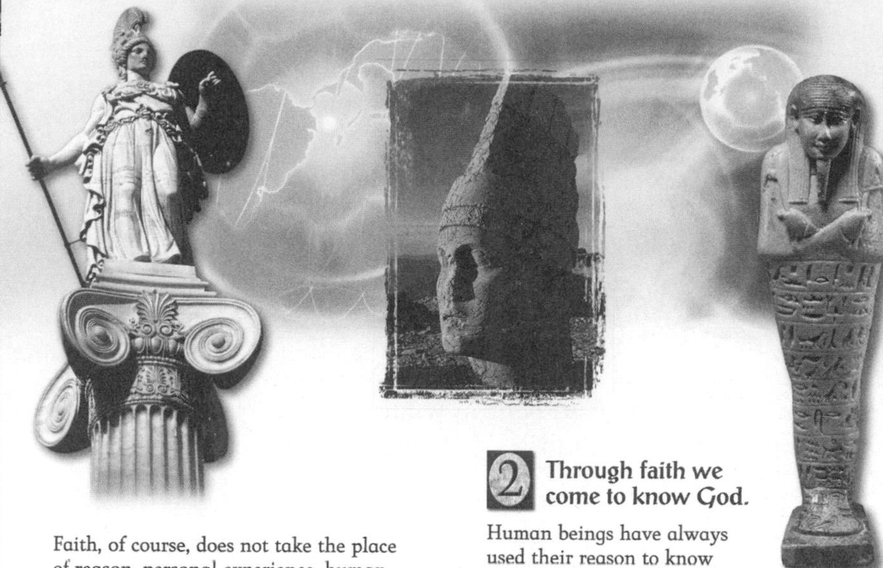

Faith, of course, does not take the place of reason, personal experience, human searching, or learning from others. Faith builds on our human abilities and works through them. We know this from experience. Throughout history, we see that some of the most creative and talented artists, educators, and scientists have been people of faith.

Faith is like a key that unlocks many doors. Our faith shows us answers we would most often be unable to discover by ourselves.

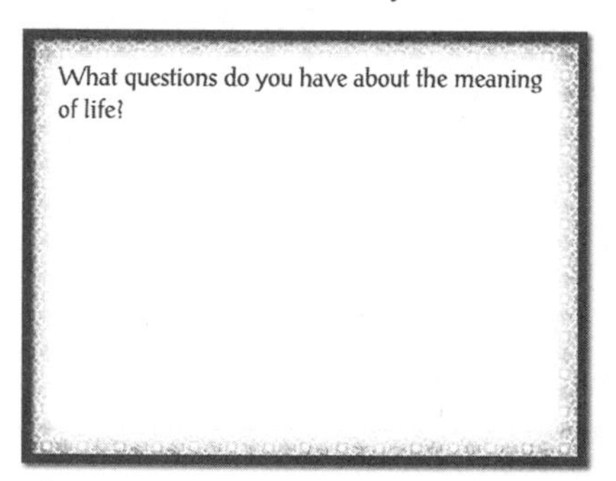

2 Through faith we come to know God.

Human beings have always used their reason to know that there must be some higher power at work in the world. When we look at ourselves and the universe around us, we realize that something so wonderful could not have come into existence or have happened by itself. So human beings search for an answer. They search for God.

In this search people living many thousands of years ago thought they had found the answer in nature. Some people named the gods they thought were at work in the terrifying clap of thunder, the flash of lightning, or the rumble of an earthquake. Others found their gods in the sun, moon, and stars.

You may know some of the fascinating stories and myths of ancient religions, such as those of Egypt, Greece, and Rome. In those religions, the gods were often pictured as animals or even as people, each in charge of some important part of life. But these creature-like gods were not the one true God. They did not satisfy the human search for the higher power at work in the world.

6

 Through faith we come to know God.

Instruct the group to read the first four paragraphs in Section Two on pages 6 and 7 silently. Ask questions such as:

◉ Did anyone ever tell you that rain and sunshine, thunder and lightning were signs from God?

Optional Activity

Invite the young people to design a comic strip or cartoon to illustrate a way our Catholic faith helps us to discover the meaning of life. If time permits, invite volunteers to share their comic strips or cartoons with the group.

Answer for page 6:

Accept all reasonable answers.

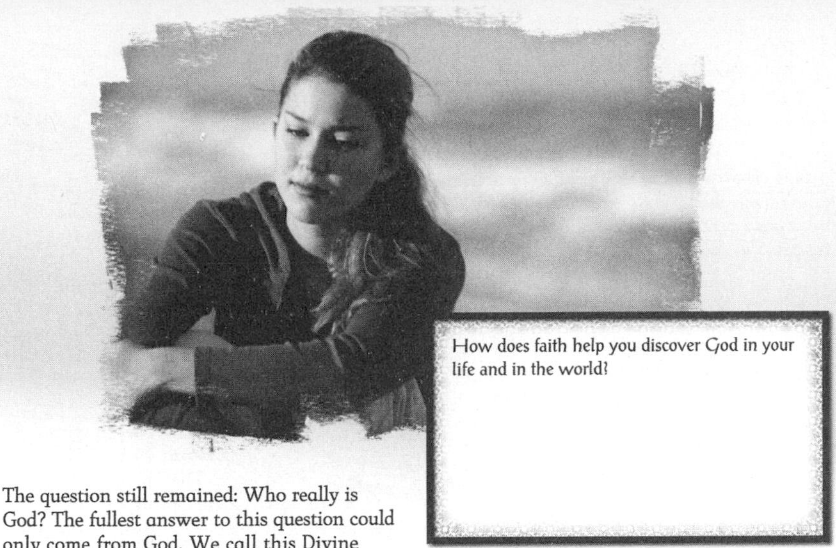

How does faith help you discover God in your life and in the world?

The question still remained: Who really is God? The fullest answer to this question could only come from God. We call this Divine Revelation. The word *divine* is used to describe God, something that comes from God, or an expression of God. The word *revelation* means "the act of making someone or something known." This is why we call God's making himself known to us **Divine Revelation**.

At a chosen time in the history of the world, God wanted to make a special Revelation to human beings. He did this through the Israelites, the ancient Jews. Out of love God gradually revealed himself and his plan through words and deeds. Some of the things the Israelites came to know and believe about God were:

- There is only one true God, not many gods.
- God is not part of nature; he created nature and all that exists.
- God is a loving and caring God.
- God is active in the world and in our lives.
- We are called into a close relationship with God and called to live as God's people in the world.

We believe these things, too. But as Catholics we also believe that the one true God offered us his complete and full Revelation in Jesus Christ, his Son. Jesus Christ, the Son of God, shows us that God is Father, Son, and Holy Spirit. Our response to this Revelation is faith.

Faith is the gift from God by which we believe in God and all that he has revealed, and all that the Church proposes for our belief. We cannot earn faith. It is God's gift to us. By faith we can believe what God has shared about himself and his Creation. Yet even though God reveals himself, he remains a mystery.

Faith is also a personal act and a choice, a free response to God's Revelation of himself and his love for us.

Our faith is the faith of the Church. Just as we do not live alone, we do not believe alone. We try to live as persons of faith, especially by turning to God in prayer and worship. We also respond to God by living our faith and doing what he asks of us, taking care of ourselves, others, and the world around us.

7

◉ Have you ever looked up at the universe and the stars and felt that there must be a God?

◉ Where do you find God now? List responses to the last question on the chalkboard or on poster board.

Have the young people continue reading the remainder of page 7. Share with them that all human beings search for God. The *Catechism of the Catholic Church* states, "the desire for God is written in the human heart" (*CCC*, 27). God created us and wants us to know him.

The Church uses the term *Divine Revelation* to describe God telling us about himself. Point out the ways that God revealed himself to the Israelites. Stress that God's full and complete Revelation is in Jesus Christ, his Son. Yet, no matter what God has revealed, we will never totally understand him. God remains a mystery. Review some of the truths God has made known to us that are listed on page 7. Highlight the response we make to God's Revelation through personal and communal prayer.

Have the young people write their responses to the question at the end of Section Two on page 7. Emphasize that our faith in God is both a gift from God and a free human act.

Optional Activity

Have the young people work in pairs or small groups to develop a lesson in order to teach the concept of faith to a group of young children. Or, have the young people draw a symbol to represent their idea of faith.

Answer for page 7:

Possible answers include:

Faith helps me to discover what God has shared about himself and his Creation. Faith helps me to turn to God in prayer and worship. Faith helps me to live as God wants me to live.

In the Bible we read about God's relationship with our ancestors in faith.

Ask the young people to recall family stories that are typically repeated at family gatherings. Discuss why families do this. Then have them read Section Three on page 8.

Review the fact that the Bible came about from the spoken word, or oral tradition. This oral tradition developed into the written word under the guidance, or inspiration, of the Holy Spirit. We call this guidance of the Holy Spirit *Divine Inspiration*.

Review the different types of writing in the Bible. Ask: How are the two main parts of the Bible different? Describe the differences.

Read the question at the end of Section Three on page 8. Instruct the group to write their responses in the space provided.

If you have time, do the following.

Hand out a Bible to each student. Invite them to look through it as you emphasize the differences between the Old Testament and the New Testament. Turn to the Table of Contents and invite the young people to read the names of the books of the Bible. Point out examples of different types of writing: historical (Exodus), poetry (Psalms), law (Leviticus), prophetic writing (Isaiah), and letters (Corinthians). You may want to refer to the section *Using the Bible* located on page 118.

In the Bible we read about God's relationship with our ancestors in faith.

The ancient Israelites were a nomadic people. Their wandering lifestyle did not allow them the time to record their special relationship with God or what God had revealed to them. Written documents were not even a part of their culture or way of life. But by word of mouth they passed on beautiful stories of faith, recounting in word and song all that God had done for them.

After many centuries the Israelites finally wrote down the oral traditions that had been passed from generation to generation. While the ancient authors chose their own words, expressions, and stories, they wrote under the guidance of the Holy Spirit. We call the special guidance that the Holy Spirit gave to the human authors of the Bible **Divine Inspiration**.

These writings were eventually collected in the book we call the **Bible**, or Scripture. The Bible is the written account of God's Revelation and his relationship with his people. The word *Bible* comes from Greek words meaning "books." The Bible is actually a collection of seventy-three smaller books divided into two main parts:

- The **Old Testament** contains forty-six books. In them we read about the faith relationship between God and the Israelites, later called the Jews.
- The **New Testament** contains twenty-seven books. They are about Jesus Christ, the Son of God, his message and mission, and his first followers.

The Bible was written over many centuries and had many human authors, all inspired by God. Because God inspired the human authors, he is also the author of the Bible. This is why all Scripture is the Word of God.

Do YOU Know?

God reveals himself to us through Scripture and Tradition. **Tradition** is the living transmission of the Word of God as entrusted to the Apostles and their successors by Jesus Christ and the Holy Spirit. It includes the Church's teachings, documents, worship, prayer, and other practices.

Catholics have deep respect for the Bible because it is God's Word to us. The Bible is a book about faith. It cannot be read as a science book or a modern history book. It is our most sacred book.

The human authors of the Bible used many different forms and styles of writing, including short stories, history, poetry, letters, and parables. Because the Bible was written so long ago and in so many different styles, we need to take time to study it carefully. Knowing the background of the human authors, the culture of the times, and the different forms and styles of writing helps us to better understand God's Word.

Belief in God's Word is a vital part of what it means to be a Catholic and to share in the beautiful faith life and tradition of our Church. What God did for our ancestors in faith, he continues to do for us.

What is the Bible? Why is it important to us?

8

Do YOU Know?

Ask the group to name various family traditions. Then read aloud the "Do You Know?" feature on page 8.

Answers for page 8:

See the Glossary, page 125. For importance of the Bible accept any reasonable answer.

GROWING IN FAITH

PRAY

As people of faith we turn to God in prayer. **Prayer** is talking and listening to God. We can pray alone, or we can join with others in communal prayer. In praising and thanking God for the gift of our lives, we also ask God for help because we trust in his love. Pray together:

✝ God be in my head,
and in my understanding;
God be in my eyes, and in my looking;
God be in my mouth, and in my speaking;
God be in my heart, and in my thinking;
God be in my end, and at my departing.

REMEMBER

The Church teaches...

- Out of love, God has revealed himself and given himself to us. He has shared with us who he is and what he asks of us.
- Faith is both a gift from God and a free human act.
- Through faith and reason we have the ability to believe all that God reveals to us and to respond to God.
- The books of the Bible were written by human authors under the inspiration of the Holy Spirit.
- The Bible is divided into two parts, the Old Testament of forty-six books and the New Testament of twenty-seven books.

Faith Words

Divine Revelation (p. 7)
faith (p. 7)
Divine Inspiration (p. 8)
Bible (p. 8)
Old Testament (p. 8)
New Testament (p. 8)
Tradition (p. 8)
prayer (p. 9)

REFLECT & ACT

Faith must be alive! We cannot just talk about what we believe. We must live it.

What do people of faith do that is different from those who do not have faith? What can you do to grow in faith, to open your mind and heart to God?

Think of someone you know and trust. What questions would you ask that person about the role faith has played in his or her life?

9

Conclusion (__ min.)

Growing in Faith

Have the young people close their books. Ask them what they have learned in this lesson about faith, Divine Revelation, Divine Inspiration, the Bible, the Old Testament, the New Testament, Tradition, and prayer. Reopen the books to page 9. Was everything from the **Remember** and **Faith Words** sections named? If not, point these out and help the group to name the remaining concepts.

Invite the young people to read the **Reflect and Act** section and to write their responses in the spaces provided. If desired, play some soft instrumental music while they do this.

Have the young people share some of the questions they will ask the person of faith they will interview.

Conclude the lesson by gathering together around the prayer table. Have a volunteer read aloud the paragraph in the **Pray** section on page 9. Then, offer the prayer together.

CATECHISM FOCUS

"Faith is a supernatural gift from God. . . . 'Believing' is a human act, conscious and free, corresponding to the dignity of the human person." (*CCC*, 179–180)

For additional reference and reflection, see *CCC*, 27–35.

Answers for page 9:

Left column:
People of faith believe what God has shared about himself. They try to respond to God in prayer and in how they live. Faith in God enables them to do good for others in his name. Help the young people to be specific in their answers to the second question.

Right column:
Accept all reasonable answers.

CHAPTER 2

GOALS

to understand God is the Creator of all life; to appreciate the unique role humans have in God's Creation

GETTING READY

■ ***Materials needed:***

Bibles—preferably one for each young person

Copies of the Genesis account of Creation (Genesis 1:1–2:4) if having different volunteers read

Adult Focus

"In the beginning, when God created the heavens and the earth. . . " (Genesis 1:1) With these opening words of the Bible, the story of Creation begins. In this chapter the young people will learn about God as the Creator of all life. They will also come to an appreciation of the ways we are called to share in the work of Creation.

It is quite likely that some of the young people hold a literal view of the Creation story, that is, that God created the world in six actual days. The second Creation narrative (Genesis 2:5–23) describes the order of Creation differently. Which account is correct? The answer, of course, is both. Without books, people who lived before the Bible was written learned by listening. Therefore, the "six-days" and other repeated phrases used in the passage

Introduction (__ min.)

Gather the group around the prayer table in the prayer space. Ask the group to reflect quietly as you lead them in prayer with the following script:

Each day we experience some part of God's Creation—the sun that warms our days, the food on our table, the people we love, the pet we take care of. It's easy to take these things for granted but each part of Creation is the handiwork of God. Let us ask God to help us become more aware of the world around us and to appreciate its wonder and beauty.

Pause briefly, and then invite the young people to name an aspect of Creation for which they are thankful. Then pray the Glory to the Father (see page 119) together.

Ask the young people to study the image on pages 10–11. Read the quote aloud. Ask the group to offer ideas about what the author meant by getting a

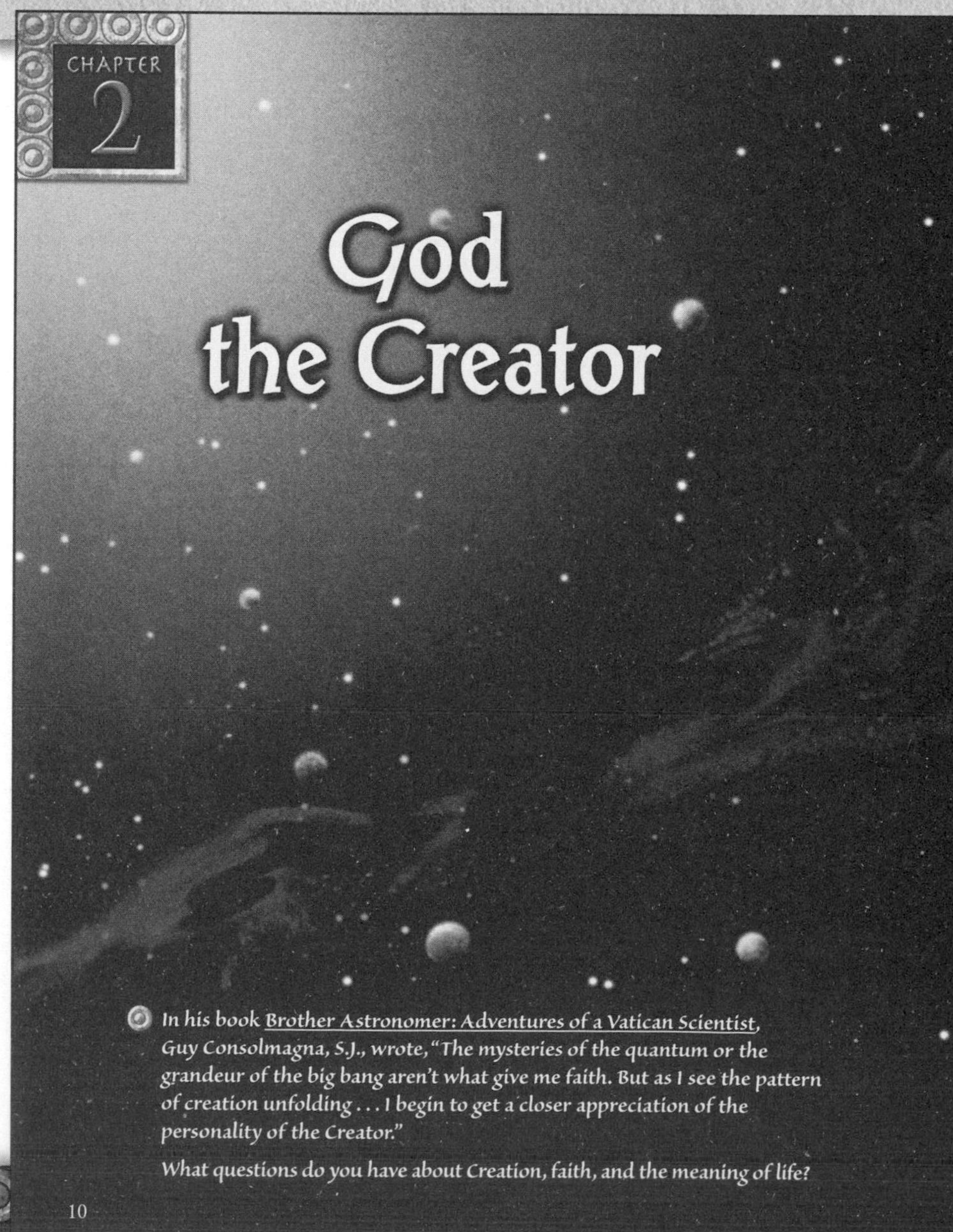

CHAPTER 2

God the Creator

In his book Brother Astronomer: Adventures of a Vatican Scientist, Guy Consolmagna, S.J., wrote, "The mysteries of the quantum or the grandeur of the big bang aren't what give me faith. But as I see the pattern of creation unfolding . . . I begin to get a closer appreciation of the personality of the Creator."

What questions do you have about Creation, faith, and the meaning of life?

were literary devices used to teach religious truth. The author of Genesis was expressing this truth in a way that people could understand and remember. The author did not intend to be scientific in the story of Creation. In the picturesque language of poetry, the author wanted to convey the truth that God created everything that exists.

"In order to discover *the sacred authors' intention*, the reader must take into account the conditions of their time and culture, the literary genres in use at that time, and the modes of feeling, speaking, and narrating then current. 'For the fact is that truth is differently presented and expressed in the various types of historical writing, in prophetical and poetical texts, and in other forms of literary expression.'" (*CCC*, 110)

Reflection

As a way to prepare for this lesson, take some time to read and reflect upon the first account of Creation, Genesis 1:1—2:4. Be aware of the ways you can help the young people "see" God through the wonders of Creation. Think, too, about how, in your daily lives, you all can be partners with God in the care of Creation.

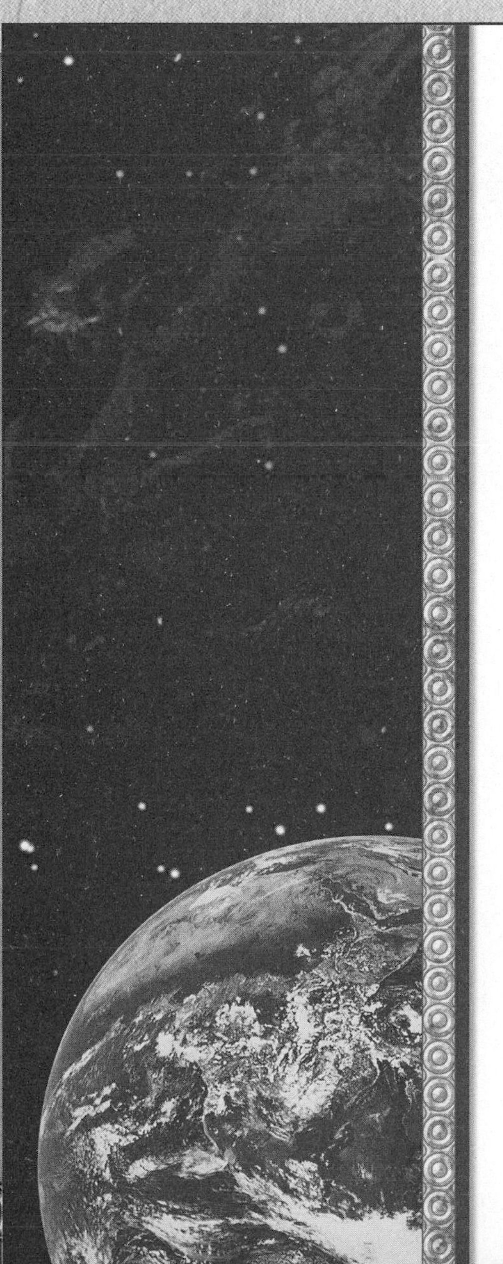

God is the Creator of the universe.

Every generation of people, young and old alike, tends to ask questions about the origin of the universe: Where did it come from? When did it start? How did it come into existence?

Scientists, historians, philosophers, and religious believers have all attempted to explain the origin of the universe. Scholars in many different areas of study have made unique and truthful contributions to our understanding of the origins of the universe. And research has raised even more questions.

People working in the fields of science and social studies try to answer important questions about how and when our world came into being. Over the centuries, as technology has advanced, our scientific theories about Creation have changed. Our knowledge has expanded.

But people do not just ask how and when. They also ask who and why: Who created the universe? Why was it created? Scientists ask where we came from, but as people of faith we also ask why we are here and where we are going. These questions can only be answered in faith.

In the Book of Genesis, the first book of the Bible, we find a beautiful and imaginative account of Creation. The Creation story is a simple, poetic story of the beginning of the universe. We read in the first Genesis account that God fashions the world in a spectacular way over a six-day period, the length of the ancient Israelites' workweek. The authors of Genesis show that God alone created everything. He begins by creating light. "Let there be light," he says (Genesis 1:3). And effortlessly—by the power of his word—God brings light into being.

11

"closer appreciation of the personality of the Creator." Ask them to consider the question at the bottom of page 10.

Presentation (__ min.)

God is the Creator of the universe.

Have volunteers read the first four paragraphs of Section One on page 11. Take some time to discuss the difference between questions of science and questions of faith as they are named in the fourth paragraph. Ask the young people what other questions of faith they can think of.

Continue reading the last paragraph on page 11 and the first two on page 12. Then have the young people underline the answers to the following questions:

- In what book of the Bible do we read about God and the Creation of the world? (Genesis)

◎ Did the author of Genesis give us a scientific explanation of how the world was created? (See second paragraph on page 12.)

◎ Why do we think the author described God as creating the world in six days? (See fifth paragraph on page 11 and first paragraph on page 12.)

◎ What religious truths are being expressed in the Creation story? (See bulleted items on page 12.)

Remind the young people that the author of Genesis is trying to teach us the great truth that God created the world. The Genesis account is not a scientific explanation of how the world came to be. Read the remaining paragraphs of Section One together, emphasizing the truths of the faith named on page 12.

Read aloud the Creation account from Genesis 1:1—2:4. If desired, divide the passage into parts and assign them to skilled readers. Encourage the young people to listen to the poetic description of God's creative work.

Have the young people write their responses to the question at the end of Section One on page 12.

Then, according to Genesis, God made the dome of the heavens—the sky. He gathered together the waters under the sky, causing dry land to appear. And "God called the dry land 'the earth,' and the basin of the water he called 'the sea.' God saw how good it was" (Genesis 1:10). On the seventh day, at the end of the workweek, the Genesis authors showed God doing just what the ancient Israelites did: resting after his labors.

From their description of Creation, we can see that the Genesis authors were not trying to answer questions of science, but questions of faith. For example, the word *day* found in the Creation account does not literally mean twenty-four hours. The seven days of Creation are simply the framework within which the Genesis authors tell the story.

Inspired by God and by the beauty and majesty of the world they saw around them, the authors wished to teach some important truths of faith:

- There is one and only one God.
- God alone created everything that is.
- God created the world and everything in it good.
- God created the world for his glory, out of his love and wisdom, and by his free choice.
- From the things God has made we can learn that he is all-powerful, all-loving, all-creative, and all-good.

The Creation story is a wonderful one. Reflect on it. How does it help you to understand the existence of the universe?

Our faith helps us to know an equally important truth about Creation. It is that Creation is the work of God the Father, God the Son, and God the Holy Spirit. And Creation is kept in existence by God the Father, his Word—the Son, and the giver of life, the Holy Spirit.

God is the Creator of all life.

In the imaginative account of Creation in the Book of Genesis, we read that God created all life: plants and trees, fish and birds, animals of every kind. Then, finally, God created humans, and made them in his own image and likeness:
"in the divine image he created him;
male and female he created them"
(Genesis 1:27).

No other creature or thing is made in the image of God. We are the crowning achievement of his Creation.

12

God is the Creator of all life.

Instruct the group to read Section Two silently. When they finish, ask the following questions:

◎ What does the Genesis account tell us about the creation of human life? (We alone are created in the "image and likeness of God.")

Answers for page 12:

Accept all reasonable answers.

We all have **human dignity** which is the value and worth we share because God created us in his image and likeness. Because of this, each of us possesses an immortal **soul**, the invisible spiritual reality that makes each of us human and that will never die. Only human beings are capable of knowing and understanding themselves and their thoughts, feelings, and motivations. Only human beings can know and love God, and thus share in his life.

God calls each of us to a relationship with him, and we are able to respond in faith and love.

One significant way that the Israelites responded to their Creator was in prayer. A collection of these prayers, known as psalms, is contained in the Old Testament. The Book of Psalms contains many references to God as the Creator of everything, and to men and women as God's special Creation. We read in the psalms:

When I see your heavens, the work
of your fingers,
the moon and stars that you set
in place—
What are humans that you are mindful
of them,
mere mortals that you care for them?
Yet you have made them little less than a
god,
crowned them with glory and honor.
Psalm 8:4–6

We alone have been given this gift of human dignity. Because of it we are free to love, to think, and to choose in God's likeness. God gives us the freedom to choose. This gift is called free will. We are responsible for our thoughts and actions. Being made in the image and likeness of God offers each of us a tremendous challenge.

Explain what it means to you to be made in the image and likeness of God.

Do YOU Know?

Throughout the pages of the Bible, in both the Old and New Testaments, there are references to angels, or messengers from God. In fact, the word *angel* comes from the Greek word meaning "messenger." Angels were created by God as pure spirits without physical bodies. As you read the Bible, you will learn that angels are servants of God that help him to accomplish his mission of Salvation. The Church teaches that the angels watch over us and pray for us.

13

What is human dignity? (the value and worth we share because God created us in his image and likeness)

What does being made in the image and likeness of God mean for us? (It means that we alone are created with an immortal soul, the invisible spiritual reality that makes each of us human and that will never die. We alone are capable of knowing and understanding ourselves and our thoughts, feelings, and motivations. We alone can know and love God, and thus share his life.)

What does God's gift of free will offer us? (the freedom to choose and to be responsible for our thoughts and actions)

Note: God gives us free will in order that we may choose what is true and good.

Have a volunteer read aloud Psalm 8 on page 13. Ask the young people to respond to the question at the end of Section Two on page 13.

Do YOU Know?

Read together the "Do You Know?" feature on page 13. If time allows, invite the young people to share their images of angels and any Biblical stories that show angels as "servants and messengers" of God.

Answers for page 13:

Accept all reasonable answers.

God calls us to share in the work of Creation.

Ask: What is our responsibility towards God's Creation?

Tell the group to use this question as a focal point as they read Section Three on page 14 silently.

In today's world there are some critical issues affecting Creation. Invite the group to list some of these issues (for example: global warming, depletion of natural resources, etc.)

Stress the responsibility we have to develop and use our talents and abilities to care for God's Creation. Have the young people think about the question at the end of Section Three on page 14. Invite them to record their thoughts.

God calls us to share in the work of Creation.

Life is a gift. In a wondrous way, God created us male and female, partners with God and equal partners with each other.

You may be surprised to learn that in the Book of Genesis, chapters two and three, there is a second account of Creation. In this story about Creation, the Genesis authors introduce Adam and Eve as the first human beings. They represent all humanity. The authors of Genesis tell us that God spoke to Adam and Eve, saying, "Be fertile and multiply; fill the earth and subdue it. Have dominion over the fish of the sea, the birds of the air, and all the living things that move on the earth" (Genesis 1:28). These words help us to understand that God invites all of us to join him as partners in the work of and care for Creation.

God entrusted us with the care of Creation. God asks us to be **stewards of Creation**—to care for his Creation and to make sure that all people share in the goodness of Creation. God made the earth, the air, and the water for all his creatures to use. As God's stewards it is our responsibility to protect all the resources of the earth from destruction, pollution, or any sort of waste. To be effective partners with God, we must develop and use our talents and abilities. By improving our world, conserving its resources, and sharing what God has given us, we build a better life for all.

God's Creation is truly a wonder. But the work of Creation is not finished, and God calls us in many ways to assist him in his work of Creation. We can study agriculture and learn to sow better crops to feed the world's hungry. We can plant new trees to preserve the world's forests. We can build devices to filter water to keep our rivers and oceans clean. We can explore the surface of the earth, the depths of the oceans, and the vastness of space in search of things to benefit all humanity. By carrying out daily acts of stewardship, large and small, we make the glory of God's name known throughout all Creation.

Think of ways that you can be a partner with God in the work of Creation. Share your ideas.

Optional Activity

Invite the young people to be mindful of the environment. For one day, have them note ways that they carry out daily acts of stewardship, large and small, to protect and care for God's Creation. Encourage them to share their experiences with the group.

Answers for page 14:

Accept all reasonable answers.

Growing in Faith

Pray

The word *Amen* is a Hebrew word meaning "It is true!" or "So be it!" In the Mass and in all prayers, when we say "Amen" we are showing our agreement with what is being said. Pray together the following prayer.

✝ Blessed are you, O God,
Creator of the Universe,
who have made all things good
and given the earth for us to cultivate.
Grant that we may always use created
things gratefully
and share your gifts with those in need,
out of love of Christ our Lord,
who lives and reigns with you
for ever and ever.
Amen.

Remember

The Church teaches...

- God created the universe. The scientific theory that the world was gradually formed over millions of years is compatible with Church teaching. Science and religion are partners in the search for truth.
- God made all the creatures of the universe, but human beings have a unique and special place in his Creation. God has created each person in his image with an immortal soul.
- From the things God has made we can learn that he is all-powerful, all-loving, all-creative, and all-good.
- God made us stewards of Creation, and we are called to respect and protect God's creatures and the environment.
- The gift of faith helps us to know that God is the source of all Creation.

Reflect & Act

The authors of the Book of Genesis never could have dreamed that we would know as much about our world as we do today. They had no idea of the vast reaches of outer space or the marvelous microscopic world of the cell. But the lessons of faith they taught are still true.

What is it about Creation that leads you to think about God? Is there any time of the day that you are especially aware of God's creative power?

How can people work together to protect and preserve the environment? Suggest some activities to help your parish, school, or neighborhood get involved in the care of Creation.

Faith Words

human dignity (p. 13)
soul (p. 13)
stewards of Creation (p. 14)

Catechism Focus

"God created the world to show forth and communicate his glory. That his creatures should share in his truth, goodness, and beauty—this is the glory for which God created them." (*CCC*, 319)

For additional reference and reflection, see *CCC*, 355–361.

Conclusion (__ min.)

Growing in Faith

Have the young people close their books. Ask them what they have learned in this lesson, prompting them to think about God as the Creator of all life, human dignity, soul, and the unique role humans have in God's Creation. Then have the young people open their books to page 15. Was everything from the **Remember** and **Faith Words** sections named? If not, offer suggestions to help the young people name the remaining concepts.

Have the group read the **Reflect and Act** section and write their responses in the spaces provided. If desired, play some soft instrumental music while they do this.

Have the young people discuss in small groups what they might do in their home, school, neighborhood, or parish to care for Creation.

Conclude the lesson by gathering the group around the prayer table. Have a volunteer read aloud the paragraph in the **Pray** section on page 15. Then, offer the prayer together.

Answers for page 15:

Left column:
Accept all reasonable answers.

Right column:
Accept all reasonable answers.

CHAPTER 3

GOALS

to understand the origin of evil; to understand that God promised to redeem his people and did so by sending Jesus Christ, his Son

GETTING READY

■ *Materials needed:*

Bibles—preferably one for each young person

Paper and markers for Section Two

Adult Focus

No one escapes suffering in life. In the face of pain—whether big or small—we look for reasons; we seek explanations; we ask, "Why?"

The realization that suffering is a part of the human condition still does not answer the deeper questions. How did suffering enter into a world created good by God? Was there an original goodness and happiness that human beings once had with God, but which was somehow lost?

Carefully read Genesis 3:1–23. Note how the author describes the first man and woman as breaking their friendship with God and shattering their own happy existence.

Introduction (__ min.)

Gather the group around the prayer table in the prayer space. Ask the group to reflect quietly as you lead them in the following prayer:

God,
we pray for ourselves,
growing up in an unsteady and confusing world.

Show us that your ways give more life than the ways of the world,
and that following you is better than chasing after selfish goals.

Help us to take failure,
not as a measure of our worth,
but as a chance for a new start.

Give us strength to hold our faith in you,
and to keep alive our joy in your Creation.

We ask this through Christ our Lord.
Amen.

Read aloud the paragraph on page 16 and lead the group in a discussion of the questions.

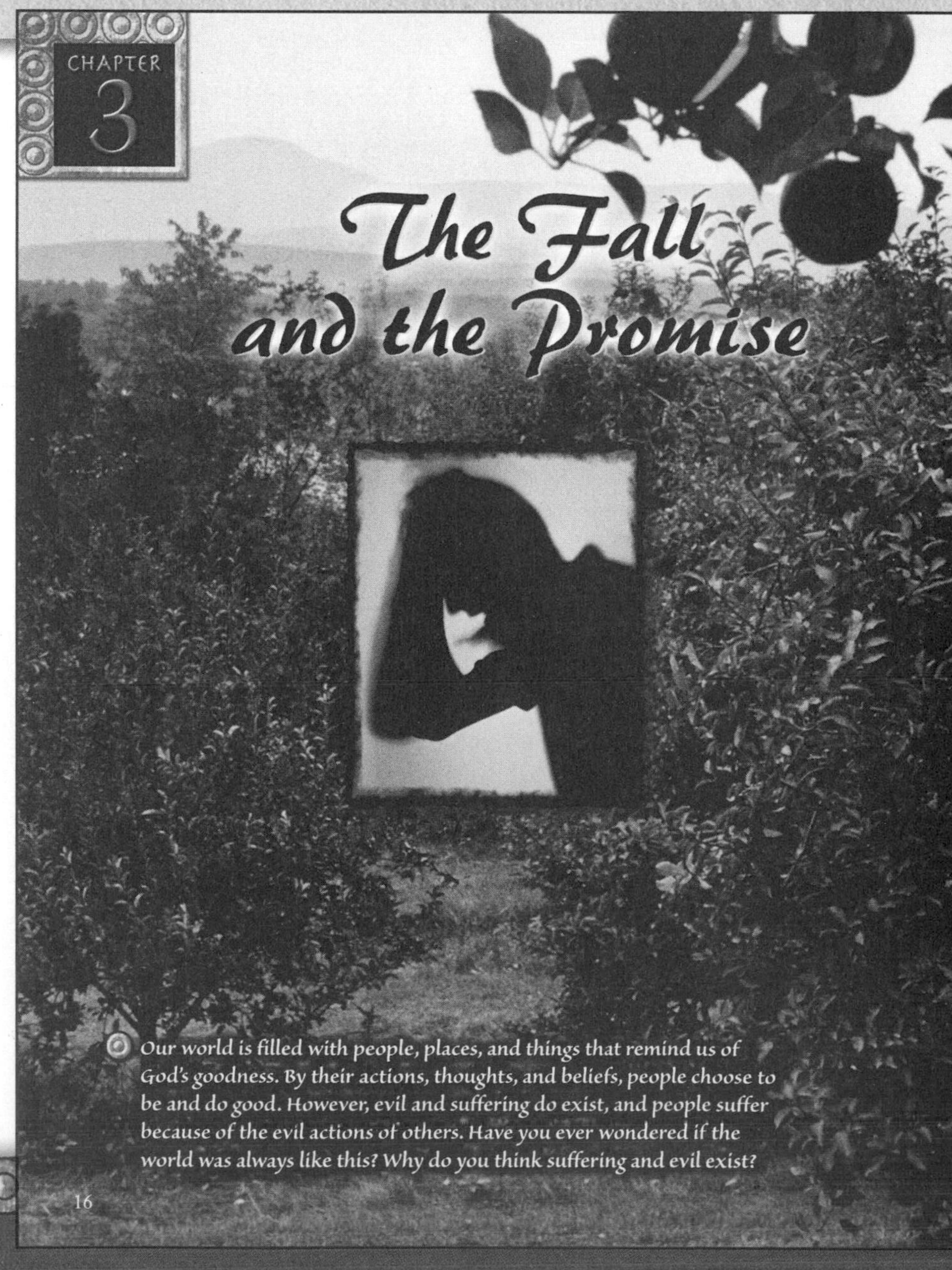

Our world is filled with people, places, and things that remind us of God's goodness. By their actions, thoughts, and beliefs, people choose to be and do good. However, evil and suffering do exist, and people suffer because of the evil actions of others. Have you ever wondered if the world was always like this? Why do you think suffering and evil exist?

In considering the topic of Original Sin, it is important to remember that we are born into a sinful condition, yet we are not personally responsible for this condition. We live in a sinful world. Because of Original Sin, we find within ourselves the tendency or inclination toward evil. We can choose evil, thereby committing personal sin, or, with the help of God, we can choose good.

The Genesis story does not end in tragedy; it ends with the promise of Salvation. Genesis 3:15 is the first promise of a Redeemer: the Messiah, or Savior, who would come to save God's people. Jesus Christ is that Savior. Through his Paschal Mystery—his suffering, Death, Resurrection, and Ascension—Jesus saves us from evil and shares God's life and love with us.

Reflection

Consider a time when you were faced with tragedy and came through it. How was God present to you? Think about how you might share this experience with your group to give them hope and a better understanding of the gracious love of God.

 **Evil and suffering entered the world through human choice.**

We do not have to live very long to know that while life is filled with hope and joy, pain and disappointment are also part of life. Humans suffer from the effects of hatred, greed, and selfishness. The daily news is filled with reports of violence, suffering, and death, often brought about by human beings themselves.

Life is a mixture of good and bad. People may have high hopes; they also may have shattered dreams. People know happiness; they also experience sorrow.

Why is life both beautiful and tragic? The writers of the Book of Genesis asked the same puzzling question. As an answer, the authors, whom God inspired, tried to explain the origins of evil in the world. The Genesis authors wanted to teach us that evil has been part of the human experience since the very beginning.

In the second Creation account found in Genesis, the first man and woman, known as Adam and Eve, lived in and cared for a beautiful garden. The garden was God's gift to them. Adam and Eve did not suffer. They did not experience loneliness, pain, or worry. They lived in harmony with God, with each other, and with all of God's Creation. The Genesis authors wanted to show that God had created human beings to be in friendship with him, and in harmony with all of his Creation.

In the story God told Adam, "You are free to eat from any of the trees of the garden except the tree of knowledge of good and bad. From that tree you shall not eat; the moment you eat from it you are surely doomed to die" (Genesis 2:16–17).

17

Presentation (___ min.)

 Evil and suffering entered the world through human choice.

Have volunteers read aloud the paragraphs in Section One on pages 17 and 18. Stress that the story is not an eyewitness account. It is intended to teach a religious truth through symbols. Ask the following questions:

- How did the author of Genesis try to answer the question "Why is life both beautiful and tragic?" (He told a story to try to explain the origins of evil in the world.)
- According to the Genesis story, how did sin and evil enter the world? (Adam and Eve listened to the serpent. They thought they would be like God if they ate the forbidden fruit.)
- What was the cause of this break in the relationship between

God and the first man and woman? (Adam and Eve disobeyed God and chose evil over good.) This first sin committed by the first human beings is called *Original Sin* (see glossary page 126).

Discuss the question at the end of Section One on page 18. Encourage the young people to write their responses in the space provided.

All of us suffer from the effects of Original Sin.

Have the young people read Section Two on pages 18–19 silently. Then divide them into four groups and assign each group a
different symbol from the story:

- garden
- serpent
- fruit of the forbidden tree
- Adam and Eve being sent out of the garden.

Then the spirit of evil appeared. Disguised as a serpent, it spoke first to the woman, asking her whether God had really told her not to eat from any of the trees in the garden. The woman replied that God had told them they could eat the fruit of any tree except the tree in the middle of the garden. If they ate or touched the fruit from that tree, they would die. The serpent assured her that she would not die if she ate the fruit. In fact, the serpent said, as soon as she and Adam ate the fruit they would be like God and know what is good and what is bad.

The woman saw how beautiful the tree was and imagined how delicious its fruit would be to eat. She thought about how wonderful it would be to become like God. So she took the fruit and ate it. Then she gave some to Adam and he ate it, too.

By doing this, Adam and Eve rejected the wonderful gifts that God had given them. Through their own actions they chose evil over good. The Genesis authors wanted to show that evil and suffering had entered into our world through the human choice to disobey God. The man and the woman had broken their friendship with God and had lost the right to be with him in the garden. The authors showed this by having God send the couple away from the garden.

What do you think led the first humans to make the choice they did in this story?

All of us suffer from the effects of Original Sin.

The story of Adam and Eve taught very important truths of faith. It was the kind of dramatic story that was easy for the ancient Israelites to remember and understand. It was built on symbols that were very familiar to them.

The Genesis authors wanted to show God's love for the first human beings by placing them in a garden filled with running water, lush plants, and trees filled with fruit. To the Israelites, who had been living in or near a desert, the garden was a symbol of happiness and of God's grace. **Grace** is a participation, or a sharing, in God's life and friendship. This free and undeserved gift of grace introduces us into the life of the Most Blessed Trinity and helps us to respond to God's call to become his children.

The garden is not the only symbol in the story of Adam and Eve. The Genesis authors used objects and actions as symbols as well:

Optional Activity

Ask the young people to brainstorm a list of current movies that are about the struggle between good and evil. Discuss the following:

How do the characters choose which way to act? How are they influenced by others? by God?

Answer for page 18:

Accept all reasonable answers.

- To the Israelites, the serpent was a symbol of evil. The Israelites worshiped only the one true God. Their pagan neighbors, however, often worshiped serpents.
- Hearing that Adam and Eve chose to eat the fruit of the forbidden tree helped the Israelites to appreciate the power they had as human beings to choose between good and evil.
- Adam and Eve's being sent out of the garden reflected the consequences of turning away from God and the loss of God's grace.

The story of the garden dramatizes how close the relationship is between God and humans. But it also tells us about the shattering of that relationship.

Adam and Eve did not respond gratefully or lovingly to God. They gave into temptation because they thought their choice would bring them happiness. Adam and Eve turned away from God, selfishly choosing what they wanted rather than what God wanted for them. This story depicts the first sin committed by the first human beings. We call this sin **Original Sin.** Every person is born with Original Sin. Because of Original Sin, each one of us is inclined to sin, and each of us is subject to ignorance, suffering, and death. The effects of Original Sin challenge us throughout life.

This simple story from Genesis offers much truth about our relationship with God and our need to be brought back into the life of grace.

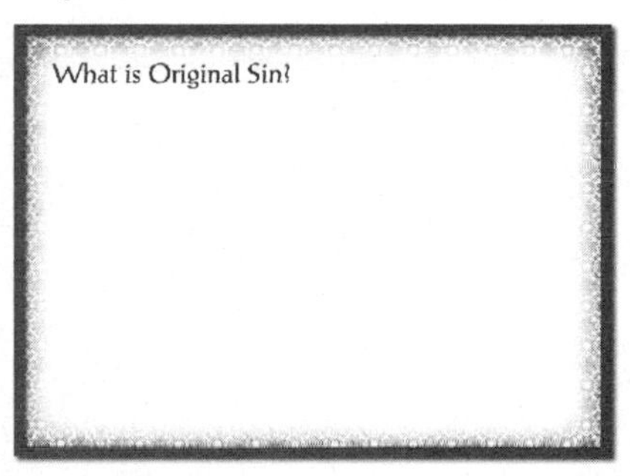
What is Original Sin?

19

Give each group a sheet of paper and some markers. Instruct them to draw the symbol and write a brief explanation of the symbol. Allow time for each group to present their symbol and explanation. Display the symbols as groups finish their presentations.

Explain that the meaning of each symbol helps us to understand a religious truth, that is, a truth that will help us to live in relationship with God. Call attention to the gift of grace, a participation, or sharing, in God's life and friendship.

Discuss the question at the end of Section Two on page 19. Have the young people write their responses in the space provided.

Optional Activity

As a group, write a prayer asking for help in facing the challenges that the effects of Original Sin bring us. Pray the prayer together.

Answer for page 19:

Allow the young people to answer in their own words. Help them to include the definition of Original Sin found in the Glossary on page 126.

God promised to send the world a Savior.

Ask the young people to silently read Section Three on page 20. Have them recall that God promised the first man and woman that he would send a Savior.

Ask the following questions. Have the young people underline the answers in their texts.

- When God's people were discouraged and without hope, whom did God inspire to give them encouragement? (The prophets reminded the people that God had not forgotten them.)
- What kind of Messiah was described by the prophets? (The Messiah would restore the people's relationship with God.)
- What did Jesus, the "New Adam," do for us? (He restored us to God's life and love.)
- At Mass, what great mystery of faith do we proclaim? (We celebrate the Paschal Mystery: Through Jesus' suffering, Death, Resurrection, and Ascension he saves us from evil and shares God's life and love with us.)

Conclude this section by having the young people write their responses to the question at the end of Section Three on page 20.

Do YOU Know?

Some of the evil that continues to be present in our world exists because people still choose to sin. It is important to remember though that God's grace can strengthen each of us to overcome evil.

God promised to send the world a Savior.

The Genesis story of Adam and Eve did not end in despair. It ended on a note of hope and mercy. The inspired authors of Genesis knew that God would never abandon human beings. In the story God had promised that sin and evil would not triumph, that the offspring of Adam and Eve would one day win over evil.

The Israelites knew that the journey back to a full and loving relationship with God was going to be a difficult one. Even though people would still sin, God would forgive them and never stop loving them.

When the Israelites felt low and hopeless, God encouraged them. He sent special people called prophets to speak for him and to remind people that he had not forgotten them. Through the prophets, God called Israel and all nations to turn to him. He promised to send them the Messiah, the Anointed One, who would restore their relationship with God. God fulfilled his promise by sending his own Son to us.

Those who first followed Christ identified him as the "New Adam"—the new Man. They believed that Jesus Christ was the Son of God who came into the world and brought victory over evil and sin. Through his obedience to God the Father unto death, Jesus Christ became the Savior of the world. Through Jesus, we are restored to God's life and love. Faith is our necessary response to the Salvation that Jesus has won for us.

The New Testament tells us about the life of Jesus, his Death on the cross, and his being raised from the dead. Through his suffering, Death, and Resurrection, Jesus Christ saves us from evil and shares God's life and love in a human way. The Church calls the suffering, Death, Resurrection, and Ascension of Jesus Christ the **Paschal Mystery**; by this great mystery of faith we are redeemed. We celebrate this great mystery each time we gather for the celebration of the Mass.

How would you explain to a younger person that God fulfilled his promise?

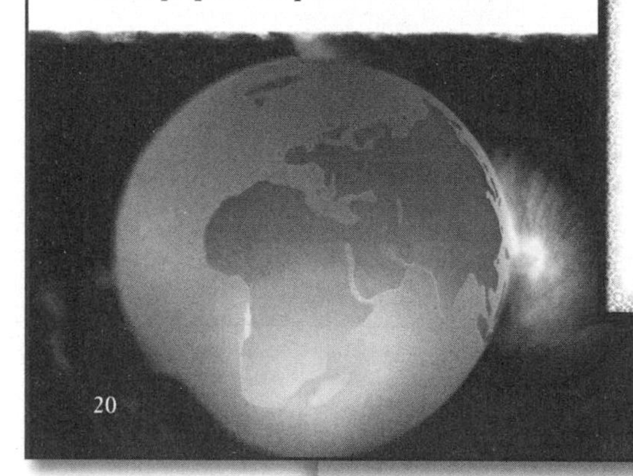

20

Do YOU Know?

Have a volunteer read aloud the "Do You Know?" feature on page 20. Emphasize that evil exists because people choose to sin. Discuss the importance of God's grace in overcoming evil.

Answer for page 20:

Possible answers include: God fulfilled his promise to send the world a Savior by sending his own Son to us, Jesus Christ. Through Jesus' suffering, Death, Resurrection, and Ascension he saves us from evil and shares God's life and love in a human way.

GROWING IN FAITH

PRAY

Just as God called us into being, he continually calls us to meet him through prayer. In prayer we respond to that call, and we raise our hearts and minds to God. Silently reflect on the following prayer:

✝ God our Creator,
You created all people out of love.
You judge us fairly and with justice,
but in mercy you redeem us
through Jesus Christ our Lord.
Amen.

REMEMBER

The Church teaches...

- God created humans to be in friendship with him and in harmony with each other and with all Creation.
- Sin entered the world through human choice.
- The first sin committed by the first human beings is called Original Sin. Every human being is born with Original Sin and suffers from its effects.
- Jesus Christ is the "New Adam" whose obedience even to death saves us from sin.
- Jesus Christ fulfills all God's promises and frees us to share in God's life and love.

Faith Words

grace (p. 18)
Original Sin (p. 19)
Paschal Mystery (p. 20)

REFLECT & ACT

What evidence of Original Sin can you find in today's headlines and news stories? Could any of these situations have been avoided?

What can you do to lessen pain and evil in the world? What actions can you take to share the Christian belief that Jesus is a sign of hope?

21

Conclusion (__ min.)

Growing in Faith

Have the young people close their books. Ask them what they have learned in this lesson about God's friendship with humans, Original Sin, Jesus as the "New Adam," grace, and the Paschal Mystery. Reopen the books to page 21. Was everything from the **Remember** and **Faith Words** sections named? If not, point these out and help the group name the remaining concepts.

Invite the young people to read the **Reflect and Act** section and to write their responses in the spaces provided. If desired, play some soft instrumental music while they do this.

When they have finished, share suggestions on how the young people can help to lessen pain and evil in the world. (Examples: avoid saying or doing hurtful things; comfort the sick; befriend the lonely; speak out against immorality in the media; say no to temptations to sin.)

Conclude the lesson by gathering the group around the prayer table. Have a volunteer read aloud the paragraph in the **Pray** section on page 21. Then, offer the prayer together.

CATECHISM FOCUS

"Although it is proper to each individual, original sin does not have the character of a personal fault in any of Adam's descendants. It is a deprivation of original holiness and justice, but human nature has not been totally corrupted." (*CCC*, 405)

For additional reference and reflection, see *CCC*, 396–412.

Answers for page 21:

Left column:
Accept all reasonable responses.

Right column:
Encourage the young people to be realistic in their planning, but prayerful in their desire to make a better world.

CHAPTER 4

GOALS

to learn about the mystery of the Incarnation; to appreciate the Blessed Trinity as the central mystery of the Christian faith

GETTING READY

- ***Materials needed:***

A simple prayer environment: Bible, decorative cloth, icon or statue of Mary

Pieces of art for optional activity in Section One

Five (5) Bibles for optional activity in Section Three

Adult Focus

The Incarnation is the truth that the Son of God, the second Person of the Blessed Trinity, became man and lived among us in order to accomplish our Salvation. The Father sent his Son so that we might be saved from sin and restored to the friendship for which God created us. Jesus Christ is the Son of God, the promised Savior.

By sending his Son, and later the Holy Spirit in the name of the Son, God revealed something truly amazing. God, although one, is not solitary. God is three Persons in one God, the Blessed Trinity: God the Father, God the Son, and God the Holy Spirit.

Introduction (__ min.)

Gather the group around the prayer table. Ask the young people: Have you ever been asked to do something that required a generous response? Did you pray for guidance?

Then, invite the young people to sit quietly for a moment and to consider any difficult decisions they are facing. Then pray the Hail Mary (see page 119) together, asking Mary's prayers for each person present.

Have them open their books to page 22. Read together the question and lead the group in a discussion. Ask them to relate the phrase "God works in mysterious ways" to their own experiences.

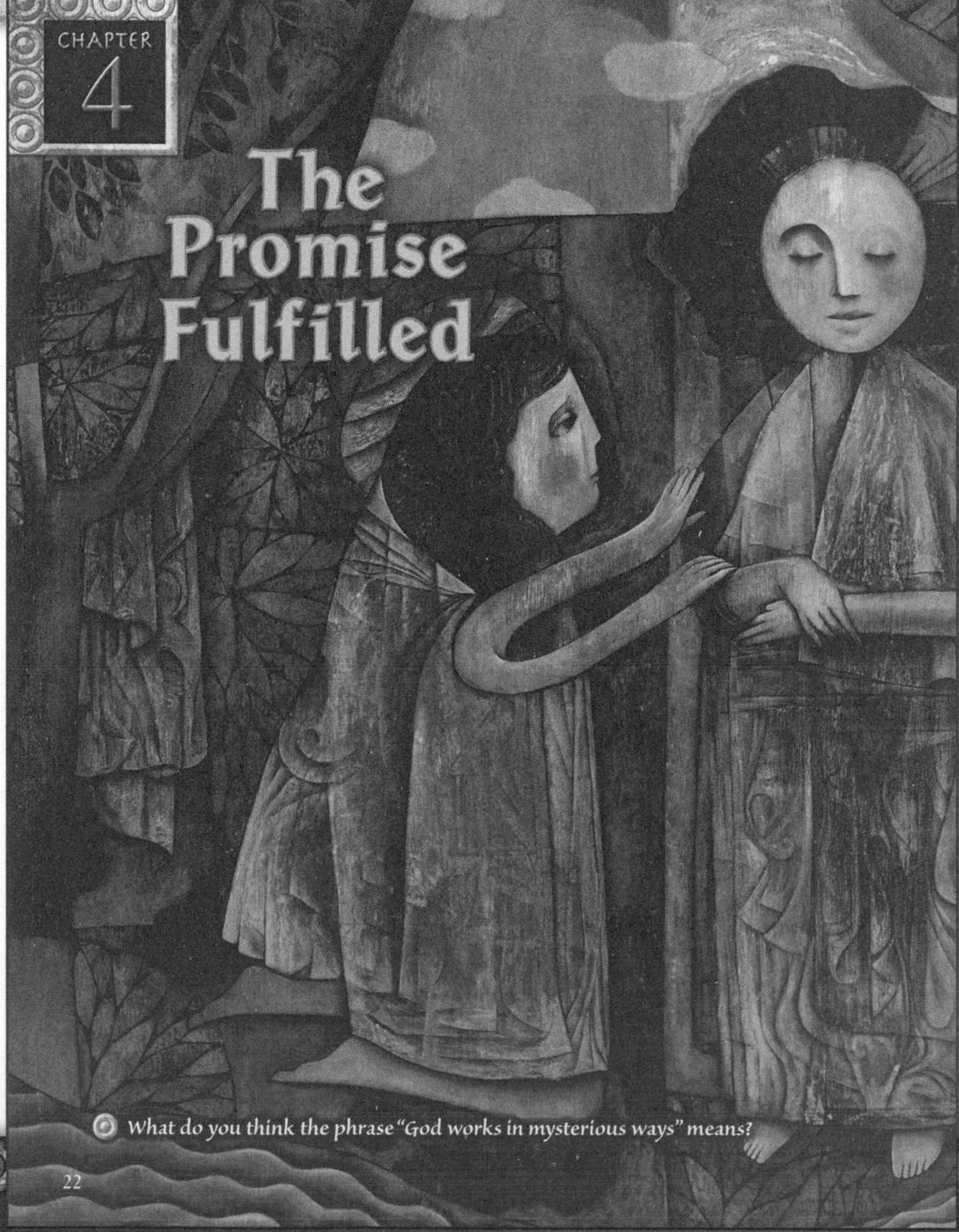

This Revelation tells us who God is, a community of love. It also tells us something about our relationship with God. For even more important than knowing about God is knowing God personally. Jesus Christ, the Son of God, leads us to the love of the Father and the Holy Spirit. Because the Son of God became one of us, we can once again share in God's life and love.

Reflection

Young people need to clarify and deepen their faith in Jesus Christ, the Son of God who became man. As you prepare for this session, write in your own words what we believe as Catholics about Jesus. This personal statement will help you share more deeply your own faith in the Incarnation.

God sent his only Son to us.

Over many centuries God prepared the people of Israel for the fulfillment of his promises. Little by little he revealed, through the words of the prophets, some insight into the Promised One to come. The prophets foretold that the Promised One would be from the family of David, the greatest king of Israel. He would be born in Bethlehem. He would be called God's Anointed One, the Messiah.

Knowing the message of the prophets, the first Christians could see that Jesus Christ fulfilled the prophets' words. The early Christians preached this Good News. Some were inspired by the Holy Spirit to record their beliefs and experiences in the pages of what we now know as the New Testament.

We read in the New Testament that over two thousand years ago God sent an angel to a young Jewish girl who lived in the town of Nazareth. Her name was Mary, and she was promised in marriage to a man named Joseph. After greeting her, the angel said, "Do not be afraid, Mary, for you have found favor with God. Behold, you will conceive in your womb and bear a son, and you shall name him Jesus. He will be great and will be called Son of the Most High" (Luke 1:30–32).

Because she had not had relations with a man, Mary questioned the angel. And then the angel told her something astonishing: "The holy Spirit will come upon you, and the power of the Most High will overshadow you. Therefore the child to be born will be called holy, the Son of God" (Luke 1:35). Mary totally accepted what God wanted her to do. She told the angel, "Behold, I am the handmaid of the Lord. May it be done to me according to your word" (Luke 1:38).

23

Presentation (__ min.)

God sent his only Son to us.

Have the young people read the first two paragraphs of Section One on page 23 and underline the clues that the prophets gave about the promised Savior. (He would be in the family of David, born in Bethlehem, the Messiah.) Review these, elaborating on the meaning of the term Messiah as "Anointed One." (Jesus was the Savior God had promised. Through his sufferings Jesus would change the world.)

Have them read the remaining paragraphs on page 23 about the Son of God's coming. Emphasize Mary's amazement at how unexpectedly God would fulfill the promise through her. Mary was troubled, yet she placed her trust in God's word and promise.

Then have the young people complete the reading of Section One on page 24. Ask volunteers to tell the story of the Annunciation and why it is so important. Have young people write their responses to the questions at the end of Section One on page 24.

 Jesus Christ is true God and true man.

Ask the young people to think of some ways we learn about Jesus. How do we know who he is, how he came into the world, what he taught, and what happened to him? Emphasize the meaning of the Gospels—the accounts found in the New Testament of God's Revelation through Jesus Christ.

We call the angel's visit to Mary and the announcement that she would be the virgin mother of the Son of God the **Annunciation**. The example of Mary's "yes" to God inspires us to work with her son as she did. Since Mary is the Mother of God and Mother of the Church, we lovingly call her Blessed Mother.

Luke chose to record the events of the Annunciation in his Gospel. This is an important indicator that the first Christians believed that God had fulfilled his promise in a way that no one had expected. The Promised One was not only a great man, he was God's own Son as well.

Why do you think Mary responded as she did to God's message? Would it be hard for you to respond as Mary did? Why or why not?

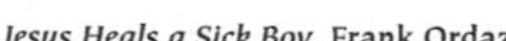
Jesus Heals a Sick Boy, Frank Ordaz

 Jesus Christ is true God and true man.

Where do we discover the truth about Jesus—about who he really is? The writings of the New Testament proclaim the Good News of Jesus Christ. The word *gospel* means "good news." The **Gospels** are the accounts of God's Revelation through Jesus Christ. The Gospels of Matthew, Mark, Luke, and John have a central place in Scripture because they are all about the Good News of Jesus. These four accounts were written after the Death and Resurrection of Jesus. They are God's Word, and they also express the faith of the early Church community.

Although they are not biographies, the Gospels are a rich source of information about Jesus. They give us a stirring picture of Jesus' humanity—who he was and what he did:

- Jesus was the son of Mary.
- He obeyed his parents, prayed, and visited the Temple.
- He labored as a carpenter, enjoyed friendship, and felt emotions like sadness, happiness, anger, and love.
- He suffered and died.

The friends of Jesus traveled the same roads as he did, sharing his joys and sorrows. Jesus' friends did not doubt that he was human, just as they were. But Jesus dared to say and do things only God could do:

- He healed the sick, restored sight to the blind, and brought the dead back to life.

24

Optional Activity

Prior to the group's meeting, compile several depictions of Mary and the Annunciation that use different forms of art (painting, sculpture, icon, etc.) and that reflect various cultures. Be sure to include the art piece on pages 22–23 of the text.

Take time to examine the different depictions and invite observations about the style of art and how the artist was trying to portray Mary.

Answers for page 24:

Accept all reasonable answers.

- He calmed raging seas. He fed thousands with a small amount of food that was meant to serve only a few.
- He forgave people's sins.

Through such words and deeds his followers came to know that Jesus was more than a mere man: Jesus was divine.

Jesus himself expressed his divinity clearly when he spoke about God his Father. One day Jesus asked his followers: "Do you not believe that I am in the Father and the Father is in me?" (John 14:10). Jesus was also establishing his own identity when he said, "The Father and I are one" (John 10:30). We learn from the very first chapter of John's Gospel one of the great truths of our faith: Jesus is the Word of God, and the Word became flesh, taking on our human nature and dwelling among us. The **Incarnation** is the truth that the Son of God, the second Person of the Blessed Trinity, became man and lived among us in order to accomplish our Salvation.

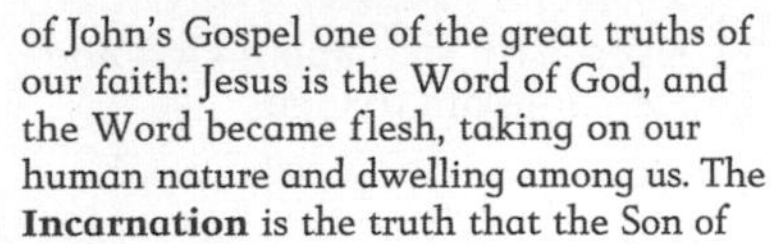

Jesus Calms the Stormy Sea, Frank Ordaz

From its beginning the Church has continually searched for a deeper understanding of Jesus. In the early days of the Church, disputes about Jesus' nature arose. Some people began to teach that Jesus was only a man. Others taught that he was the Son of God but not fully human.

In the fifth century all the bishops met to discuss the issue of Jesus' humanity and divinity. With the guidance of the Holy Spirit, the bishops proclaimed this great truth of faith: Jesus Christ is true God and true man. This means that Jesus is both fully human and fully divine.

Do YOU Know?

We learn from the Gospels of Luke and Matthew that God's promises were fulfilled in the birth of Jesus. However, in Matthew's Gospel the story is told from Joseph's perspective rather than Mary's. In this Gospel we read that an angel came to Joseph in a dream and spoke these assuring words: "Joseph, son of David, do not be afraid to take Mary your wife into your home. For it is through the holy Spirit that this child has been conceived in her. She will bear a son and you are to name him Jesus, because he will save his people from their sins" (Matthew 1:20–21). The very name *Jesus* means "God saves."

What do we mean by the Incarnation? What does it tell us about the humanity and divinity of Christ?

Have volunteers read the paragraphs in Section Two on pages 24–25. Elaborate on the meaning of the word *Incarnation*—the truth that the Son of God, the second Person of the Blessed Trinity, became man and lived among us in order to accomplish our Salvation. Stress that the Incarnation is a central truth of our Catholic faith. Ask: What does the art on pages 24 and 25 tell us about Jesus?

Have the young people write their responses to the questions at the end of Section Two on page 25.

After reading the **Do You Know?** feature, you may want to do the following:

Read together the sections in Matthew's Gospel that deal with Joseph's dreams (Matthew 1:18–25 and Matthew 2:13–15). Ask the young people to imagine what it would be like if they could interview Joseph about his life. Brainstorm together a list of questions they would want to ask him. Then divide the young people into smaller groups and assign each group a question or two. How do they think Joseph would respond? On what would they base their answers? Come together, and listen to each group's responses.

Do YOU Know?

Read the "Do You Know?" feature on page 25 and discuss how Joseph was called to be part of the plan for the Incarnation.

Explain that in the Bible we read about people having "prophetic dreams"—dreams that reveal something to someone called to be an important part of God's plan.

Answers for page 25:

See Glossary, page 125. The Incarnation tells us that Christ is true God and true man.

Jesus teaches us about God and the Kingdom of God.

Have the young people read Section Three on page 26 silently. Then:

◎ Have the young people identify the Blessed Trinity by asking: Who are the three divine Persons in the Blessed Trinity? (God the Father, God the Son, God the Holy Spirit)

Reiterate the importance of the Blessed Trinity in Catholic belief (see page 26).

◎ Talk about the Kingdom of God as the power of God's love active in our lives and in our world. Emphasize that the Kingdom of God is present now and will come in its fullness at the end of time. Have the young people describe how the Kingdom of God is referred to in the parables (see page 26). In groups of three, have the young people discuss what each one can do to help bring about God's Kingdom of justice, peace, and love in their home, school, and neighborhood.

Have the young people write their descriptions in the space provided at the end of Section Three on page 26.

Answer for page 26:

Accept all reasonable answers.

Jesus teaches us about God and the Kingdom of God.

Jesus' followers knew about and believed in the one true God. But Jesus taught them more. Jesus taught them about God his Father, and he spoke to his followers about the Holy Spirit: "The Advocate, the holy Spirit that the Father will send in my name—he will teach you everything and remind you of all that [I] told you" (John 14:26).

We learn from Jesus that God is Father, Son, and Holy Spirit. This teaching of Jesus' does not mean that there are three gods. It means that there are three Divine Persons in one God: the Father, the Son, and the Holy Spirit. This is what we call the **Blessed Trinity**:

- God the Father is the first Person of the Blessed Trinity.
- God the Son is the second Person of the Blessed Trinity.
- God the Holy Spirit is the third Person of the Blessed Trinity.

God is one community of three Divine Persons, and these three are one and share a single mission.

Some people ask, "How can there be three Persons in one God?" This is a matter of faith. It is, in fact, the central mystery of our faith, revealed in the Incarnation and in the sending of the Holy Spirit. Belief in the Blessed Trinity is at the very root of our faith. We celebrate the relationship of Father, Son, and Holy Spirit in our prayer and in our worship. We can see this most particularly in our Baptism: We are all baptized in the name of the Father, and of the Son, and of the Holy Spirit.

Jesus told us more about God in his teaching on the Kingdom of God. Jesus spoke constantly about the Kingdom, or Reign, of God. He invited us all to enter the Kingdom, to follow God's will through our words and deeds.

Jesus never defined the Kingdom of God. Instead, he used beautiful stories called parables to describe the Kingdom, how important it is, and how it grows. Many of these parables begin with the words, "the kingdom of heaven is like. . . ." In the thirteenth chapter of Matthew's Gospel, we read that the Kingdom can be compared to:

- a tiny seed that will blossom into a large bush
- the yeast that makes bread rise
- a buried treasure or a pearl of great price
- a net thrown into the sea that collects fish of every kind.

The Kingdom of God is not a place or a political state. **The Kingdom of God** is the power of God's love active in our lives and in our world. Through his teaching, his miracles, and his healing ministry, Jesus brought about God's Kingdom in a unique way. Jesus himself is the Good News of God's Kingdom—a Kingdom that is here now and yet is growing until the end of time. We believe that the Church is the seed and beginning of the Kingdom of God on earth.

Describe the Kingdom of God in your own words.

26

Optional Activity

Review how to locate a chapter and verse in the Bible (see page 118). Divide the young people into five groups and have each group look up the following passages in the Bible:

- **Matthew 13:31–32 (mustard seed)**
- **Matthew 13:33 (yeast in the dough)**
- **Matthew 13:44 (buried treasure)**
- **Matthew 13:45–46 (pearl of great price)**
- **Matthew 13:47–48 (net)**

Ask each group to explain what Jesus is trying to teach us about the Kingdom of God.

GROWING IN FAITH

PRAY

The priest's greeting to the gathered assembly at Mass expresses our relationship to the Trinity in this way: "The grace of our Lord Jesus Christ, and the love of God, and the communion of the Holy Spirit be with you all." Our prayer, both personal and communal, draws us into the life of the Trinity. Pray together:

✝ Glory to the Father,
and to the Son,
and to the Holy Spirit:
as it was in the beginning, is now,
and will be for ever.
Amen.

REMEMBER

The Church teaches...

- The Blessed Virgin Mary conceived by the power of the Holy Spirit and gave birth to the Son of God.
- The Blessed Trinity is the three Divine Persons in one God: the Father, the Son, and the Holy Spirit.
- God the Father is the first Person of the Blessed Trinity; God the Son is the second Person of the Blessed Trinity; God the Holy Spirit is the third Person of the Blessed Trinity.
- Jesus Christ is the Son of God, the second Person of the Blessed Trinity who became one of us. He is true God and true man.
- The Kingdom of God is the power of God's love active in our lives and in our world. It is present now and will come in its fullness at the end of time.

Faith Words

Annunciation (p. 24)
Gospels (p. 24)
Incarnation (p. 25)
Blessed Trinity (p. 26)
Kingdom of God (p. 26)

REFLECT & ACT

What does Jesus' teaching on the Kingdom of God mean for us? When we follow Jesus, when we live by his example and are guided by the Holy Spirit, we help to build God's Kingdom. We are called to bring God's love to the world, to all people, and to all Creation.

Think of some things you can do to further the Kingdom of God on earth.

How would you explain to a friend the Church teaching that Jesus is both fully human and fully divine?

27

CATECHISM FOCUS

"The unique and altogether singular event of the Incarnation of the Son of God does not mean that Jesus Christ is part God and part man. . . . He became truly man while remaining truly God." (*CCC*, 464)

For additional reference and reflection, see *CCC*, 464–483.

Conclusion (__ min.)

Growing in Faith

Have the young people close their books. Ask them what they have learned in this lesson about the Annunciation, the Gospels, the Incarnation, the Blessed Trinity, and the Kingdom of God. Reopen the books to page 27. Was everything from the **Remember** and **Faith Words** sections named? If not, point these out and help the group name the remaining concepts.

Invite the young people to read the **Reflect and Act** section and to write their responses in the spaces provided. If desired, play some soft instrumental music while they do this. Then, have volunteers share how they will explain that Jesus is truly man (like us in all things except sin) and truly God (one with the Father and the Holy Spirit).

Gather around the prayer table. Have a volunteer read aloud the paragraph in the **Pray** section on page 27. Then, offer the prayer together.

Answers for page 27:

Left column:
Accept all reasonable answers.

Right column:
Possible answers include:

I would tell my friend stories from the life of Jesus Christ that show that he is true God and true man.

CHAPTER 5

GOAL

to learn about Jesus' suffering, Death, and Resurrection

GETTING READY

■ ***Materials needed:***

prayer table environment: Bible, decorative cloth, and crucifix

Bibles—preferably one for each young person

drawing paper and markers for optional activity in Section One

poster board or chalk for Section Three

Adult Focus

To some of the Jewish people, Jesus was the Messiah for whom they had waited. He held them spellbound with the message that the Kingdom of God was theirs. Jesus spoke to the crowds in a way that no one else had done. He did not protect them from the harsh truth that following him would include suffering. These stark words did not sit well with the crowd, or even with Jesus' closest followers. Yet the prophets had hinted at the idea that the Messiah would have to suffer.

Jesus did not live up to some people's expectations of the Messiah. Instead, he chose to follow the single purpose of his mission: to do the will of his Father. Jesus' mission ran counter to these people's expectations, so he was rejected. Outright rejection of Jesus came quickly on the heels of his triumphant

Introduction (__ min.)

Gather the group with their books around the prayer table. Draw attention to the crucifix you have placed on the prayer table and explain that today we will be learning that Jesus died and rose from the dead. If desired, pass the crucifix around the circle and invite each person to hold it for a moment and to consider what he or she needs to ask of Jesus in this time of prayer. Then pray the following:

"Save us, Savior of the world,
for by your Cross and Resurrection
you have set us free. "

Have them open their books to page 28. Read together the story of Pedro Calungsod on page 28 and discuss the questions that follow.

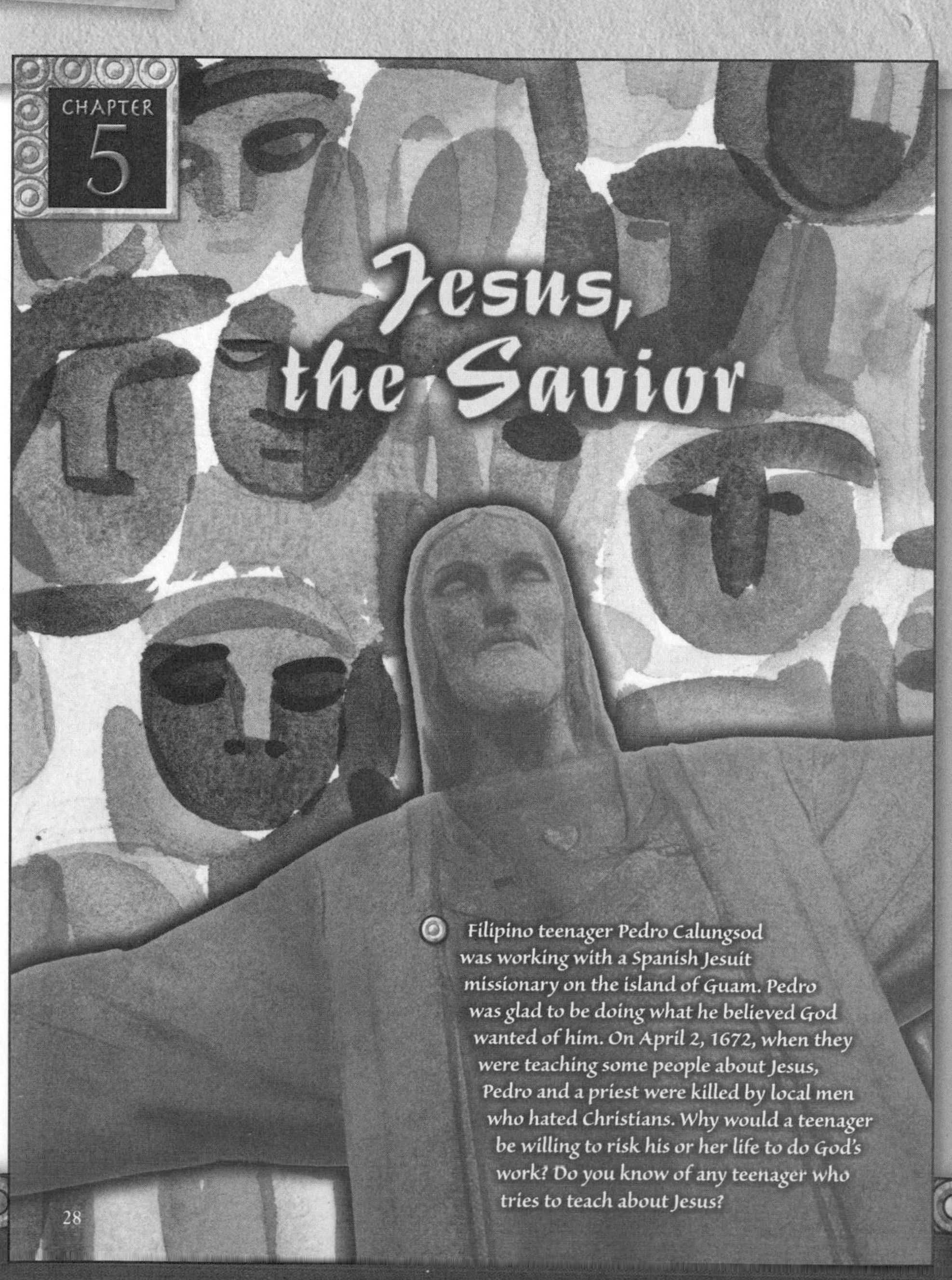

entry into Jerusalem. Jesus' Crucifixion and Death confirmed the belief of many that Jesus could not have been the Messiah. But those who experienced the risen Christ believed in his victory over death. The forces of sin and evil did not have the final word.

Suffering is not an end in itself. Hope keeps us from being overwhelmed by our present sufferings. For Christians, the basis of hope is our faith in the power of Jesus' Resurrection and his promise that we will rise with him. As Saint Paul said, "If Christ has not been raised, then empty [too] is our preaching; empty, too, your faith. . . . If for this life only we have hoped in Christ, we are the most pitiable people of all" (1 Corinthians 15:14, 19).

Reflection

Reflect on Saint Paul's words so that you will be able to share more deeply the meaning of Jesus' mission. What message of hope do you want to leave with your class after this lesson?

Jesus faithfully did the work God his Father gave him.

One of the central beliefs of the people of Old Testament times was that of a **Messiah**—a person God planned to send to save the people from their sins. God fulfilled his promise by sending his own Son, Jesus Christ, to be the Savior and Messiah. In the time that Jesus lived on earth, there was a great deal of speculation about when this Messiah, or Savior, would come and what he would be like. Authors of the books of the Old Testament had described the Messiah as anointed king, just ruler, liberator, and Savior. He would restore Israel to its rightful place as a kingdom ruled only by God and influential over other nations.

Most Jews hoped for a powerful king who would free Israel from domination by foreigners and bring prosperity to the people. The symbol of this new kingdom was a great banquet at which the king would preside and the people of Israel would celebrate their victory over their oppressors. For this reason many of the people were not prepared for the kingdom that Jesus announced.

According to the Gospels a large crowd often followed Jesus, but Jesus was never controlled by the whims of the crowd. When they wanted to make him king, Jesus fled. When they asked him, "Are you the one who is to come or should we look for another?" (Matthew 11:3), Jesus answered by using the words of the prophet Isaiah to describe the time of the Messiah: "The blind regain their sight, the lame walk, lepers are cleansed, the deaf hear, the dead are raised, and the poor have the good news proclaimed to them" (Matthew 11:5).

From the Gospel accounts we learn that early Christians believed that Jesus was the Messiah. The word *messiah* comes from the Hebrew word for "anointed." In the New

Presentation (__ min.)

Jesus faithfully did the work God his Father gave him.

Discuss the following with the group:

- Why didn't Jesus please all of the people?
- What guided and directed Jesus' life?

Distribute Bibles to the young people. Have them use the Bibles to find the following passages from the Gospels in which Jesus seems to be acting contrary to the crowd or, in some cases, contrary to those in authority:

- Matthew 9:1–8 (healing of a paralytic)
- Mark 14:60–64 (Jesus before the Sanhedrin)
- Luke 4:14–30 (teaching in the synagogue)

◎ John 6:1–15 (multiplication of the loaves)

Then have the young people read silently Section One on pages 29–30.

Discuss Section One by asking the following questions:

◎ How did Jesus avoid being controlled by the crowd? (Jesus, at times, fled. At other times, he refused to be the kind of Messiah the crowd expected.)

◎ What kind of Messiah did most of the crowd expect? (They looked for a political king who would help them overthrow the Romans.)

◎ What do the titles *Messiah* and *Christ* mean? (Both mean *Anointed One* and both apply to Jesus.)

◎ What does it mean to be a disciple of Jesus, the Messiah? (A disciple is one who says yes to Jesus' call to follow him.)

Have the young people write their responses to the questions at the end of Section One on page 30.

Testament, which was written in Greek, the word *christos* was used to translate *messiah*. In English this word is *Christ*. The titles Messiah, Christ, and Anointed One all mean the same thing. We call Jesus—Christ, Messiah, and Anointed One.

Jesus did not deny that he was the Messiah, but Jesus was not the kind of Messiah that the people expected. His mission was not directed toward himself or earthly kingship and prosperity, but toward his Father. The Son of God came to earth to do his Father's will: to save us from sin and unite us with himself so that we could share in God's life and love. We read in the Gospel of John that Jesus describes himself as "the way and the truth and the life. No one comes to the Father except through me" (John 14:6).

Jesus' friends realized how faithfully he had done God's will by denying himself and serving the needs of all. All of Jesus' life was a constant teaching. He:

Christ Healing the Withered Hand, James J. Tissot, circa 1870

30

- fed the hungry and helped the poor
- forgave sinners and healed the sick
- taught people about God and what he asked of them
- called all people, women and men alike, to share God's life and love.

The followers of Jesus would have to obey God's will as Jesus himself did in order to become disciples. A **disciple** is one who says yes to Jesus' call to follow him. All were welcome, but they would have to put aside selfishness to become disciples.

Did Jesus fit the people's idea of the Messiah? Why or why not?

Jesus died on the cross for us.

Jesus was completely faithful to God and to the customs and laws of his people. But Jesus dared to interpret the Law of Moses with divine authority. Such acts brought him into conflict with the religious and civil leaders of his time.

In Mark's Gospel we read that Jesus predicted that certain leaders would put him to death, but that he would rise three days later. One of Jesus' followers took him aside and urged him to see things as others did. But Jesus told his disciple that God's thinking is not like ours.

All four Gospels record the details of Jesus' Passion—his suffering and Death. Jesus and his disciples had traveled to Jerusalem for the Jewish Feast of Passover. Every year faithful Jews of Jesus' time—as well as those

Answer for page 30:

Possible answers include: Jesus did not fit the people's idea of the Messiah. The people were expecting a king who would lead them into prosperous times. Instead, Jesus preached a Kingdom of the Spirit.

Optional Activity

Read the explanation and description of the Stations of the Cross found on page 123. Assign each young person a different station (have them work in pairs if young people outnumber the stations). Give them paper and markers to illustrate their assigned station.

Instead of, or in addition to this activity, take your group to see your parish's Stations of the Cross.

today—prepared a special meal to celebrate God's delivering them from slavery in Egypt. Jesus knew that this would be his last Passover meal because he would be betrayed.

At what we now call the Last Supper, Jesus taught his disciples about love and promised them that the Father would send the Holy Spirit. Jesus went with his disciples to pray in the Garden of Olives, a beautiful garden on a hill overlooking the city of Jerusalem. There Jesus agonized over his coming death. He fell to the ground and prayed, "My Father, if it is possible, let this cup pass from me; yet, not as I will, but as you will" (Matthew 26:39).

The Agony in the Garden (Christ in the Garden of Olives), Paul Gauguin, 1889

Jesus' fear of death was very real, but his faith was rooted in his Father. He was able to face suffering and death knowing how much his Father loved him. While Jesus prayed in the garden, he was betrayed by his disciple Judas. Jesus was then arrested and brought to trial, and his other disciples deserted him, fleeing from the area.

Jesus was brought before Pontius Pilate, the Roman governor of Judea. Pilate asked Jesus whether he was the king of the Jews. Pilate knew that Jesus did not claim to be an earthly king, but Pilate still believed that any talk of kingship was a threat to Roman authority. So Jesus was condemned to die.

The Roman soldiers led Jesus to the place where he would be crucified. Crucifixion was a form of execution the Romans used for common criminals. Jesus did not struggle, protest, or resist as he was nailed to the cross. With trust and love he placed his life in his Father's care: "Father, into your hands I commend my spirit" (Luke 23:46). Jesus said this and died. Good Friday is the name we give to the day Jesus died for us.

How did Jesus' determination to do the will of his Father affect his disciples?

Do YOU Know?

We learn from many religious and political situations today that an entire nation, people, or religious group cannot be held responsible for the actions of some of its members. Blessed Pope John Paul II reminded us of this during his visit to a Roman synagogue in 1986. The Pope stated that in no way can Christians blame "the Jews as a people for what happened in Christ's passion."

31

2 Jesus died on the cross for us.

Have volunteers read the paragraphs in Section Two on pages 30 and 31. Discuss the question at the end of Section Two and encourage the young people to write their own responses in the space provided.

Then, have the young people reflect on the art on page 31. Ask them to try to identify with Jesus in the garden. What might Jesus have been thinking and feeling?

Ask the group to imagine the following scenario: You are one of Jesus' disciples. Jesus has just been crucified. How would you explain to some friends who did not know Jesus why he had been crucified?

Have them write their responses in the form of a letter.

Do YOU Know?

Explain to the young people that, over the past several centuries, groups of Christians have placed blame for Jesus' death on all Jewish people. It has led to great prejudice against and hatred toward the Jewish people. That, in turn, has resulted in terrible acts of violence and persecution. Emphasize that these kinds of behavior and attitudes are completely counter to Christian values. Read the "Do You Know?" feature on page 31. What makes this statement by Blessed Pope John Paul II so important?

Answers for page 31:

Possible answers include: When they realized that Jesus was determined to follow his Father's will and be crucified, the disciples ran away. His disciple Judas betrayed him.

By rising from the dead, Jesus Christ brings us new life.

Write the following words on the board or poster board: *abandonment*, *pain*, *ridicule*, and *rejection*.

Ask the group to suggest ways people might respond to situations of abandonment, pain, ridicule, or rejection.

Have volunteers read Section Three on page 32. Then, ask the young people to compare the possible responses they just named to the feelings with those of the first disciples. Discuss how the women at the tomb may have felt when they discovered that Jesus was not there. Ask:

- What did the women at the tomb first assume happened to Jesus? (They thought his body had been stolen.)
- How did they react when they saw that Jesus was alive? (They were amazed. They honored him and ran to tell the disciples.)

Stress how the Resurrection of Jesus helped these and the other disciples to be more courageous and capable of spreading the message of Jesus. Explain that it gave them a new vision of life, pain, suffering, ridicule, rejection, even death. The Resurrection can do the same for us today when we place our faith in the risen Lord.

Ask the group to think about experiences of ridicule and rejection in their own lives. How does Jesus' response in the face of ridicule and rejection make a difference in the way they can now face such experiences?

Help your young people to understand that we celebrate Christ's saving Death and Resurrection throughout the liturgical year. Refer to pages 116–117 for information on the liturgical year, and the significance of the Easter Triduum. Note that the

Resurrection Icon, Sophie Hacker/Bridgeman Art Library

By rising from the dead, Jesus Christ brings us new life.

For a short time Jesus' Death crushed the disciples' hopes that he was their Messiah. The disciples hid for fear of death or imprisonment because of their association with Jesus. Then, as the Gospels record it, the unexpected happened. Some women followers of Jesus went to his burial place, expecting to anoint his body. But the large stone at the tomb's entrance had been rolled away. The tomb was empty!

The women's first thoughts were that someone had stolen the body. Then they saw an angel robed in white and became frightened. The angel told them, "Do not be afraid! I know that you are seeking Jesus the crucified. He is not here, for he has been raised just as he said. Come and see the place where he lay" (Matthew 28:5–6).

The women were amazed, and they ran to tell the disciples. As they made their way, the risen Jesus met them. He spoke to them, and they honored him by embracing his feet. When the women told the disciples what they had seen and heard the disciples did not believe.

Later, on the day we now celebrate as Easter Sunday, the risen Jesus appeared to his disciples. Even though they were behind locked doors, Jesus came among them and said, "Peace be with you" (John 20:19). Jesus' disciples were filled with joy at seeing their Lord among them, truly risen from the dead.

After Jesus' **Resurrection**, the mystery of Jesus' rising from Death to new life, the empty tomb and Christ's appearances as the Risen One awakened the disciples' faith in the power of God. We share the disciples' faith that Jesus is risen. Jesus' Resurrection is a central belief of our faith. Because of his Resurrection Jesus' life and death have meaning. The power of sin and evil was broken for all time.

Through his Death Christ opened the gates of Heaven and freed us from the power of sin and evil. By his Resurrection we are restored to new life. Through Jesus Christ humanity was reunited with God. As Saint Paul reminds us, "For just as in Adam all die, so too in Christ shall all be brought to life" (1 Corinthians 15:22).

Why is belief in the Resurrection of Jesus Christ so important to our faith?

32

Optional Activity

Have the young people work together in small groups to write and perform a skit based on one of the following stories of Jesus' Resurrection from Scripture:

- **Matthew 28:1–10**
- **Mark 16:1–10**
- **Luke 24:1–12**
- **John 20:1–10**

Allow time for each group to perform their skit.

Growing in Faith

PRAY

The Easter joy of Jesus' Resurrection is captured in one word—*Alleluia*. The word *Alleluia* comes from the Hebrew for "Praise the Lord!" The Alleluia is most often used as an acclamation. Pray together:

✝ Jesus Christ
is risen from the dead,
Alleluia!

REMEMBER

The Church teaches...

- Jesus' mission was directed toward his Father. He came to do his Father's will.
- Jesus is the Messiah, the promised Savior. *Messiah* is a word that means "Christ," or the Anointed One of God. That is why we say that Jesus is the Christ.
- Jesus died to save us from sin, and his Resurrection restores us to new life.
- The Resurrection of Jesus is a central belief of our faith. We share the belief of the first disciples that Jesus is risen.

Faith Words

Messiah (p. 29)
disciple (p. 30)
Resurrection (p. 32)

REFLECT & ACT

Jesus did the will of the Father despite opposition. Do you know anyone who did what he or she believed was right in spite of opposition? What consequences did the action have for that person?

In what ways can you live out the meaning of the life of Jesus? What can you do to share the hope of Jesus' Resurrection with others?

33

liturgical year is built around the Easter Triduum.

Then, have the young people write their responses to the question at the end of Section Three on page 32.

Conclusion (__ min.)

Growing in Faith

Have the young people close their books. Ask them what they have learned in this lesson about Jesus' mission, the Messiah, Jesus' disciples and Jesus' suffering, Death, and Resurrection. Reopen the books to page 32. Was everything from the **Remember** and **Faith Words** sections named? If not, point these out and help the group name the remaining concepts.

Invite the young people to read the **Reflect and Act** section and to write out their responses in the spaces provided. If desired, play some soft instrumental music while they do this.

When they have finished, call for responses to the questions about ways the young people can live out the meaning of the life of Jesus. Name specific ways they can do God's will by helping to feed the hungry, by forgiving those who offend them, by sharing their faith with those who need a sign of hope.

Explain the meaning of the word *Alleluia* as described under **Pray** on page 32. Then, offer the prayer together, singing the Alleluia if desired.

Answer for page 32:

Possible answers include: The Resurrection is the central belief of our faith, because of it Jesus' life and Death have meaning. The power of sin and evil was broken for all time.

Answers for page 33:

Left column:
Accept all reasonable answers.

Right column:
Be sure they understand the meaning of "the hope of Jesus' Resurrection." What can they do besides tell the story of Jesus?

CATECHISM FOCUS

"The Paschal mystery of Christ's cross and Resurrection stands at the center of the Good News that the apostles, and the Church following them, are to proclaim to the world." (*CCC*, 571)

For additional reference and reflection, see *CCC*, 606–623.

Unit 1 Assessment

A. Choose the correct term to complete each statement.

Incarnation	**Grace**	**stewards of Creation**
Resurrection	**Divine Revelation**	**Blessed Trinity**
Gospels	**Original Sin**	**Paschal Mystery**
Old Testament	**Kingdom of God**	**New Testament**
Messiah	**Faith**	**Annunciation**

1. The ______Resurrection______ is the mystery of Jesus' rising from death to new life.
2. The first sin committed by the first human beings is known as ______Original Sin______.
3. Those who take care of everything that God has given them are called ______stewards of Creation______.
4. ______Faith______ is the gift from God by which we believe in God and all that he has revealed, and all that the Church proposes for our belief.
5. ______Divine Revelation______ is God's making himself known to us.
6. In the ______Old Testament______ we read about the faith relationship between God and the Israelites.
7. The ______Messiah______ is the person God planned to send to save people from their sins.
8. The ______Blessed Trinity______ is the three Divine Persons in one God: God the Father, God the Son, and God the Holy Spirit.
9. The accounts found in the New Testament of God's Revelation through Jesus Christ are known as the ______Gospels______.
10. The ______Kingdom of God______ is the power of God's love active in our lives and in our world, which is present now and will come in its fullness at the end of time.
11. The ______Incarnation______ is the truth that the Son of God, the second Person of the Blessed Trinity, became man and lived among us in order to accomplish our Salvation.
12. ______Grace______ is a participation, or sharing, in God's life and friendship.
13. The ______Paschal Mystery______ refers to the suffering, Death, Resurrection, and Ascension of Jesus Christ.
14. The ______Annunciation______ is the name given to the announcement to Mary that she would be the Mother of the Son of God.
15. In the second part of the Bible, the ______New Testament______, we read about Jesus Christ, his message and mission, and his first followers.

B. Circle the response that does *not* belong.

1. Our Catholic faith helps us
   a. discover the meaning of life.
   (b.) have all the answers.
   c. come to know God.
   d. give a free response to God's Revelation of himself.

2. This is what the Church teaches about the fall and the promise:
   a. evil and suffering entered the world through human choice.
   b. Jesus Christ fulfills God's promise to free human beings to share in God's life.
   c. every human being suffers the effects of Original Sin.
   (d.) the first humans did not sin.

3. From the Book of Genesis we learn that
   (a.) Creation was completed in seven years.
   b. God alone created everything that is.
   c. the world God created is good.
   d. we are made in the image and likeness of God.

4. We find in the four Gospel accounts that Jesus
   (a.) worked no miracles.
   b. is the Son of God and the long-awaited Messiah.
   c. is both divine and human.
   d. is one with the Father.

5. Jesus fulfilled his Father's will by
   a. feeding the hungry and healing the sick.
   b. suffering and dying on the cross.
   (c.) avoiding contact with the poor.
   d. rising from the dead to bring us new life.

C. Share your faith by responding thoughtfully to these questions.

1. How does your faith make a difference in your life? How can you strengthen your faith?
   (Accept all reasonable answers.)

2. In what ways can you live out your responsibility to take care of Creation?
   (Accept all reasonable answers.)

3. What meaning do these symbols from the story of Adam and Eve have for you?
   the garden: God's gift—Adam and Eve lived there in harmony with God, with each other, and with all Creation.
   the serpent: the spirit of evil
   being sent from the garden: Evil and suffering entered our world through human choice.

4. Why is it important to help build up the Kingdom of God? What can you do to spread the Kingdom? (Encourage serious thought, but accept all reasonable answers.)

5. How does the suffering and Death of Jesus help you to cope with the sorrows in your own life? Why does Jesus' Resurrection give you hope?
   (Accept all reasonable answers.)

CHAPTER 6

Adult Focus

At the end of his public ministry, Jesus promised to send the Holy Spirit to his disciples. He explained to them that it was only through his suffering, Death, Resurrection, and return to the Father that they would receive the Holy Spirit.

When the Holy Spirit came to Jesus' followers, the world knew that Jesus' Death was not the end. This dynamic concept runs throughout the New Testament. An important theme of this chapter is that today, more than two thousand years after Jesus' Death and Resurrection, the Holy Spirit is still present and active in the Church.

As with the Apostles long ago, the Holy Spirit urges each one of us toward a more complete union with God and others. The Holy Spirit brings "love, joy, peace, patience, kindness, generosity, faithfulness, gentleness, self-control" (Galatians 5:22–23).

GOALS

to realize that the Holy Spirit strengthens each of us to be Christ's witnesses; to understand the role of the Holy Spirit in the establishment and growth of the Church

GETTING READY

- ***Materials needed:***

Prayer table environment: Bible, decorative cloth, candle, crystal or glass bowl, small pieces of paper, and pens

Bibles—preferably one for each young person

Chalkboard or poster board for several of the sections

Scripture task cards for Section One

Current world map for Section Two

Introduction (__ min.)

Gather the young people around the prayer table. Encourage them to think about an occasion on which they were proud of their actions. Offer suggestions such as an act of kindness, or a goal that they had reached. Ask: Who or what inspired them to do this thing? How did this action affect them?

Offer the prayer of the Holy Spirit on page 41. After a moment of silence, explain that this prayer asks the Holy Spirit to inspire us in every aspect of our lives.

Recall that a martyr is someone who dies for the faith. Explain that Sister Ita Ford was a missionary who served the poor in El Salvador. Talk about her love for God and commitment to her work, which led to her martyrdom in 1980 along with three other Catholic churchwomen.

Read the passage on page 36. It is from one of Sister Ita's letters. Discuss the questions that follow.

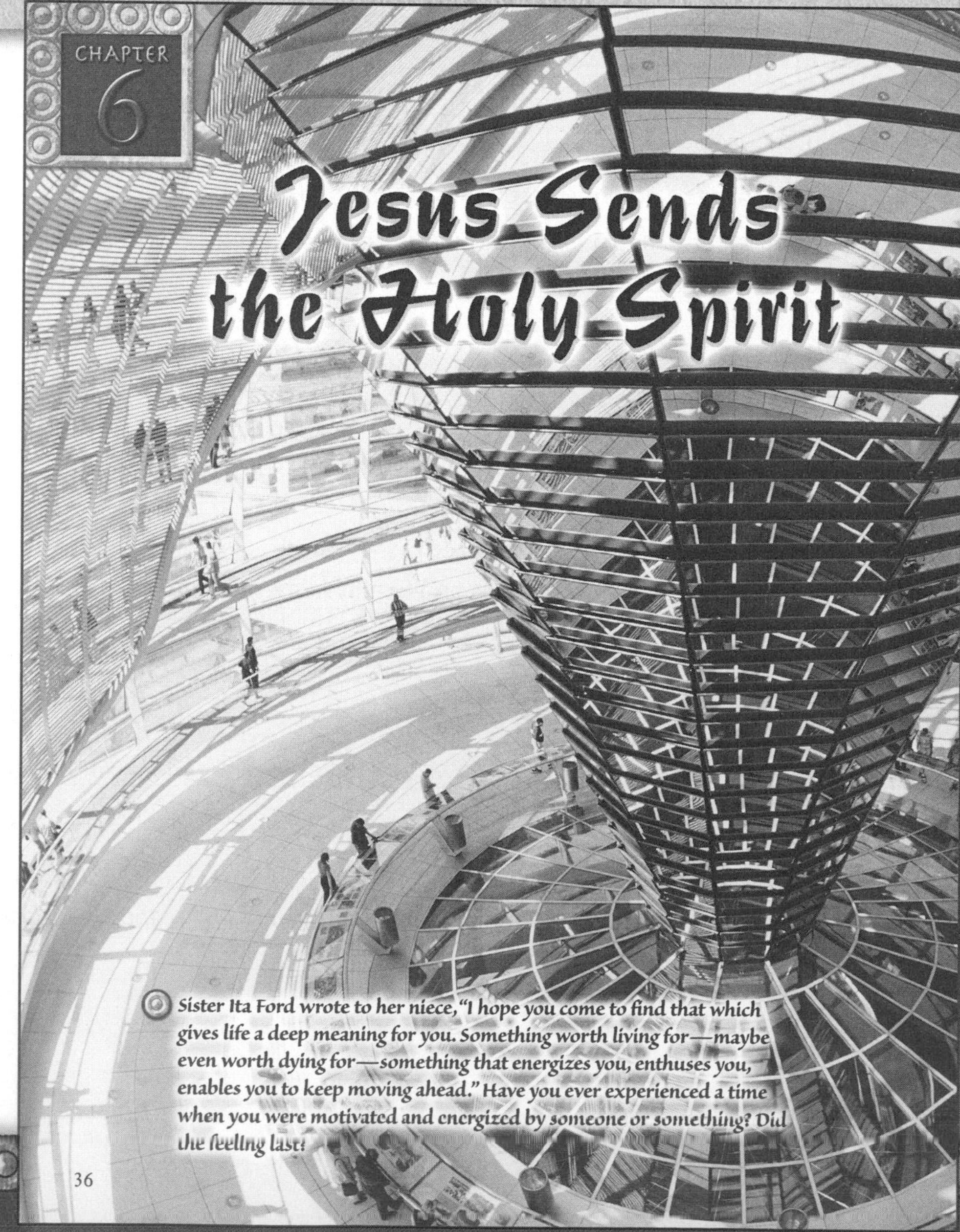

CHAPTER 6

Jesus Sends the Holy Spirit

Sister Ita Ford wrote to her niece, "I hope you come to find that which gives life a deep meaning for you. Something worth living for—maybe even worth dying for—something that energizes you, enthuses you, enables you to keep moving ahead." Have you ever experienced a time when you were motivated and energized by someone or something? Did the feeling last?

36

To be a Christian means to be identified by these characteristics.

The Holy Spirit is the source of all activity in the Church. The Holy Spirit unites the members into one living body with Christ as head, allowing each person to grow according to his or her gifts. "There are different kinds of spiritual gifts but the same Spirit. . . . To each individual the manifestation of the Spirit is given for some benefit." (1 Corinthians 12:4, 7)

Read Acts of the Apostles 2:1–4, the passage concerning the first Pentecost. Consider that through the active presence of the Holy Spirit, the Apostles were given the strength and courage to carry out the mission they had been given by Jesus.

Reflection

Reflect for a moment on the presence of the Holy Spirit in your life and in the lives of your young people. Ask for guidance as you prepare to share with them this great news of the coming of the Holy Spirit and the building of the Church.

Jesus promised to send the Holy Spirit.

We all need vision and goals to give us direction. We need courage and hope and someone to help guide us if we get off track. Jesus has given these things to us in a way we never could have imagined.

Jesus provided a sense of purpose, strength, and direction for his followers. His presence among his disciples, his teachings, and his way of life united them. Among these followers were a special group we know as the *Apostles*, a word meaning "those sent on a mission." The **Apostles** were twelve men chosen by Jesus to share in his mission in a special way.

Jesus promised his Apostles that he would be with them always. He would do this by sending the Holy Spirit to guide and encourage them. Jesus assured his Apostles with these words, "You will receive power when the holy Spirit comes upon you, and you will be my witnesses in Jerusalem, throughout Judea and Samaria, and to the ends of the earth" (Acts of the Apostles 1:8). The Holy Spirit would help them find the way to bring Jesus' message of God's love to the entire world.

Jesus told his Apostles, "When the Advocate comes whom I will send you from the Father, the Spirit of truth. . . . he will testify to me. And you also testify, because you have been with me from the beginning" (John 15:26–27). The Advocate is God the Holy Spirit, the third Person of the Blessed Trinity. The Holy Spirit would:

- remain with them and in them
- teach them and help them to remember all that Jesus had said

37

Ask the young people what motivated Sister Ita Ford. Discuss the ways in which she can be an example of someone who motivates others.

Presentation (__ min.)

Jesus promised to send the Holy Spirit.

Have young people read silently Section One on pages 37–38. Then discuss:

- If a person lacks goals or vision, how does that affect him or her? (They have no direction; they lose a sense of purpose in their lives.)
- What did Jesus promise to do to help his followers maintain a sense of purpose, strength, and direction? (Jesus said he would remain with them always and send the Holy Spirit to guide and encourage them.)

◉ What did Jesus say the Holy Spirit would do for them? (Jesus said the Holy Spirit would remain with them and in them; the Holy Spirit would teach them and help them remember what he had taught them; the Holy Spirit would lead them to the truth and give them strength.)

Have the young people write their responses to the questions at the end of Section One on page 38.

In advance, prepare task cards with one of the following Scripture passages on each card. Give each person, or pair of young people, a task card and a Bible. Instruct them to look up the passages and report on what each tells about the role of the Holy Spirit. Use these passages:

◉ Ephesians 3:14–21 (strengthened through the Holy Spirit)

◉ 1 Peter 1:10–12 (preaching Good News through the Holy Spirit)

◉ 1 John 5:5–12 (the Spirit is truth)

- lead them to the truth of the Gospel, that Jesus Christ is the Son of God who brings us Salvation and redemption
- give them the strength to be Jesus' witnesses.

Advocate is a word with many meanings: helper, friend, consoler, teacher, guide, and defender. The Holy Spirit is all of these things for us—our intercessor, consoler, and teacher.

God the Holy Spirit guides and strengthens us today as members of God's family. Because the Holy Spirit is unseen, like the wind, we know the Holy Spirit only by what he does to us and for us in the Church. At all times the Holy Spirit is in us and with us, drawing us together as God's people, making the Church one in truth and love.

Who were the Apostles? Why did Jesus promise to send them the Holy Spirit?

The Holy Spirit came at Pentecost.

Forty days after Jesus had risen from the dead, he returned to his Father in Heaven. We celebrate this event on the Feast of the Ascension. The Apostles then went back to Jerusalem, where they often came together to pray. We read an account in the New Testament of the earthshaking day on which the Holy Spirit came upon them:

> When the time for Pentecost was fulfilled, they were all in one place together. And suddenly there came from the sky a noise like a strong driving wind, and it filled the entire house in which they were. Then there appeared to them tongues as of fire, which parted and came to rest on each one of them. And they were all filled with the holy Spirit and began to speak in different tongues, as the Spirit enabled them to proclaim.
> Acts of the Apostles 2:1–4

38

The Holy Spirit came at Pentecost.

Read aloud the paragraph and passage from the Acts of the Apostles under Section Two on page 38. Talk about how the disciples might have reacted (fearfully, excitedly, and joyously) to the events that happened on that first Pentecost. Have the young people finish reading Section Two on page 39. Ask:

◉ How were the Apostles different after the Holy Spirit had come to them?

Answers for page 38:

See definition of Apostles in the Glossary on page 125. See names of the Apostles on page 39.

For second question see bulleted items on page 37.

Do YOU Know?

Read the "Do You Know?" feature on page 39. Ask the group to share anything they know about any of the Twelve Apostles. For example: Peter was a fisherman with Andrew, James, and John. When Peter confessed his belief in Jesus as the Son of God, Jesus made Peter the leader of the Apostles.

After Jesus was arrested, Peter denied three times that he even knew Jesus.

The day on which the Holy Spirit came to Jesus' first disciples as Jesus promised is known as **Pentecost**. We read further in the Acts of the Apostles that the Apostle Peter began to preach to the crowds that filled Jerusalem. He declared that Jesus of Nazareth had worked amazing wonders and deeds and had been raised from the dead by God the Father. And Jesus had indeed sent the Holy Spirit, as he had promised.

Peter continued his speech, telling the crowds that all who were gathered there had seen and heard the coming of the Holy Spirit. They had to know that the crucified Jesus had been raised up. Jesus was truly Lord and Messiah!

The community of Jesus' disciples was called to share this message that Peter proclaimed. They would be the witnesses of Jesus Christ in the world, and the Holy Spirit would guide them. At first they had been a timid and fearful group: They had run away when Jesus was arrested, tried, and put to death. With the help of the Holy Spirit, however, they became strong and fearless. The Holy Spirit filled them with the fire of faith and the courage to proclaim the Good News of the risen Christ.

What happened at Pentecost? If you had been there, how do you think you would have acted?

Do YOU Know?

Jesus went alone to a mountain and prayed all night before he chose his Apostles. When he was commissioning the Apostles, Jesus said, "As the Father has sent me, so I send you" (John 20:21). Because they were sent by Jesus, the Apostles had the power to act in Jesus' name. The Twelve Apostles were:

Simon, later called Peter
Andrew, Simon Peter's brother
James, son of Zebedee
John, James' brother
Philip, a fisherman
Bartholomew, also known as Nathanael
Thomas, whose name means "twin"
Matthew, a tax collector
James, son of Alphaeus
Thaddeus, also known as Jude
Simon the Zealot
Judas Iscariot, Jesus' betrayer

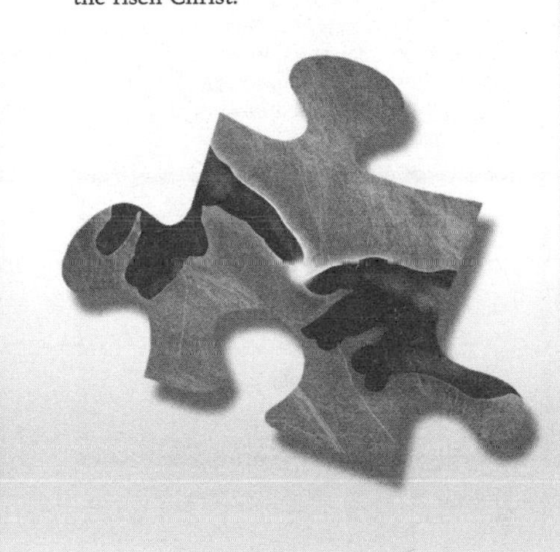

39

◉ How did the Holy Spirit both comfort and challenge the Apostles?

◉ After receiving the Holy Spirit, what did the Apostles do?

◉ What is the Good News that the Apostles preached?

Emphasize the dramatic nature of the story of Pentecost. Have the young people respond to the questions at the end of Section Two on page 39. Share responses.

Remind the young people that Jesus had asked the Father to send the Holy Spirit to help the disciples proclaim the Good News of the risen Christ. At Pentecost, the people who listened to the disciples were able to understand them in their own languages.

Show the group a map of the world. Point out places in the world where missionaries are working to spread the Gospel. On the chalkboard or poster board, make a list of obstacles, other than language, that these missionaries might face.

Explain to the group that there are people where they live who are working to spread the Gospel to others. Ask the young people to think about which obstacles these missionaries might face. How are these obstacles the same or different from those faced in other countries?

John stayed with Mary at the foot of the cross when all of the other Apostles had run away. Jesus asked John to take care of Mary. John was the only Apostle not to be martyred. Thomas was not with the other Apostles when Jesus first appeared to them. Therefore, he did not believe that Jesus had risen from the dead. Jesus came the next Sunday and told Thomas to put his fingers into the wounds in his hands and side.

Answers for page 39:

Accept all reasonable answers.

The Holy Spirit helped the disciples to be Christ's witnesses.

Ask the group to think about situations that would make someone almost too afraid to do or try something. Make a list of these fears on the chalkboard or poster board. Then ask the group to describe how they would try to calm someone's fear in each of these situations.

Have the group read silently Section Three on page 40. Ask:

- What difference did the Holy Spirit make in the lives of the Apostles?
- How did the early Christians show that they were witnesses of Jesus Christ?

Reiterate that the Holy Spirit empowers and transforms people, changing them from people of fear to people of courage. Recall that the Holy Spirit appeared to the disciples in the form of fire. Discuss the characteristics of fire and why fire is an appropriate symbol for the Holy Spirit. Explain that people who are disciples of Christ are often described as "on fire" with love of God. Ask: What aspect of discipleship does this refer to? Have you ever met anyone you would describe as being "on fire" with love of God?

Discuss characteristics of someone who is a true witness of Jesus Christ. Then have the young people write their description of a true witness at the end of Section Three on page 40.

The Holy Spirit helped the disciples to be Christ's witnesses.

Peter's proclamation of Jesus as Lord was very powerful. Lord was a title reserved only for God, and Peter truly believed in Jesus' divinity. Peter told the people gathered, "Repent and be baptized, every one of you, in the name of Jesus Christ for the forgiveness of your sins; and you will receive the gift of the holy Spirit" (Acts of the Apostles 2:38).

The Holy Spirit was at work through the Apostles. Through the power of the Holy Spirit, thousands of people changed their lives:

- They were baptized.
- Their sins were forgiven.
- They shared in the Gift of the Holy Spirit.
- The Holy Spirit made them one in their love for God and one another.

We read in the Acts of the Apostles about the way the early Christians tried to live. They committed themselves to the Apostles' teachings about Jesus. They lived together in fellowship and prayer. The early Christians ate together and shared their possessions. They cared for the needy as best they could. In what they said and what they did, they were witnesses of Jesus Christ.

To witness is to provide evidence for or to testify to the truth or validity of something. The word *witness* means "someone who has seen or heard something, or someone who gives evidence." This word brings up images of an eyewitness to a crime or a character witness in a court hearing. Being a witness or giving witness in these situations is not a life long task. But being a life long witness is exactly what Jesus calls us to. **Witnesses** are people who speak and act based upon what they know and believe about Jesus Christ.

To be a Christian is not just to believe in Jesus Christ. We must give witness to Christ in all that we say and do. We need to share the Good News of Jesus with others. When people see us, they should see the power of Christ in our lives. If they do, they may come to believe, too.

The Apostles were the first witnesses of Jesus—they saw, touched, and spoke with him. The early Christians were called to give witness to the life and mission of Jesus. Many practiced their faith in spite of persecution from the government and from people who were not Christians.

We, too, are called to be Christ's witnesses through the actions, words, and thoughts of our daily lives. Sometimes this requires courage; sometimes it requires sacrifice; but through it all the Holy Spirit is with us, assisting us in living as followers of Jesus Christ.

Describe someone who is a true witness to Christ's life and teachings.

40

Optional Activity

Encourage the young people to make a list of popular or religious songs that inspire them or give them courage. Discuss the specific elements of the songs that "speak" to the young people, for example: the powerful lyrics, the upbeat tempo of the music, etc. Compare the answers of the group. Is there any song or lyrics that they all find inspiring?

Answer for page 40:

Accept all reasonable answers.

GROWING IN FAITH

PRAY

Jesus prayed at all times of the day. He asked his Father's blessing before he acted, and he thanked his Father afterward. Jesus prayed for strength and direction, and he taught his disciples to do the same. Jesus told them, "Ask and you will receive; seek and you will find; knock and the door will be opened to you" (Luke 11:9).

✝ Breathe into me Holy Spirit,
that my thoughts may be all holy.
Move in me, Holy Spirit,
that my work too, may be holy.
Attract my heart, Holy Spirit,
that I may love only what is holy.
Strengthen me, Holy Spirit,
that I may defend all that is holy.
Protect me, Holy Spirit,
that I always may be holy.
Amen.

REMEMBER

The Church teaches...

- God the Holy Spirit is the third Person of the Blessed Trinity.
- The Apostles were twelve men chosen by Jesus to share in his mission in a special way.
- Jesus Christ sent his disciples the Gift of the Holy Spirit.
- The Holy Spirit is the Advocate: the helper, consoler, and teacher who strengthens and guides us.
- The Holy Spirit is in us and with us at all times, drawing us together as God's people, making the Church one in truth and love.

Faith Words

Apostles (p. 37)
Advocate (p. 38)
Pentecost (p. 39)
witnesses (p. 40)

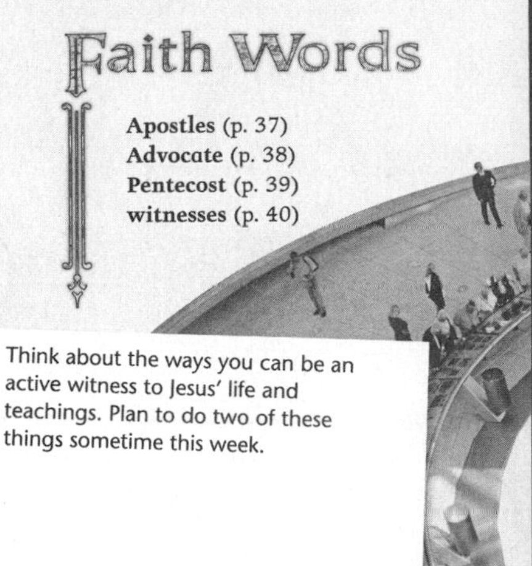

REFLECT & ACT

Do you prefer to think of the Holy Spirit as a helper, teacher, consoler, or defender? Why? When you are in need of help, do you ever ask the Holy Spirit to guide or help you?

Think about the ways you can be an active witness to Jesus' life and teachings. Plan to do two of these things sometime this week.

Conclusion (__ min.)

Growing in Faith

Have the young people close their books. Ask them what they have learned in this lesson about the Holy Spirit, the Apostles, Pentecost, and witnesses. Reopen the books to page 41. Was everything from the **Remember** and **Faith Words** sections named? If not, point these out and help the group name the remaining concepts.

Invite the young people to read the **Reflect and Act** section and to write out their responses in the spaces provided. If desired, play some soft instrumental music while they do this.

Then, share the ways in which the young people can be active witnesses to Jesus. (Suggestions: communicating with and supporting missionaries in foreign lands; joining parish peace and social justice groups; teaching or enacting Gospel stories for young children or in nursing homes.)

Have a volunteer read aloud the paragraph in the **Pray** section. Invite the young people to use the prayer to the Holy Spirit as an opportunity to ask for strength, guidance, direction, and comfort.

Close by offering the prayer to the Holy Spirit in the **Pray** section on page 41 together.

CATECHISM FOCUS

"The Holy Spirit, whom Christ the head pours out on his members, builds, animates, and sanctifies the Church." (*CCC*, 747)

For additional reference and reflection, see *CCC*, 687–690.

Answers for page 41:

Left side:
Accept all reasonable answers.

Right side:
Accept all reasonable answers.

CHAPTER 7

GOALS

to identify the Church founded by Christ;
to understand the four Marks of the Church

GETTING READY

Tape a piece of poster board to a wall or chalkboard for the Introduction

Mark Bible passages for the Opening Prayer, John 17:20–23

■ *Materials needed:*

Prayer table environment: Bible, decorative cloth

CD or tape of "Anthem" by Tom Conry and CD player/tape player (optional)

Poster board and markers for all sections

Adult Focus

From among his followers, Jesus chose Twelve Apostles to be the nucleus of the new community that would continue his mission. After Jesus' Death and Resurrection, the Apostles experienced the power of the Holy Spirit. From that moment on they lived their mission to preach about Jesus to all people.

Jesus' community was open to all who believed and were baptized in his name. It is from this one apostolic community, characterized by its universal call to holiness, that the Catholic Church grew.

In the Nicene Creed, we profess that "I believe in one, holy, catholic and apostolic church." These are the Marks of the Church. They describe realities of the Church's nature, and as identifying elements of the Church's mission, they are tasks and goals to be

Introduction (__ min.)

Gather the group around the prayer table. Read John 17:20–23 to the group. Explain that these Scripture passages were part of a prayer offered by Jesus for all people. Ask the young people to think about what it means to be one in Christ.

Explain that part of being one is praying together. Encourage the young people to share intentions for which they would like to pray. Ask everyone to stand, join hands, and pray the Lord's Prayer (see page 119) together.

Tell the young people that Christ is the source of unity for all believers. Draw a circle on poster board, or the chalkboard, with the name *Christ* written in the middle. Encourage the young people to think of aspects of our faith that come from our belief in Jesus Christ and list them in the circle (possible answers: Mass, faith, Bible, Tradition, Church, love, respect, understanding,

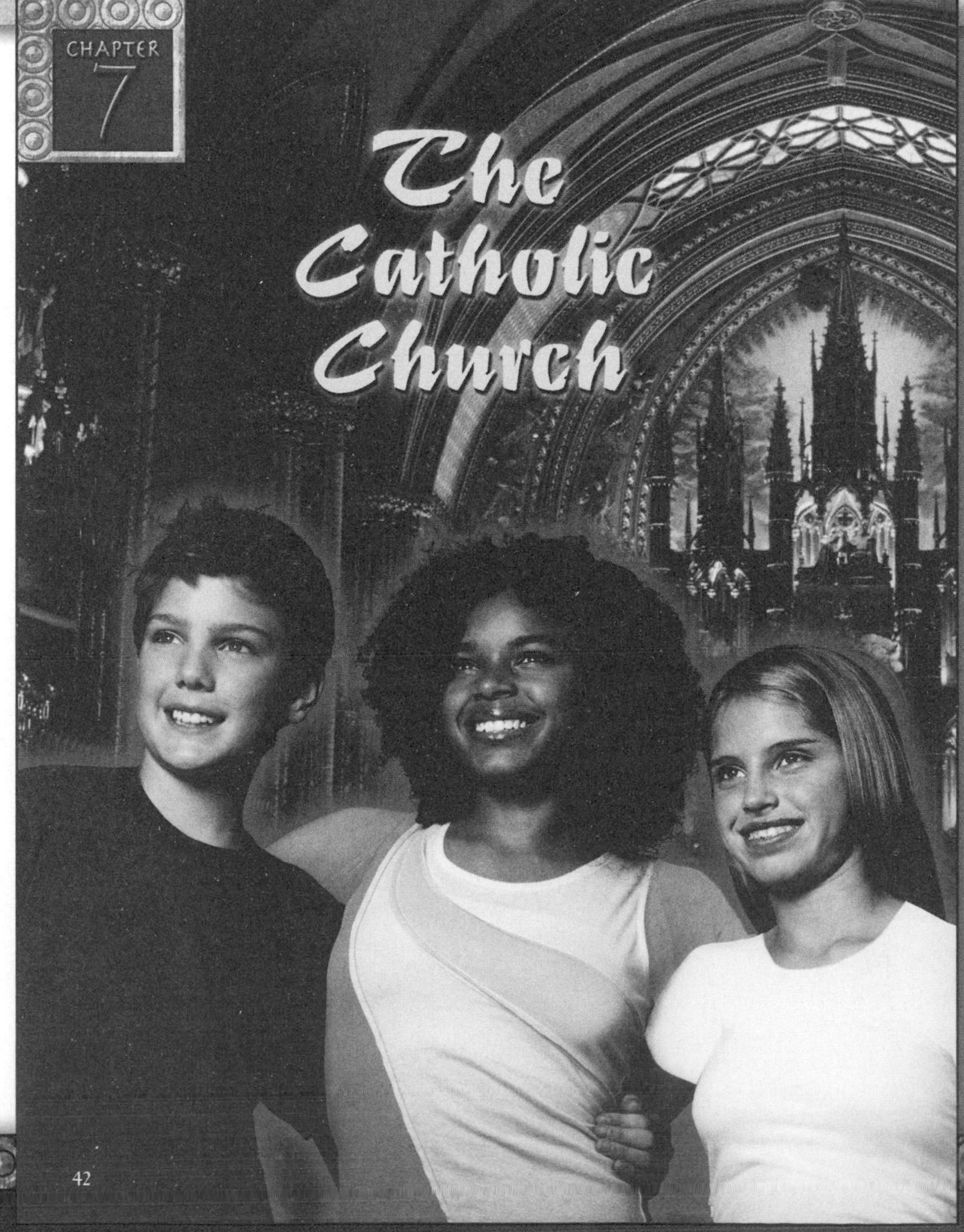

worked toward. In other words, these four Marks of the Church are not only identifying characteristics already possessed but also dynamic challenges and ideals towards which we strive.

It is through striving together that we strengthen our bond of unity in the Lord and our witness to the world that Christ is present. Through his Spirit, Jesus is fashioning us, the Church, into his people.

Reflection

Meditate on these words of Saint Paul in preparation for this session:

"Striving to preserve the unity of the spirit through the bond of peace: one body and one Spirit, as you were also called to the one hope of your call; one Lord, one faith, one baptism; one God and Father of all, who is over all and through all and in all" (Ephesians 4:3–6).

What do you appreciate most about the Catholic Church?

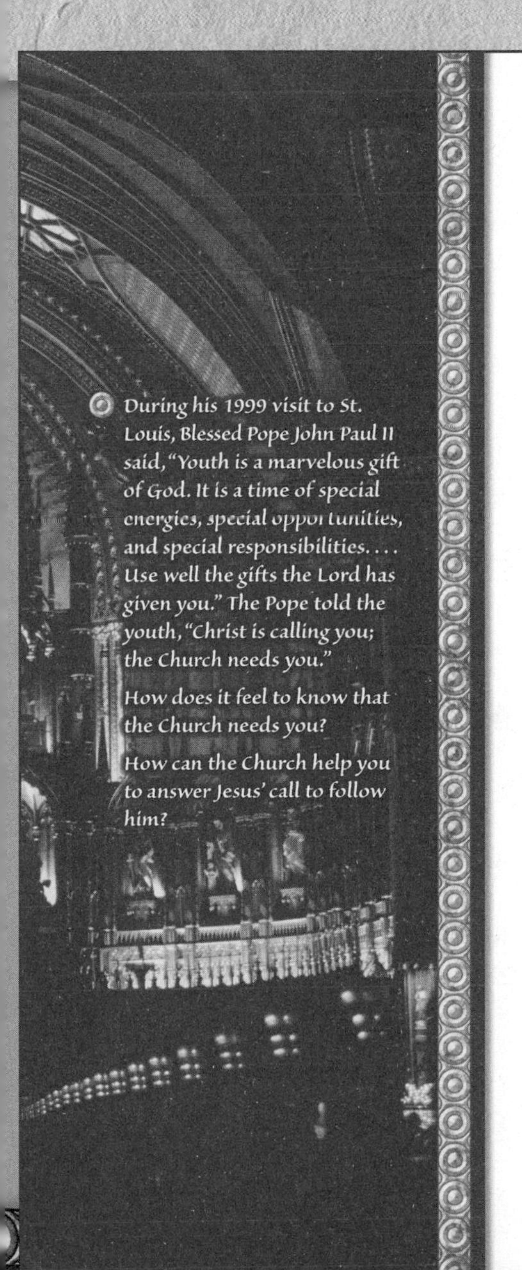

During his 1999 visit to St. Louis, Blessed Pope John Paul II said, "Youth is a marvelous gift of God. It is a time of special energies, special opportunities, and special responsibilities.... Use well the gifts the Lord has given you." The Pope told the youth, "Christ is calling you; the Church needs you."

How does it feel to know that the Church needs you?

How can the Church help you to answer Jesus' call to follow him?

1 Jesus invites us to follow him in his Church.

From the very beginning of his public ministry, Jesus called people to follow him. People listened to his message about God the Father and the coming of his Kingdom. They heard his promise of new life.

More and more people responded to Jesus' invitation to follow him. Among his followers, the Apostles were a special group handpicked by Jesus. They stayed with Jesus and traveled together. They got to know Jesus and one another. The Apostles shared in Jesus' mission and authority, and Jesus gave them the power to continue his preaching and healing. With them Jesus formed the community we call the Church.

The **Church** is the community of people who believe in Jesus Christ, have been baptized in him, and follow his teachings. Members of the Church are called Catholics. The Catholic Church is rooted in beliefs, sacraments, and ministry that go back through the centuries to Jesus and the Apostles.

Jesus Christ, the Son of God, is the cornerstone of the Church and the source of our identity as its members. But God the Holy Spirit is our unending life force:

- making us one, preserving the Church in its true identity as the faith community founded by Christ
- calling us to worship and pray
- leading the Church in teaching, serving, and governing.

At the Sunday celebration of the Eucharist we pray this ancient profession of faith: "We believe in one holy catholic and apostolic Church." This is our belief, and it is a good description of the Church.

43

teachings, justice, etc.) Point out that everything we believe comes through Christ, which is why he is the source of our unity.

Ask a volunteer to read aloud the quotation on page 43. Discuss the questions that follow Blessed Pope John Paul II's words.

Presentation (__ min.)

1 Jesus invites us to follow him in his Church.

Have young people read the first four paragraphs in Section One on page 43. Stress that if we accept our Baptism as a sign of belonging to Jesus Christ and his Church, we are also called to live as Jesus did.

Write the following expressions on the chalkboard or poster board:

- mark my words
- make one's mark
- miss the mark

Ask what each expression means. Then ask what all the expressions have in common. (They all contain the work *mark*.) Discuss what the word *mark* means in each expression. Focus on the meaning of the word *mark* as an indicator, something that points out something specific that distinguishes one thing from another.

Explain the four Marks of the Church as essential characteristics of the Church founded by Jesus Christ. Add that *one, holy, catholic,* and *apostolic* are the Church's identifying marks, or characteristics.

Finish reading Section One aloud on pages 43–44. Have the group name the four Marks of the Church. As they do so, list them as headings on a piece of poster board.

Discuss the questions at the end of Section One on page 44. Have the young people write their responses in the space provided.

One, holy, catholic, and apostolic—these are the four identifying **Marks of the Church**, or essential characteristics of the Church begun by Jesus Christ. Through these characteristics the Church is known and recognized. But we, the members of the Church, could not bring about these characteristics alone. It is by Christ and through the Holy Spirit that the Church is one, holy, catholic, and apostolic.

Describe the Church. What role does the Holy Spirit play in the life of the Church?

The Church is one and holy.

At the Last Supper Jesus prayed to his Father for his followers "that they may be one just as we are" (John 17:11). In the first letter to the Corinthians, Saint Paul also spoke of the Christian community as one. He spoke of the Church in terms of the body. The body has a marvelous unity. Each part has its own function, and all parts work for the good of the whole body.

Saint Paul wrote, "Now you are Christ's body, and individually parts of it" (1 Corinthians 12:27). Being *one*, then, is a Mark of the Church. She is one, brought into unity by the unity of the Father, Son, and Holy Spirit. Her members together form the one Body of Christ, with Jesus Christ as the head, and with the Holy Spirit as the source of its life, unity, and gifts.

In his letter to the Ephesians, Saint Paul identified some of the things that make us one. This is how he encouraged his fellow Christians to live as one:

> I . . . urge you to live in a manner worthy of the call you have received, with all humility and gentleness, with patience, bearing with one another through love, striving to preserve the unity of the spirit through the bond of peace: one body and one Spirit, as you were also called to the one hope of your call; one Lord, one faith, one baptism; one God and Father of all, who is over all and through all and in all.
> Ephesians 4:1–6

As Catholics we celebrate our unity in the Eucharist. As a community we are nourished by the Sacrament of the Eucharist, the Body and Blood of Christ, and are strengthened in our one common faith. We also celebrate the other sacraments and have as our leaders the bishops.

Do YOU Know?

The pope and the bishops sometimes come together to discuss and make decisions on issues of faith, morals, and the life of the Church. These gatherings are called **Ecumenical Councils**. When Ecumenical Councils solemnly define a doctrine as being divinely revealed, they do so with the gift of infallibility. *Infallibility* is the Gift of the Holy Spirit that keeps the Church free from error—in her beliefs and teachings—in matters concerning Divine Revelation and the Deposit of Faith. The pope also has the gift when he specifically defines a doctrine pertaining to faith and morals.

44

Do YOU Know?

Read the "Do You Know?" feature on page 44. Help the young people to understand what is meant by "doctrine." (official Church beliefs and teachings)

Answers for page 44:

Use definition on page 125 of the Glossary as a basis for this answer. Also, see bulleted items on page 43.

Holiness is another mark by which we identify the Church. People are not born holy. Only God is holy. Our holiness is always a share in God's holiness. But by his Death and Resurrection, Jesus prepared the way for people to become holy. He calls us to be a holy people dedicated to God, the Holy One, and dedicated to one another.

In our lives, we are called to carry out our loving relationship with God and with one another. One way we do this is through prayer, especially the celebration of the sacraments, and by serving others.

Holiness describes those who listen to the Gospel message and respond to it. Our daily challenge is to live as Jesus taught. Only by trying consciously to do what is right can we begin to grow in holiness. Throughout the ages the Church has guided many people to lead holy lives. Holiness is an essential characteristic of the Church.

What are some signs that the Church is one? that the Church is holy?

The Church is catholic (universal) and apostolic.

Another identifying Mark of the Church is that it is *catholic*—universal and worldwide. This means that the Church welcomes everyone equally to hear and accept the Good News of Jesus' Salvation for all. The Church is everywhere, including people of every race, color, nationality, and economic status. The Church exists in all cultures and languages, celebrating the one mystery of Jesus Christ in diverse liturgical traditions, or rites.

45

The Church is one and holy.

Have volunteers read aloud the first five paragraphs in Section Two on page 44.

Brainstorm ways in which the Church is *one* and list these on the poster board under the corresponding heading. Draw upon specific examples of the unity of the Church as they exist in your parish.

Have the young people finish silently reading Section Two. Together name signs of the Church's *holiness* and list them on the poster board.

Ask the young people to write their responses to the questions at the end of Section Two on page 45.

Answer for page 45:

The Church is one because we are nourished by our one common faith, share the same sacraments, and have the pope and bishops as our leaders. (See page 44.)

Possible answers include: We can see that the Church is holy because through prayer, especially the celebration of the sacraments, and through service to others, we carry out our call to live in loving relationships with God and with each other.

The Church is catholic (universal) and apostolic.

Read aloud the first paragraph under Section Three on page 45. Stress the meaning of the word *catholic* as "universal" and discuss what this means.

Together name ways that the Church is *catholic* or universal and list them on the poster board.

For additional information about the diverse liturgical traditions referred to on page 45, see *CCC*, 1201–1203.

Have the group finish reading Section Three silently. Ask what it means to say that the Church is *apostolic*. List the signs of how the Church is *apostolic* on the poster board chart.

Ask the young people to write their responses to the question at the end of Section Three on page 46.

Recall the challenge that is posed to young people by the words of Blessed Pope John Paul II (see page 42). If time allows, have the young people work together in small groups to make posters portraying ways in which young people can respond to his challenge. Display the posters in prominent places within your parish.

People of God, like *Body of Christ*, is an image of the Church that we find in the New Testament. This image comes from Old Testament times. God chose the people of Israel to be his people. The early Christians saw themselves as part of the continuing story of God's people, growing into the Church of Christ. The People of God are spread throughout the world, and all enter into the People of God in the same way: by faith and Baptism.

Jesus entrusted his Church to his Apostles, his chosen leaders whom he had formed in faith. Jesus had confidence in his Apostles, and he assured them that the Holy Spirit would always be with them. The Holy Spirit would help them preach the Good News to the whole world. From its beginning, the Church has been missionary.

Jesus told his Apostles:

> All power in heaven and on earth has been given to me. Go, therefore, and make disciples of all nations . . . teaching them to observe all that I have commanded you. And behold, I am with you always, until the end of the age.
> Matthew 28:18–20

With the coming of the Holy Spirit on Pentecost, the Church became the visible sign of Christ's continuing work in the world. Jesus had handed over the roles of leadership and service in his community to Peter and the other Apostles. As the Church grew, it was built on the faith of the Apostles. This is why we say the Church is *apostolic*, another identifying Mark of the Church.

The Apostles' authority and call to service have been handed down to their successors, the pope and bishops of the Catholic Church. This is what we call **apostolic succession**. The pope, the bishop of Rome, is the successor to Saint Peter. The pope leads the whole Church with his brother bishops. The pope and bishops are the authentic teachers of the Church. They teach the People of God the faith which is to be believed and applied in moral life. The Church continues to be taught, sanctified (made more holy), and guided by the pope and bishops.

There are other Christian communities in the world besides the Catholic Church. As Catholics we respect these communities and recognize Christ working in them. With them we pray that unity among all who believe in Jesus will be realized.

All Christian churches are not the same, however. The fullness of Christ's action and the working of the Holy Spirit are realized in the Catholic Church. All Salvation comes from Christ, the head through the Church, his Body. And to every generation the Church shares all that she believes through her teaching, worship, and her life.

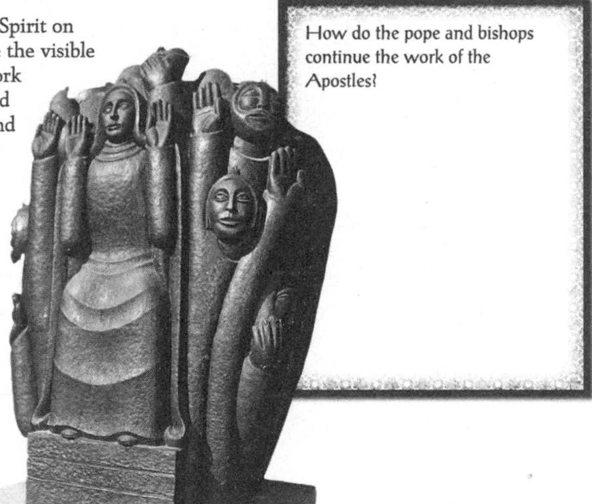

How do the pope and bishops continue the work of the Apostles?

46

Optional Activity

Divide the young people into four groups. Ask each group to research one Mark of the Church. Ask them to use various multimedia to show how the Church is one, holy, catholic, or apostolic. For example, one group could design a pictorial essay depicting ways the Church is one or use magazine clippings illustrating ways the Church is catholic. Encourage creativity. Allow time for the groups to share their presentations.

Answer for page 46:

See column 2, paragraph 1.

GROWING IN FAITH

PRAY

✝ We are called, we are chosen.
We are Christ for one another.
We are promised to tomorrow,
while we are for him today.
We are sign, we are wonder.
We are sower, we are seed.
We are harvest, we are hungry.
We are question, we are creed.
"Anthem"
Tom Conry

REMEMBER

The Church teaches...

- The Church is the community of people who believe in Jesus Christ, have been baptized in him, and follow his teachings.
- The Church has four identifying marks: The Church is one, holy, catholic, and apostolic. By these four essential characteristics Jesus' Church is known and recognized.
- The Holy Spirit guides and preserves the Church in its true identity as the faith community founded by Christ.
- Christ is the cornerstone of the Church. All Salvation comes from Christ through the Church.
- Peter and the Apostles were the first leaders of the Church. The apostolic authority and call to service are handed down to their successors: the pope and bishops who teach, sanctify, and govern the Catholic Church.

Faith Words

Church (p. 43)
Marks of the Church (p. 44)
Ecumenical Councils (p. 44)
apostolic succession (p. 46)

REFLECT & ACT

We all share in the mission to bring Christ to all people. We are called to share who Christ is and why he is so important.

What actions can you take in your neighborhood or school to share what you know and how you feel about Jesus?

How is your life different from the lives of those who are not Catholic?

47

Conclusion (__ min.)

Growing in Faith

Have the young people close their books. Ask them what they have learned in this lesson about the Church, the Marks of the Church, Ecumenical Councils and apostolic succession. Reopen the books to page 47. Was everything from the **Remember** and **Faith Words** sections named? If not, point these out and help the group name the remaining concepts.

Invite the young people to read the **Reflect and Act** section and to write out their responses in the space provided. If desired, play some soft instrumental music while they do this.

Sing or pray the words to "Anthem" found in the **Pray** section on page 47. Close by offering the Apostles' Creed on page 119 together.

CATECHISM FOCUS

"The Church is the Body of Christ. Through the Spirit and his action in the sacraments, above all the Eucharist, Christ, who once was dead but is now risen, establishes the community of believers as his own Body." (*CCC*, 805)

For additional reference and reflection, see *CCC*, 781–795.

Answers for page 47:
Accept all reasonable answers.

CHAPTER 8

GOALS

to learn that the Church is a sign and instrument of God's life and love among us; to understand the meaning of the sacraments

GETTING READY

■ ***Materials needed:***

Prayer table environment: flower, Bible, decorative cloth, sacramental symbols—bread, goblet filled with red wine or grape juice, oil in a small glass bottle or dish, water in glass bowl or pitcher

Poster board and markers for optional activity in Section Three

Adult Focus

One of the most appealing requests in the New Testament comes from Greek pilgrims who have arrived in Jerusalem to celebrate the Passover. They go directly to Philip and say, "Sir, we would like to see Jesus" (John 12:21).

More than two thousand years later our hearts still resonate with that request. We want to see Jesus and to be reassured that he remains with us always.

Christ and the Church respond to our need with seven grace-filled and effective signs called the sacraments. By these signs we are nourished, healed, and transformed as members of the faith community.

"What was visible in our Savior has passed over into his mysteries," observed Pope Leo the Great, suggesting why the sacraments are so vital in the lives of those who desire to see and follow Christ

Introduction (__ min.)

Point out the symbols on the prayer table and ask the group to identify all the symbols and their origin in nature. Emphasize that these are all symbols that come from the earth and part of ordinary life. Next, encourage the young people to think about what each might represent. Explain that today's lesson will focus on the Seven Sacraments of the Church.

Ask the young people to consider God's presence in their lives. Allow quiet time in which the young people may volunteer to offer a simple prayer thanking God for a specific way in which they experience his presence. Conclude with a short prayer of your own, and join with the young people in saying "Amen!"

Gather the group with their books around the prayer table. Read the poem on page 48 and discuss what the poet is saying about God's goodness and the beauty of Creation. Discuss the contrast

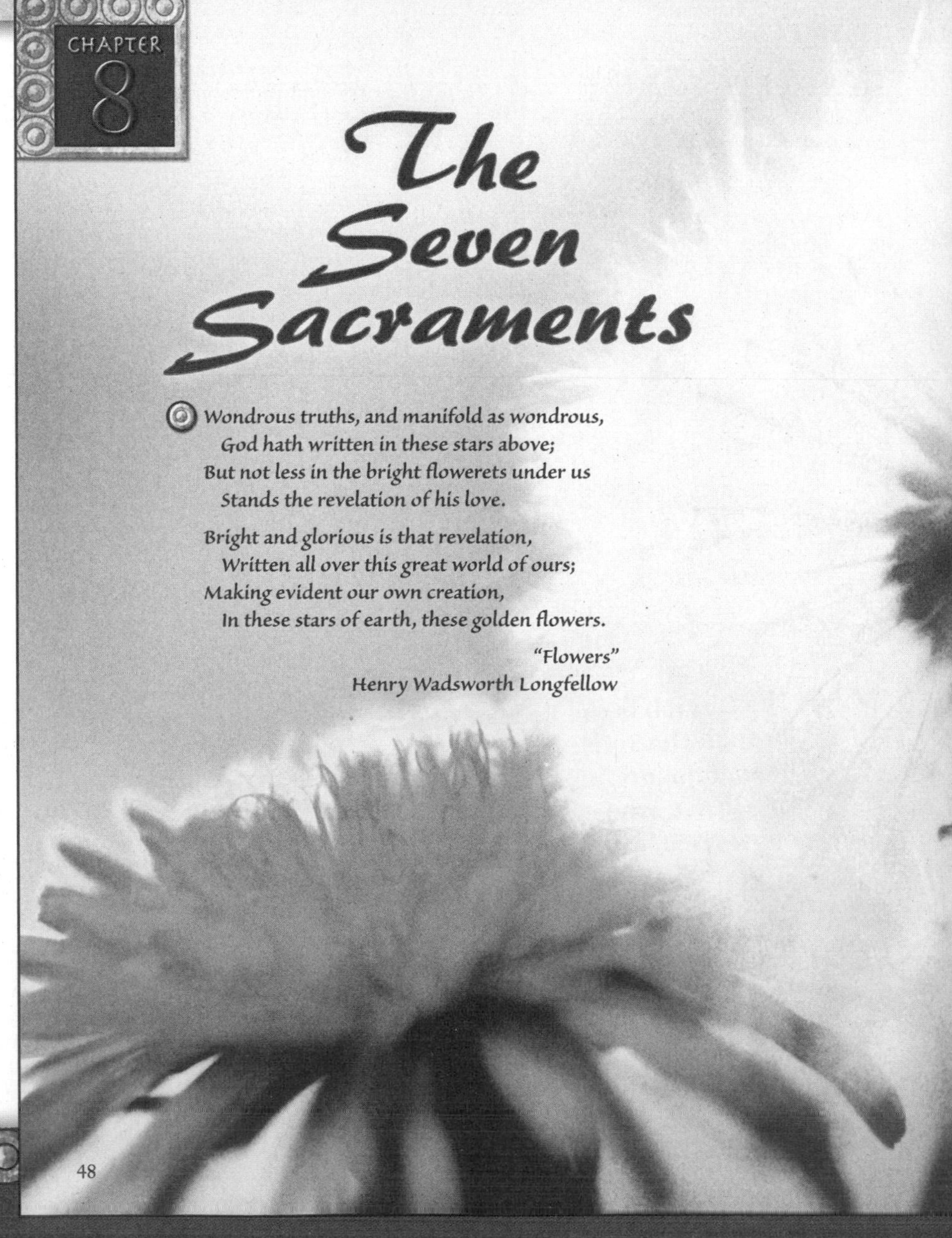

CHAPTER 8

The Seven Sacraments

Wondrous truths, and manifold as wondrous,
God hath written in these stars above;
But not less in the bright flowerets under us
Stands the revelation of his love.

Bright and glorious is that revelation,
Written all over this great world of ours;
Making evident our own creation,
In these stars of earth, these golden flowers.

"Flowers"
Henry Wadsworth Longfellow

48

(see *CCC*, 1115). What Jesus did and said in the Gospels, we now encounter him doing in our own lives.

Each sacrament marks a particular time of growth for us as Christians and invites us to share God's grace in a special way. The three Sacraments of Christian Initiation (Baptism, Confirmation, and Eucharist) initiate us as members of the Church. As members, we are thus charged with carrying out the mission of Jesus Christ in the world. The two Sacraments of Healing (Reconciliation and Anointing of the Sick) restore us when we experience "brokenness" in our physical or spiritual lives. The two Sacraments at the Service of Communion (Matrimony and Holy Orders) strengthen those who receive them to live out a particular mission in the building up of the Church.

Reflection

Consider what the sacraments mean to you. How do they enable you to see Jesus and to live a life of love? How can you share this with your young people?

 **God uses signs to show us his love and power.**

A sign is something visible that tells us about something that is often invisible. From the pages of the Old Testament we learn that God's chosen people lived by signs. These signs showed that God was acting among his people and shaping their lives. People interpreted even the ordinary things that happened as signs of God's action in their lives. The rain, the light and warmth of the sun, a growing family, a long life, and a homeland all signified God's care.

God met both the physical and spiritual needs of his people. He knew that the Israelites were suffering greatly while they were enslaved in Egypt. God called Moses to lead the Israelites out of Egypt and slavery. As they wandered in the desert in search of a place to live, God protected them. When they cried for water and food, God made water flow from a rock and sent them *manna*, "bread from heaven." These were signs to the chosen people that they could always depend on God because he was always with them.

An event, a community tradition, or a person can be a sign. God sent prophets to the Israelites to speak for him and to remind the people of his love. We read in the Old Testament about such prophets as Isaiah, Ezekiel, and Jeremiah—men who sometimes scolded the people, calling them to change their ways. These prophets were signs of God's concern for the people.

49

between the grandeur of the stars and the simplicity of the flower. What is the poet expressing about his experience of God in nature?

Ask: What is an extraordinary way in which you have experienced God? What is an ordinary way you have experienced God?

Presentation (__ min.)

God uses signs to show us his love and power.

In preparation for Section One you may wish to refer to the Book of Exodus to refresh your memory about Moses, the Passover, and the Exodus.

Have the group read Section One on pages 49–50 silently. Ask for responses to the following questions:

- What are some specific signs that God gave his people to show his love and care for them?

Why do you think the Israelites interpreted ordinary signs such as light and rain as signs of God's action in their lives?

How is Jesus a sign of God's love?

Discuss the questions at the end of Section One on page 50. Have the young people write their responses in the space provided.

The Church is a sign and instrument of God's life and love among us.

Have volunteers read the paragraphs under Section Two on pages 50–51.

Ask the group to imagine being a first-time visitor to a Catholic parish. What "signs" might they see that indicate this faith community works together to carry out Jesus' mission of service? Some areas that could be considered:

- how newcomers are welcomed
- how children and young people are treated
- how those who are poor are cared for
- how those who are sick are tended
- how special events are celebrated
- how people pray together.

Encourage the young people to be creative in their responses.

Answer for page 50:

See left column. Accept all reasonable answers.

Jesus Christ himself is the greatest gift of the Father's love. In his interactions with people, Jesus always showed God's love. Like a parent bending to comfort or feed a child or to soothe a family's fears, Jesus was there caring for people in need. In his life and his teaching, Jesus made it clear to us that he was concerned about the needs of everyone.

- Jesus fed the hungry, taught the ignorant, and brought people back to God's love and friendship.
- Jesus met the blind, the deaf, the lame, and the sick—and healed them. He showed them God's power and mercy, and saved them.

These works showed Jesus' compassion, but they also showed more. By his words and his actions, Jesus showed that he was divine. Jesus Christ is the Son of God, the second Person of the Blessed Trinity who became man. In him we see, hear, and touch God. He is the greatest gift of God's love because he is God.

The Church is a sign and instrument of God's life and love among us.

After Pentecost the Apostles and first disciples set about the task of spreading the Good News of Jesus Christ. Since that time, men and women of faith have sought to establish the Church in every nation throughout the world.

By proclaiming and living out the Gospel message, the Church continues what Jesus began. In the community of the Church, we meet the Blessed Trinity. We meet Father, Son, and Spirit when we pray and worship together, and when we follow Jesus' way of living.

It is in the Church that God shares his grace, or life and friendship, with us. The Church, therefore, is an instrument of God's grace. Through the Church we can be united

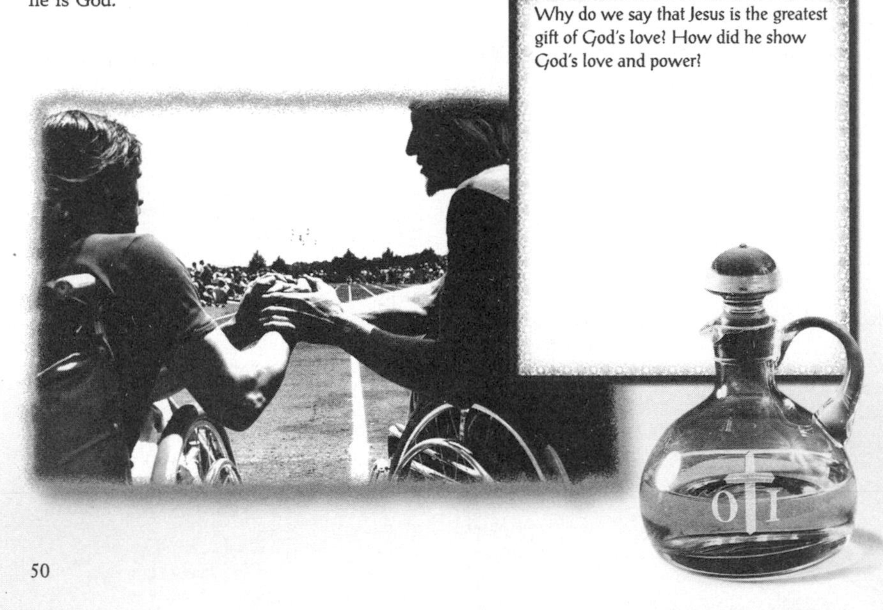

Why do we say that Jesus is the greatest gift of God's love? How did he show God's love and power?

50

with God. The Church is also a sign of God's grace among us. Through the Church we can be united with one another. We are united in carrying out Jesus' mission of service to others. The Church helps us to help others and to live as Jesus did.

Among the ways that the Church is a sign of God's grace are particular acts of worship, or community celebrations, that we call sacraments. Sacraments are events that are signs, too. **Sacraments** are effective signs given to us by Jesus Christ through which we share in God's life. God acts through the sacraments to effect, or cause to happen, the very thing for which these signs stand.

By the power of the Holy Spirit, Jesus is present in the Church in a unique way in his sacraments. The sacraments help us to grow in holiness, to build up the Body of Christ, and to give worship and praise to God.

Describe how the Church is a sign and an instrument of God's love in the world.

Through the Seven Sacraments we share in God's grace.

There are Seven Sacraments, and in each one God invites us to share in his life in a special way. Each of the Seven Sacraments —Baptism, Confirmation, the Eucharist, Penance and Reconciliation, the Anointing of the Sick, Holy Orders, and Matrimony— marks a particular time in our growth as a Christian.

The Church invites us to full participation in Christ's life through the *Sacraments of Christian Initiation*: Baptism, Confirmation, and the Eucharist. Through these three sacraments we are welcomed into the Church, strengthened in faith by the Holy Spirit, and nourished by Christ himself.

- Baptism is the first sacrament of our initiation into the Church. To be baptized means to be born anew, to share in Christ's life. Through Baptism, we become children of God, are freed from sin, and are welcomed into the Church.
- In Confirmation, we receive the Gift of the Holy Spirit in a special way.
- Through the Eucharist we complete our initiation into the Church. The Eucharist is the Sacrament of Christ's Body and Blood. For the rest of our lives we will be nourished, and our life of grace will be sustained, when we receive Holy Communion.

51

Go back over the text on page 51 and have the young people find and underline the definition of sacraments (effective signs given to us by Jesus Christ through which we share in God's life). Stress the role the sacraments play in bringing us together as the Church, the Body of Christ.

Have the young people respond to the closing questions at the end of Section Two on page 51.

Through the Seven Sacraments we share in God's grace.

After the young people have read Section Three on pages 51 and 52, ask for responses to these questions:

- In which sacraments do we share God's life of grace? (all of them)
- What do the sacraments invite us to do? (to share in the life of Christ, each in a special way)

Explain the three groupings of the sacraments and the purpose for each (initiation, healing, and service). You may want to use the sacrament chart on pages 114–115 as you explain each grouping and sacrament.

Have young people write their responses to the questions at the end of Section Three on page 52.

Optional Activity

Arrange for a priest, deacon, or other pastoral leader to take the group on a tour of the parish church in order to see various sacramental objects: baptismal font, holy oils, chalice, etc. Or, invite this person to bring some of these items to class for a presentation.

Answer for page 51:

It is in the Church that God shares his love with us. God especially shares his grace, or life and love, with us when we join together to carry out Jesus' mission to others and when we celebrate the sacraments.

If you have time, do the following.

On a separate sheet of paper, have the young people answer the following questions:

- What sacraments have you received?
- How have you participated in the celebration of these sacraments?
- What signs of the sacraments did you see?
- How does your parish celebrate these sacraments?

Two other sacraments, Penance and the Anointing of the Sick, are known as *Sacraments of Healing*. Even though we begin a new life of grace through the Sacraments of Initiation, we are still subject to suffering, illness, and sin. These two Sacraments of Healing restore and strengthen our life of grace.

In the celebration of the Sacrament of Penance, also known as the Sacrament of Reconciliation, the Church experiences God's loving forgiveness. Those who are truly sorry for their sins and are firmly committed to sin no more, turn back to God. Their relationship with God and the Church is restored, and their sins are forgiven.

The Sacrament of the Anointing of the Sick calls upon the whole Church to care for its sick or aged members. In this sacrament God's grace and comfort are given to those who are seriously ill, or who are suffering because of their old age. Through this sacrament they are united to the suffering of Christ and receive God's grace.

Finally, the Church has two *Sacraments at the Service of Communion*: Holy Orders and Matrimony. These two sacraments are concerned with the Salvation of others. These sacraments give those who receive them a particular mission, or role, in the building up of the Church.

In the Sacrament of Holy Orders, baptized men are ordained to serve the Church as bishops, priests, and deacons.

What is a sacrament? Why are the sacraments important?

Do YOU Know?

It is in the **parish** that we gather as a community of believers who worship and work together. In the parish we celebrate the sacraments, participate in the education of the faith, and grow in love for God and one another through good works. A **pastor** is the priest who leads the parish in worship, prayer, and teaching. Each parish is part of a large group of parishes that make up a diocese. A **diocese** is a local area of the Church led by a bishop.

Bishops, priests, and deacons have different roles and responsibilities in their service to the community, but they all receive the Sacrament of Holy Orders. Only bishops, however, receive the fullness of Holy Orders.

In the Sacrament of Matrimony, a man and a woman become husband and wife and promise to be faithful to each other for the rest of their lives. The priest and community witness to their vows to love each other as Christ loves his Church. This sacrament perfects the love the spouses share and strengthens their unity. Through this sacrament the married couple help each other to live holy lives in service to each other and to the community. They welcome children into their lives and create a home of faith, prayer, and love.

The sacraments are truly sources of life for us. They nourish and strengthen our faith, and in them the faith-filled community of the Church meets the risen Christ.

Do YOU Know?

Read the "Do You Know?" feature on page 52. Talk about your own parish. Help the young people to name the pastor, priests, and deacons who serve there. Then, ask if they know the name of your local bishop. If not, perhaps someone could do a Web search for the Web site of your diocese. You might be able to plan a trip to see the diocesan cathedral.

Answers for page 52:

See Glossary, page 126.

The sacraments are important because they are truly sources of life for us. They nourish and strengthen our faith, and in them the faith-filled community of the Church meets the risen Christ.

Growing in Faith

PRAY

In the sacraments, we begin with signs we can see, feel, or hear: water, oil, bread and wine, human words and gestures. God acts through the ordinary to make our lives extraordinary. Blessing and praising God is one way we respond to God's action in our lives. Pray together the following psalm:

✝ Sing to the LORD a new song;
sing to the LORD, all the earth.
Sing to the LORD, bless his name;
announce his salvation day after day.
Tell God's glory among the nations;
among all peoples, God's marvelous deeds.
Psalm 96:1–3

REMEMBER

The Church teaches...

- Jesus Christ is God's greatest gift. In Jesus we meet the invisible God in a visible way.
- The Church is the visible sign and instrument by which we meet God.
- The Seven Sacraments are effective signs given to us by Jesus Christ through which we share in God's life.
- The sacraments help us to grow in holiness, to build up the Body of Christ, and to give worship to God.

Faith Words

sacraments (p. 51)
parish (p. 52)
pastor (p. 52)
diocese (p. 52)

REFLECT & ACT

Have you ever seen God through the actions of someone else? Describe that person and tell how he or she acted.

What sacraments have you received? How can receiving those sacraments help you to bring Jesus' message to your neighborhood or community?

53

Conclusion (__ min.)

Growing in Faith

Have the young people close their books. Ask them what they have learned in this lesson about the Church, the Seven Sacraments, and the role of a pastor, a parish, and a diocese. Reopen the books to page 53. Was everything from the **Remember** and **Faith Words** sections named? If not, point these out and help the group name the remaining concepts.

Invite the young people to read the **Reflect and Act** section and to write out their responses in the spaces provided. If desired, play some soft instrumental music while they do this.

Then, share specific ways in which receiving the Sacraments of Baptism, Confirmation, Eucharist, and Penance enable the young people to be effective witnesses of Jesus to their community.

Read the paragraph under **Pray** on page 53 and offer the prayer together.

CATECHISM FOCUS

"A sacramental celebration is woven from signs and symbols. In keeping with the divine pedagogy of salvation, their meaning is rooted in the work of creation and in human culture." (*CCC*, 1145)

For additional reference and reflection, see *CCC*, 1113–1130.

Answers for page 53:

Left side:
Accept all reasonable answers. Encourage the young people to be specific in their responses.

Right side:
Accept all reasonable answers.

CHAPTER 9

GOALS

to understand the process of Christian Initiation; to learn about the Gifts of the Holy Spirit

GETTING READY

■ ***Materials needed:***

Place symbols of Baptism and Confirmation on the prayer table. Include water; a dish of oil; a baptismal garment; a white candle for Section Two

Bibles—preferably one for each young person

Pictures of water shown as powerful, refreshing, cleansing, and life-giving for Section Two

7 tagboard sheets with a different Gift of the Holy Spirit listed on each one for optional activity in Section Three

Adult Focus

"Those who are moved by grace to decide to follow Jesus are 'introduced into the life of faith, of the liturgy and of the charity of the People of God.'" (*General Directory for Catechesis*, 51)

Adults who have come into the Church through the Rite of Christian Initiation of Adults (RCIA) experience the process of initiation as a unified journey into a community of faith. This journey culminates in the celebration of the Sacraments of Baptism, Confirmation, and Eucharist usually at the Easter Vigil.

Those who were baptized as infants and celebrated First Eucharist and Confirmation as children or young teens need the witness of these committed adults. They help us to appreciate the power and importance of the Sacraments of Initiation. These

Introduction (__ min.)

Invite the young people to sit quietly while they listen to the reading. Read aloud or ask a volunteer to read 1 John 3:1–2.

Have the young people reflect on the fact that they are children of God. Play music softly while you allow a few minutes for private meditation.

Conclude by praying the Glory to the Father on page 119 together.

Gather the group with their books around the prayer table. Read and discuss the questions on page 55.

Explain that today's lesson will focus on Baptism and Confirmation, two of the three Sacraments of Initiation. They lead us to the Eucharist, the third Sacrament of Initiation. These sacraments have to do with becoming a member of the Church.

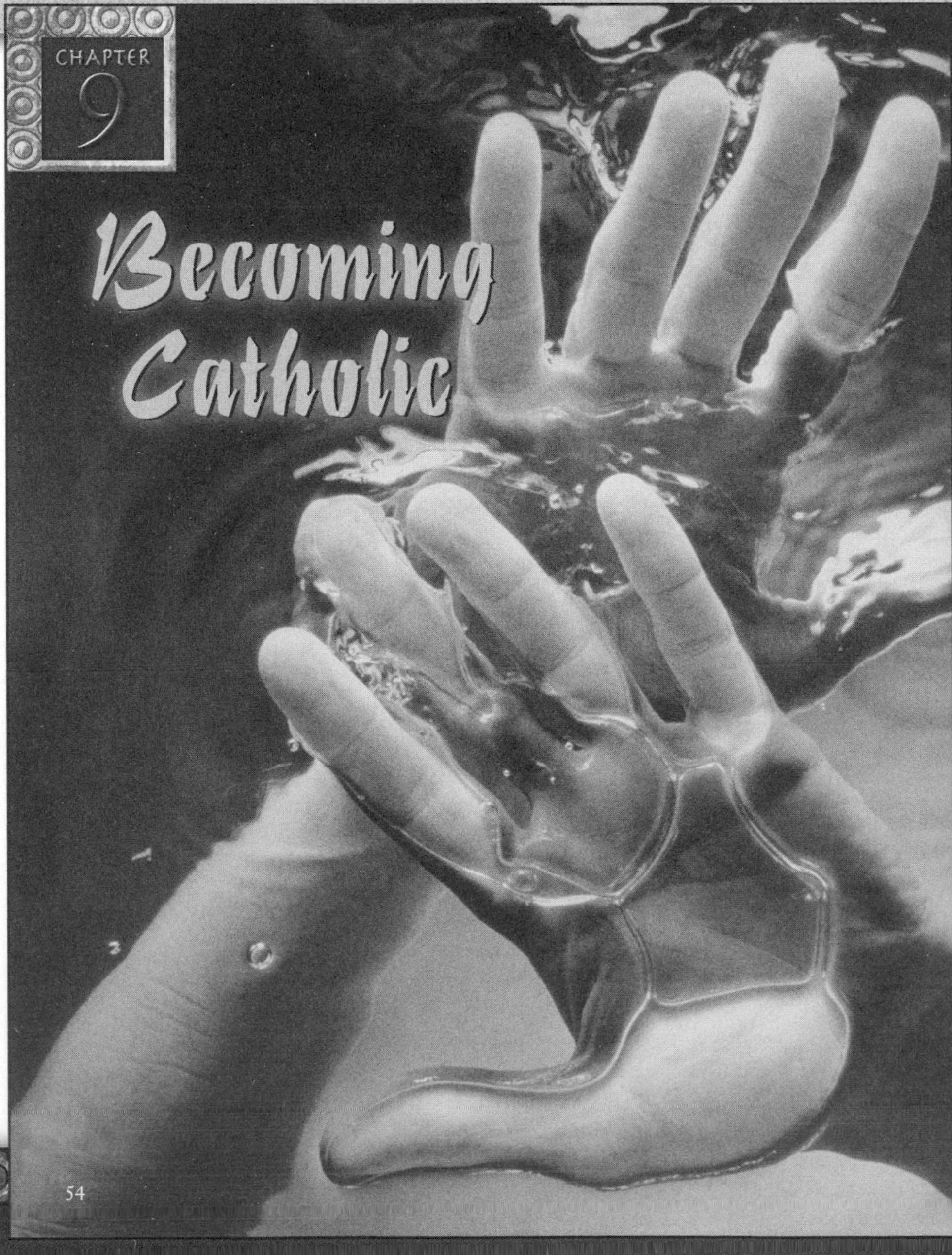

initiated adults remind us of our own call to evangelize others by sharing our stories of how God has been present to us.

How should initiation into the Church, by whatever path, change us? "The three sacraments of Christian initiation closely combine to bring us, the faithful of Christ, to his full stature and to enable us to carry out the mission of the entire people of God in the Church and in the world." (*Rite of Christian Initiation of Adults*, Christian Initiation, General Introduction, 2).

When we respond to the grace of Baptism, Confirmation, and Eucharist our lives show it and others are drawn to Christ and the Church. As sons and daughters of the Most High, we are commissioned to "go, therefore, and make disciples of all nations" (Matthew 28:19).

Reflection

How have you been changed by your initiation into the Church?

Now that you are halfway through *One Faith, One Lord,* name one or two ways you have seen your young people growing in their faith.

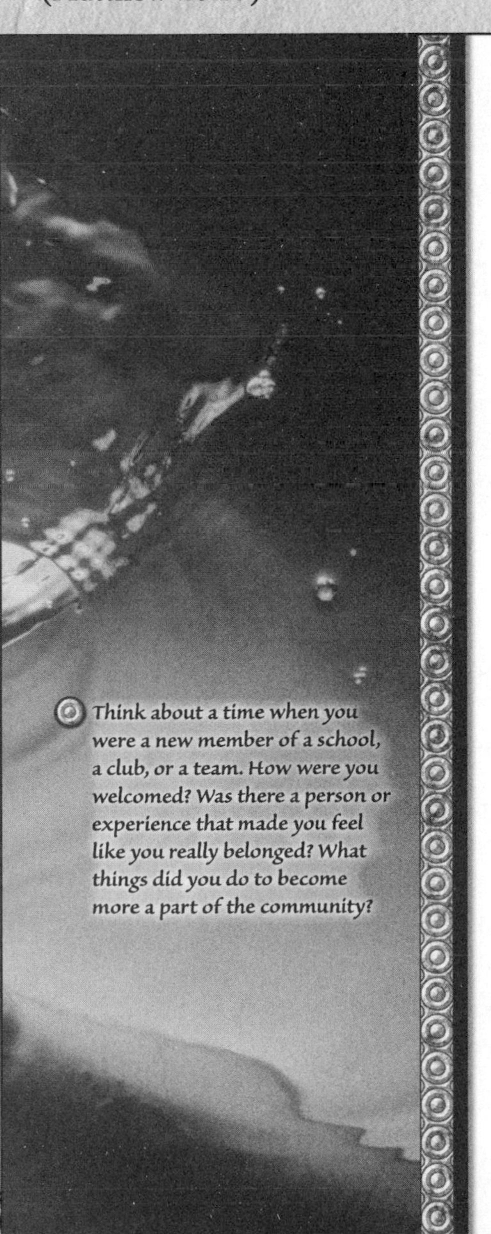

Think about a time when you were a new member of a school, a club, or a team. How were you welcomed? Was there a person or experience that made you feel like you really belonged? What things did you do to become more a part of the community?

In the Sacrament of Baptism we are welcomed into the Church.

The Gospel of Matthew concludes with Jesus telling his first disciples, "Go, therefore, and make disciples of all nations, baptizing them in the name of the Father, and of the Son, and of the holy Spirit" (Matthew 28:19).

These words show us some very important things about the Church and about our life in the Church. They show us that the Church is universal—it is open to all people, everywhere, and all are invited to be one with Christ. These words show us that we begin our life in the Church through the Sacrament of Baptism; we share this sacrament with every member of the Church.

Each of us in the Church is welcomed in Baptism, and each of us is called to welcome others. In our world today people are too often left out, cut off, or held back. Some are even favored at the expense of others. The Church tries to welcome all without distinction. This, after all, is what Jesus did.

Some of the first words we hear from the priest or deacon at Baptism are words of welcome. These words are a part of our initiation into the Church. We call the process of becoming a member of the Church *Christian Initiation*. We are initiated into the Church through the Sacraments of Baptism, Confirmation, and Eucharist.

While our full initiation into the Church always consists of these three sacraments, the process of initiation can vary. Many people are baptized as infants. If we were baptized as babies, we were baptized in the faith of the Church. Our parents and godparents affirmed their own faith and promised to help us grow as faithful Christians.

55

Presentation (__ min.)

In the Sacrament of Baptism we are welcomed into the Church.

Help the group understand that the Sacrament of Baptism includes a special way of welcoming us as members of the Church. Ask volunteers to read aloud Section One on pages 55–56.

Discuss the concept of Christian Initiation and the connection among the Sacraments of Baptism, Confirmation, and Eucharist. Then ask: How does the process of Christian Initiation vary? (Answers will vary; for example: some people are baptized as infants and some people go through RCIA as adolescents or adults)

The Catholic Church today consists of twenty-two Churches: the Roman Catholic Church and twenty-one Eastern Catholic Churches. (See *CCC*, 1201–1203.)

The celebration of Christian Initiation varies among the Churches.

Read the question at the end of Section One on page 56 and have the young people write their responses in the space provided.

Baptism frees us from sin and gives us God's life and love.

Before reading Section Two, show the group a variety of pictures of water as cleansing, refreshing, powerful, life-giving, etc. Then read Section Two on pages 56–57.

Stress that *original* means "first." Recall that Original Sin refers to the first sin committed by the first human beings, who are known to us as Adam and Eve. Original Sin is not something we do ourselves. Each of us is born with Original Sin, but Baptism frees us from this sin. Any personal sins we may have committed before Baptism are forgiven, and we receive a share in God's life, which we call *grace*. Encourage the young people to decide how they can best express their thanks for the gift of Baptism.

When adults are initiated into the Church, they participate in a process of formation through the Rite of Christian Initiation of Adults (RCIA). They receive all three Sacraments of Initiation at the Easter Vigil on Holy Saturday. In the Eastern Church, Confirmation is administered immediately after Baptism and followed by the reception of the Holy Eucharist. The practice also highlights the unity of these sacraments.

No matter when we receive the Sacraments of Initiation, they are celebrated in our parish, which welcomes and provides for us.

Baptism frees us from sin and gives us God's life and love.

In Baptism we are called by name to begin a lifelong relationship with God in the Church. **Baptism** is the first and foundational sacrament by which we become sharers in God's divine life, are freed from Original Sin and all personal sins, become children of God, and are welcomed into the Church. Because a number of important things happen to us in Baptism, this sacrament is necessary for Salvation.

- We receive the Holy Spirit.
- Our sins are forgiven, and we are reborn as children of God.
- We become members of the Body of Christ, the Church.
- We begin our journey in faith, filled with God's life, presence, and favor. This is a journey that will continue throughout our lives.

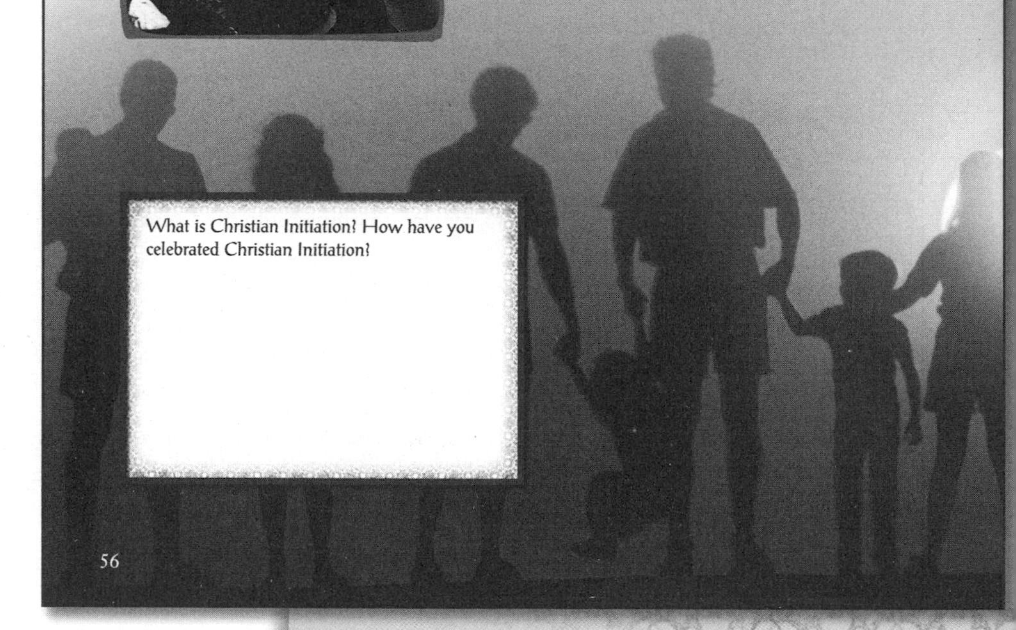

What is Christian Initiation? How have you celebrated Christian Initiation?

56

Have the young people gather around the prayer table. Point out the symbols used for Baptism and briefly explain each one:

- Water is a symbol of cleansing, showing that Original Sin and any personal sins we may have committed are washed away. Water is also a sign of life.

Optional Activity

Imagine that someone was interviewing you about the Church. What are some questions they might ask? What would your answers be?

Members of the group can take turns asking and responding to the questions.

Answers for page 56:

Christian Initiation is the process of becoming a member of the Church.

Some members of your group may not have received all of the Sacraments of Christian Initiation.

Think for a moment about the precious gift of water. Without water we could not live. Water makes things grow. It nourishes and restores. Water cleanses things, too, making them bright and new.

In the water of Baptism, the Holy Spirit cleanses and makes us new, giving us new life and rebirth. The very word *baptize* means "to immerse," or plunge. Through the waters of Baptism, we participate in the Paschal Mystery: Christ's suffering, Death, Resurrection, and Ascension. We rise with him to new life through this sacrament.

Baptism also breaks our ties to sin. All of us have been born into this world with Original Sin, that first sin of humans that separated us from God and brought suffering and evil into the world. Through Baptism we are freed from this sin.

However, we still need to overcome the effects of Original Sin, most particularly our inclination to sin. With God's grace and the help and support of our family and parish, we can choose to do what is right as baptized followers of Christ.

In Baptism we are marked with an indelible character, or spiritual mark, that claims us as belonging to Christ. Because no action on our part can erase this character, Baptism does not need to be, nor can it be, repeated. Baptism is a once-in-a-lifetime sacrament.

What is Baptism?

Do YOU Know?

The ordinary minister of Baptism is a bishop, priest, or deacon. But in an emergency, any person with the right intention can baptize. This is done by pouring water on the person's forehead and saying the words that are always used in the Sacrament of Baptism: "(Name), I baptize you in the name of the Father, and of the Son, and of the Holy Spirit."

57

Do YOU Know?

Have a volunteer read the "Do You Know?" feature on page 57. Stress that it is only in an emergency that anyone can baptize. It is the responsibility of a baptized Christian to do this if they are present at this time. And the words and ritual action, as it is in other baptisms, are used in this case also.

- Oils: the Oil of Catechumens is used as a symbol of strengthening and preparation for the new life ahead. Chrism is a sign of sealing of the Gifts of the Holy Spirit.
- The white garment symbolizes new life in Christ.
- The white candle symbolizes Christ, the Light of the World. It is lit from the Paschal Candle that stands near the altar during the Easter season.

Have the young people write their understanding of Baptism in the space provided at the end of Section Two on page 57.

If you have time, do the following.

Discuss what it means to welcome all without distinction as Jesus did. Have the group work in groups to research the following Gospel stories. How does Jesus treat and interact with the people in each story?

- Mark 12:41–44 (poor widow's contribution)
- Mark 10:13–16 (blessing of the children)
- Mark 1:40–41 (cleansing of a leper)
- Matthew 15:29–31 (healing of many people)
- Luke 14:12–14 (invite the poor to your table)

Answer for page 57:

See Glossary, page 125.

Confirmation seals us with the Holy Spirit and strengthens the grace received at Baptism.

Read Section Three on page 58 with the group. Discuss the connection between Baptism and Confirmation. Discuss the following questions:

- What does it mean to be "sealed" with the Gift of the Holy Spirit? (to be marked with an indelible character, strengthened in our baptismal grace, and to receive the seven special Gifts of the Holy Spirit)

- What are the requirements for the candidates to receive the Sacrament of Confirmation? (candidates must profess the faith, be in a state of grace, desire the sacrament, and be prepared to be a disciple and witness to Christ)

Explain that being in a state of grace means being without unforgiven mortal, or serious sin. Mortal sin is forgiven through the Sacrament of Penance.

Have volunteers read the descriptions of the Gifts of the Holy Spirit on page 58. Have the young people share what each gift might mean in their lives.

Read and discuss the question at the end of Section Three on page 58. Have the young people write their responses in the space provided.

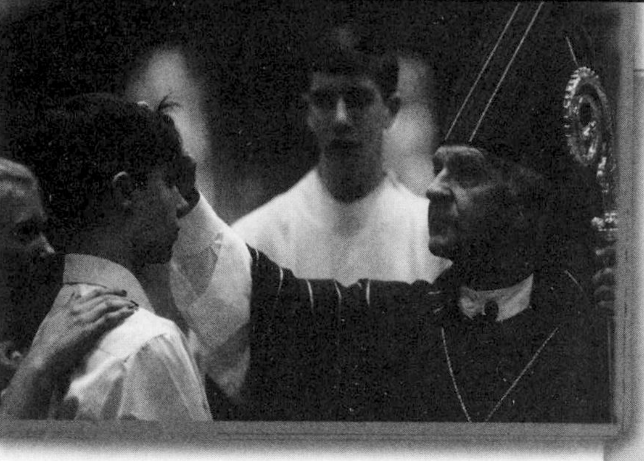

GIFTS OF THE HOLY SPIRIT

Wisdom—the knowledge and ability to recognize and follow God's will in our lives

Understanding—the ability to love others as Jesus calls us to

Counsel (right judgment)—the ability to make good choices

Fortitude (courage)—the strength to give witness to our faith in Jesus Christ

Knowledge—the ability to learn more about God and his plan, leading us to wisdom and understanding

Piety (reverence)—a love and respect for all that God has created

Fear of the Lord (wonder and awe)—a recognition that God's presence and love fills all Creation

Confirmation seals us with the Holy Spirit and strengthens the grace received at Baptism.

In the Sacrament of **Confirmation**, we receive the Gift of the Holy Spirit in a special way. Confirmation continues the life of grace begun in Baptism and strengthens us to be Christ's witnesses. We are sealed with the Gift of the Holy Spirit, the Spirit of truth whom Jesus promised to send and who would guide us always.

A candidate for Confirmation must profess the faith, be in a state of grace, desire the sacrament, and be prepared to be a disciple and witness to Christ. In this sacrament the bishop extends his hands over the candidates for Confirmation and prays that the Gift of the Holy Spirit will be sent to them. The bishop then anoints each candidate with holy oil called Chrism. He does this by laying his hand on the head of the candidate and at the same time making the Sign of the Cross on the person's forehead while saying: "(Name), be sealed with the Gift of the Holy Spirit." The candidate responds, "Amen." Holy oil is a sign of being sealed, or confirmed, with the Holy Spirit.

When we are confirmed, the Holy Spirit strengthens us with seven special gifts. The **Gifts of the Holy Spirit** help us to live as faithful followers and true witnesses of Jesus Christ, strengthening our minds and our wills to do what Christ asks of us.

Like Baptism, Confirmation marks each of us with an indelible character. And, like Baptism, Confirmation is a special moment in our Catholic faith that we only celebrate once. Confirmation cannot be repeated. And both of these sacraments must always be thought of in relation to the third Sacrament of Initiation, the Eucharist.

How can you use the Gifts of the Holy Spirit to show that you are a follower of Christ?

58

Optional Activity

Give each young person a note card with a Gift of the Holy Spirit written on it. Instruct the young people to hold the card so that they cannot see it but others can. Then, have them take turns giving each other clues concerning the Gift of the Holy Spirit that each one is holding. Guessing continues until each young person has guessed his/her Gift of the Holy Spirit. If time permits, exchange cards and repeat the activity.

Answer for page 58:

Have the young people study the chart of the Gifts of the Holy Spirit as they reflect on their answers. Accept all reasonable answers.

Growing in Faith

PRAY

✝ God our Father,
Complete the work you have begun in us.
Keep the Gifts of your Holy Spirit alive
in our hearts.
Unite us in living your Son's Gospel
message and make us eager to do his will.
May we always bless and thank you
for your gifts to us.
Amen.

REMEMBER

The Church teaches...

- Baptism, Confirmation, and the Eucharist are the three Sacraments of Initiation.
- Baptism is the first and necessary sacrament by which we are freed from sin, become children of God, and are welcomed into the Church.
- In Confirmation, we receive the Gift of the Holy Spirit in a special way. We experience, affirm, and receive in a deeper way the life of the Holy Spirit that we first received at Baptism.
- Both Baptism and Confirmation mark us with an indelible character, or spiritual mark. We can receive these sacraments only once.

Faith Words

Baptism (p. 56)
Confirmation (p. 58)
Gifts of the Holy Spirit (p. 58)

REFLECT & ACT

Who are your godparents? What questions might you ask them or your family members about your own Baptism?

Do you know anyone who is preparing to become a Catholic? Think of some questions to ask that person.

59

Conclusion (__ min.)

Growing in Faith

Have the young people close their books. Ask them what they have learned in this lesson about Baptism, Confirmation, and the Gifts of the Holy Spirit. Reopen the books to page 59. Was everything from the **Remember** and **Faith Words** sections named? If not, point these out and help the group name the remaining concepts.

If possible, connect the young people with catechumens from your parish (along with their sponsors). Ask the group of catechumens to share insights into why people choose to become Catholics.

Invite the young people to read the **Reflect and Act** section and to write out their responses in the spaces provided. If desired, play some soft instrumental music while they do this.

Turn to the **Pray** section on page 59. Offer the prayer together.

CATECHISM FOCUS

"Christian initiation is accomplished by three sacraments together: Baptism which is the beginning of new life; Confirmation which is its strengthening; and the Eucharist which nourishes the disciple with Christ's Body and Blood for his transformation in Christ." (*CCC*, 1275)

For additional reference and reflection, see *CCC*, 1262–1274 and 1302–1305.

Answers for page 59:

Left side:
Some young people might not be sure who their godparents are. Allow some time for family discussion at home so that they will be comfortable when the question is raised.

Right side:
Accept all reasonable answers.

Unit 2 Assessment

A. Choose the correct term to complete each statement.

Confirmation	**Pentecost**	**Gifts of the Holy Spirit**
Apostles	**Baptism**	**diocese**
Christian Initiation	**Holy Spirit**	**Holy**
One	**Apostolic**	**Catholic**
Sacraments of Initiation	**Infallibility**	**Church**

1. The ____Holy Spirit____ is the third Person of the Blessed Trinity who guides and strengthens the Church.
2. A ____diocese____ is a local area of the Church led by a bishop.
3. The ____Sacraments of Initiation____ is a name given to the Sacraments of Baptism, Confirmation, and Eucharist.
4. ____Pentecost____ is the day on which the Holy Spirit came to Jesus' first disciples as Jesus promised.
5. ____One____ is the Mark of the Church that describes the unity of the Church.
6. The ____Church____ is the community of people who believe in Jesus Christ, have been baptized in him, and follow his teachings.
7. ____Baptism____ is the first and foundational sacrament by which we become sharers in God's divine life, are freed from Original Sin and all personal sins, become children of God, and are welcomed into the Church.
8. ____Apostles____ is the name given to the twelve men chosen by Jesus to share in his mission in a special way.
9. The Church is ____holy____ because she shares in the holiness of God.
10. ____Christian Initiation____ is the process by which we become members of the Church.
11. ____Confirmation____ is the sacrament in which we receive the Gift of the Holy Spirit in a special way.
12. ____Infallibility____ means that the pope and bishops are guided in truth when defining the doctrines of faith and morals.
13. ____Catholic____ is the Mark of the Church that identifies the Church as universal, open to all who believe.
14. The ____Gifts of the Holy Spirit____ help us to live as faithful followers and true witnesses of Jesus Christ.
15. ____Apostolic____ is the Mark of the Church that identifies the Church as founded by Christ on the Apostles.

B. Circle the response that does *not* belong.

1. Jesus told his followers that the Holy Spirit would
   a. remain with them forever.
   (b.) come to them on Good Friday.
   c. lead them to the truth.
   d. strengthen them to be his witnesses.

2. The Marks of the Church identify it as
   (a.) an exclusive closed community.
   b. a community dedicated to God and one another.
   c. based on apostolic authority.
   d. welcoming to all people.

3. The sacraments are
   a. life-giving signs of Christ's presence.
   b. acts of worship.
   c. seven in number.
   (d.) personal and private.

4. Through the Sacrament of Baptism we
   a. receive the Holy Spirit.
   (b.) are kept from sin forever.
   c. are reborn as children of God.
   d. become members of the Church.

5. Through the Sacrament of Confirmation we
   a. are anointed with holy oil.
   b. receive the Holy Spirit in a new way.
   (c.) have water poured on our head as a sign of cleansing.
   d. are strengthened with special Gifts of the Holy Spirit.

C. Share your faith by responding thoughtfully to these questions.

1. What signs do you see that show you God is truly present and active in our world today?
   Answers may vary. Answers may include mention of people, sacraments, Creation, the Church.

2. How is the Church a sign and an instrument of God's life and love among us?
   Through the Church we are united in carrying out Jesus' mission of service to others. (See page 51.) It is in the Church that God shares his life and love with us. (See page 50.)

3. Explain in your own words how Jesus acts in and through the sacraments.
   Accept all reasonable responses. (See page 51 for content that should be included in answer.)

4. What does it mean to you to be a witness to Christ? What would a person see or hear or sense in you that would show that you are a Catholic?
   We must give witness to Christ in all we say and do. People should see the power of Christ in our lives. (See page 40.)

5. Reflect for a moment on a problem or decision you and other young people must face or make in today's world. How can your faith help you to make right choices?
   Be sure the problem or decision is stated. Allow for individual personal responses to the second part of the question. Accept all reasonable responses.

Semester 1 Assessment

A. Choose the correct term to complete each statement.

sacraments	**Divine Inspiration**	**Divine Revelation**	**Bible**	**Apostles**
Grace	**Gospels**	**Church**	**Paschal Mystery**	**Messiah**

1. The ____Church____ is the community of people who believe in Jesus Christ, have been baptized in him, and follow his teachings.

2. The ____Apostles____ are the twelve men chosen by Jesus to share in his mission in a special way.

3. ____Messiah____ means "God's Anointed One," the Savior.

4. The accounts found in the New Testament of God's Revelation through Jesus Christ are known as the ____Gospels____.

5. ____Divine Revelation____ is God making himself known to us.

6. ____Divine Inspiration____ is the special guidance that the Holy Spirit gave to the human authors of the Bible.

7. The ____Bible____ is the written account of God's Revelation and his relationship with his people.

8. The ____Paschal Mystery____ refers to the suffering, Death, Resurrection, and Ascension of Jesus Christ.

9. ____Grace____ is a participation, or sharing, in God's life and friendship.

10. ____Sacraments____ are effective signs given to us by Jesus Christ through which we share in God's life.

B. Describe in your own words these mysteries and beliefs of the Catholic Church.

1. The Incarnation: The Son of God took on our human nature and lived with us. (Also see Glossary, p. 125.)

2. The Blessed Trinity: the mystery of three Persons in one God: Father, Son, and Holy Spirit (Also see Glossary, p. 125.)

3. The Annunciation: the name given to the angel's visit to Mary and the announcement that she would be the virgin mother of the Son of God (Also see Glossary, p. 125)

4. Pentecost: the name given to the day on which the Holy Spirit came upon the Apostles, fifty days after Easter (Also see Glossary, p. 126)

5. Easter: the name given to the day that Jesus rose from the dead—the Resurrection of Jesus is a central belief of our faith

C. Circle the letter beside the correct response.

1. We become members of the Church through the Sacrament of
   a. Holy Orders.
   b. Grace.
   (c.) Baptism.
   d. Eucharist.

2. The part of the Bible in which we read about God and the early Israelites is the
   (a.) Old Testament.
   b. New Testament.
   c. Gospels.
   d. Revelation.

3. Faith is
   a. just another way of looking at life.
   (b.) a belief in things unseen.
   c. one of the sacraments.
   d. a feast of the Church.

4. Because we are made in God's image
   a. we are the same as all of his creatures.
   b. we have no soul.
   (c.) we can know and love God.
   d. we are not free to make choices.

5. By his actions, Jesus showed that he is
   a. only divine.
   b. only human.
   (c.) fully divine and fully human.
   d. half human and half divine.

D. Answer as completely and thoughtfully as you can.

1. What do we learn from the New Testament about Jesus Christ being truly human? about Jesus Christ being truly God's Son?
   Jesus was born of Mary; was obedient to his parents; experienced hunger, thirst, sadness, happiness, and death. Jesus always did the will of God, his Father, forgave sins; worked miracles; restored life to the dead; rose from the dead.

2. What are some images that Jesus used to describe the Kingdom of God? a tiny seed that grows into a great tree; yeast that makes bread rise; a buried treasure; a pearl; a net that catches many fish

3. How do the sacraments help us to grow in faith and become stronger witnesses to Jesus Christ?
   See page 51, left column.

4. What does the story of Jesus' Resurrection mean to you? What hope does it give you?
   Accept all reasonable responses.

5. How did the Holy Spirit help the first followers of Jesus? How is the Holy Spirit helping you?
   The Holy Spirit strengthened and encouraged the disciples to follow Jesus. Accept reasonable responses for the second question.

CHAPTER 10

GOALS

to appreciate that Jesus gives himself to us in the Eucharist; to understand the Eucharist as both a meal and a sacrifice

GETTING READY

■ *Materials needed:*

Prayer table environment: loaf of bread, wineglass filled with grape juice or wine, Bible, decorative cloth

Poster board and markers

Bible for the optional activity in Section Two

Adult Focus

The African Masai word for *Eucharist* means "food for the heart." When we recall how Jesus celebrated the Eucharist with his friends at the Last Supper, we can appreciate how well the Masai word expresses Jesus' intention.

The Gospel accounts make it clear that Jesus fully intended and eagerly expected to provide his disciples with "food for the heart" before he returned to his Father. He had made detailed preparations well in advance. When the hour finally arrived, he told them, "I have eagerly desired to eat this Passover with you before I suffer" (Luke 22:15).

Introduction (__ min.)

Gather the young people around the prayer table. Ask the group to think about the various titles of Jesus. Make a list of these titles on the chalkboard or poster board (for example: *Word of God, Savior of the World, Messiah, Bread of Life, Sacred Heart*). Explain that these titles of Jesus can be made into a prayer called a *litany*. Pray the litany by having the group respond, "Have mercy on us," after each title of Jesus is prayed. When you reach the end of the litany, join with the young people in saying, "Amen."

Have a volunteer read aloud the paragraph on page 65. Discuss the questions that follow. Encourage the young people to name the special words, actions, and symbols that are used in specific celebrations. Examples are singing to someone on his or her birthday, fireworks on the Fourth of July, the preparing a meal on Thanksgiving.

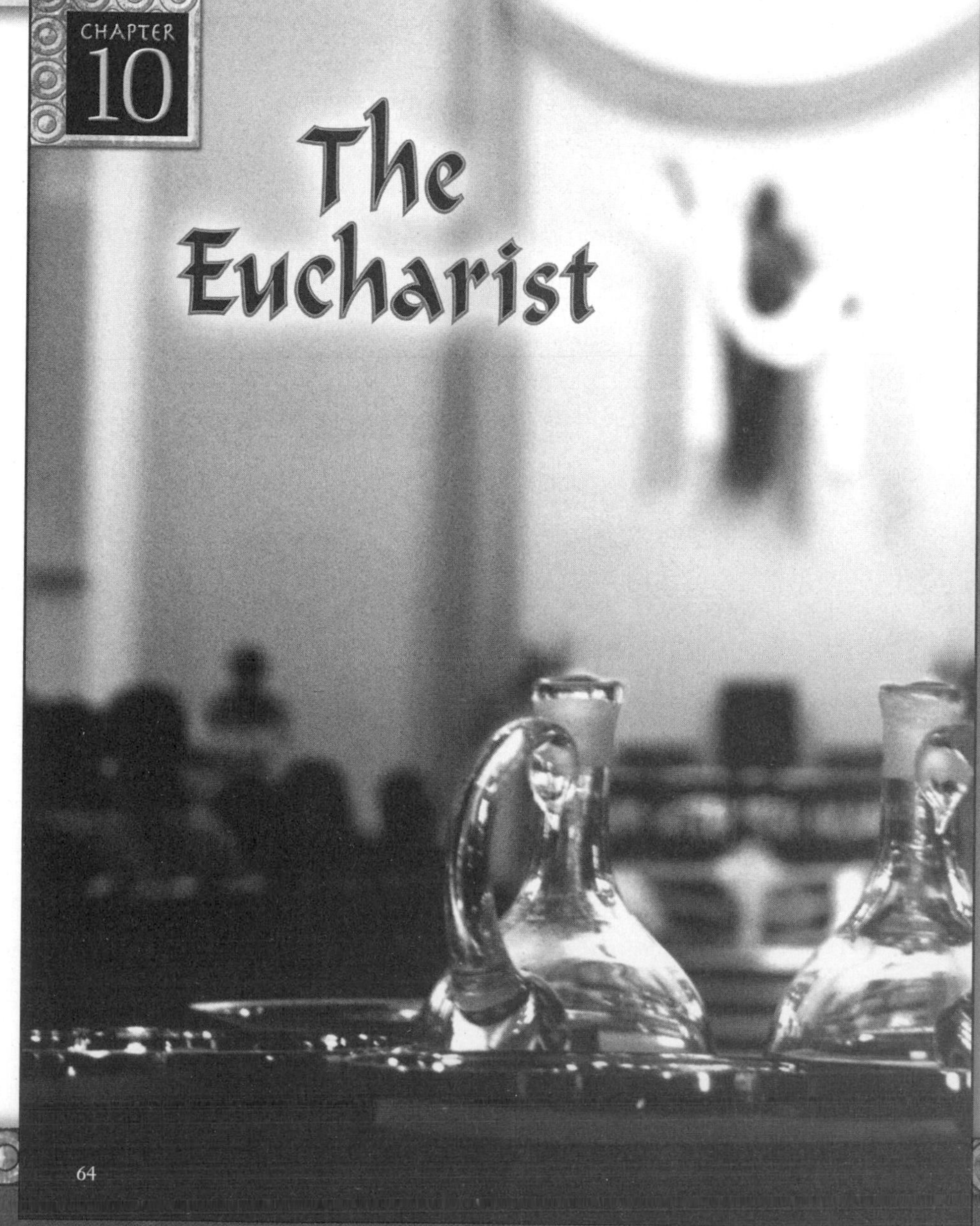

Jesus knows that the food he is about to offer will give life to the world. He knows that the giving will cost no less than his life. Yet as we read in John's Gospel, "He loved his own in the world and he loved them to the end" (John 13:1).

When we celebrate the Eucharist, we remember how Jesus gave himself, Body and Blood, to provide us with this "food for the heart."

By this Sacrament of Initiation, we are made one with Christ whom we receive in Holy Communion. We are also made one with the Body of Christ in the assembled community. We are nourished, and sent to be the Body of Christ in the world.

Reflection

How is the Eucharist food for your heart?

The word *eucharist* means "to give thanks to God."

In the spirit of eucharistic love, offer a prayer of thanksgiving for each young person in your class.

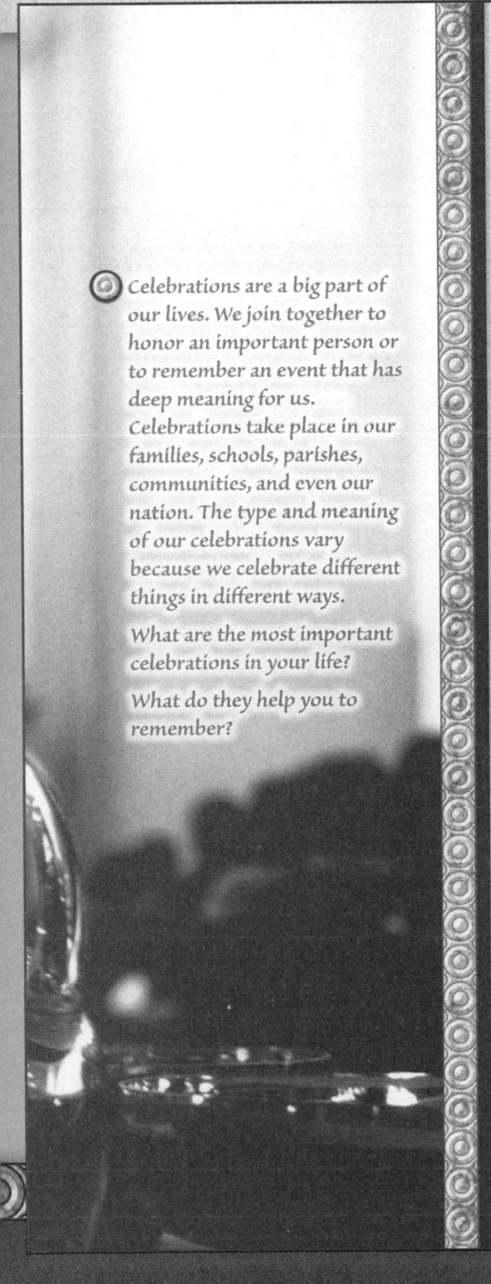

Celebrations are a big part of our lives. We join together to honor an important person or to remember an event that has deep meaning for us. Celebrations take place in our families, schools, parishes, communities, and even our nation. The type and meaning of our celebrations vary because we celebrate different things in different ways.

What are the most important celebrations in your life?

What do they help you to remember?

1 Jesus gave us the Eucharist at the Last Supper.

In the Bible we read of many celebrations among the Israelites. Sacrifice was one of their chief forms of celebrating and worshiping the one true God. At their celebrations the Israelites remembered their past great moments of victory and deliverance. One celebration was more important to them than all others. In this celebration they remembered that God had freed them from slavery in Egypt by helping them to escape from their Egyptian masters.

On the night before this escape, the Israelites would save their newborn children from death if they did as their leader, Moses, told them. Speaking in God's name Moses ordered each Israelite family to kill a young lamb and to sprinkle its blood on the doorposts and frames of their homes. The people were then to have a special meal of roasted lamb, unleavened bread, wine, and bitter herbs:

> This is how you are to eat it: with your loins girt, sandals on your feet and your staff in hand, you shall eat like those who are in flight. It is the Passover of the LORD. For on this same night I will go through Egypt, striking down every first-born of the land. . . . But the blood will mark the houses where you are. Seeing the blood, I will pass over you.
> Exodus 12:11–13

This great event is known as the **Passover**, the feast on which Jewish people remember the miraculous way that God saved them from death and slavery in ancient Egypt. God also instructed Moses to tell the people to remember and celebrate this saving event always:

65

Talk about other rituals that the young people may have experienced. Ask: why do you think rituals are an important part of many celebrations? What purpose do the rituals serve in the celebration? (Rituals should direct attention to the reason for the celebration.) Remind the young people that it is important in any celebration to keep an understanding of the meaning and focus of its rituals.

Presentation (__ min.)

1 Jesus gave us the Eucharist at the Last Supper.

Have volunteers read the first five paragraphs of Section One on page 65. Write *Passover* on the chalkboard or poster board and have volunteers list words and phrases that describe this celebration (for example: *sacrifice*, *blood*, *lamb*, *liberation*, *salvation*).

Finish reading the remaining paragraphs of Section One on

page 66. Write *Last Supper* on the chalkboard or poster board. Ask the young people to list words or phrases that describe this celebration (for example: *sacrifice, covenant, bread and wine, Body and Blood,* etc.).

Next, compare the list of words for Passover and Last Supper. How are the celebrations similar? How are they different?

Discuss the question at the end of Section One, top of page 67, and have the young people write their responses in the space provided.

We celebrate the Eucharist at Mass.

Recall the meaning of the word *eucharist* and ask, "For what do we give thanks at Mass?"

Explain how the early Church first celebrated the Eucharist in people's homes. Only gradually, as the Church grew, did the ritual of the Eucharist take on a different style. However, the basic elements of the Eucharist have not changed throughout the ages: giving thanks to God in the assembly, proclaiming the Word of God, remembering what Jesus did, sharing in the breaking of the bread, and being sent out to do Jesus' work.

The Last Supper, Andy Warhol, 1986

This day shall be a memorial feast for you, which all your generations shall celebrate with pilgrimage to the LORD, as a perpetual institution. . . . Keep, then, this custom of the unleavened bread. Since it was on this very day that I brought your ranks out of the land of Egypt. . . .
Exodus 12:14,17

Centuries later Jesus celebrated this same Passover meal every year with his family and friends. On the night before he died, Jesus shared the Passover meal with his Apostles. At that meal, which Christians now call the Last Supper, Jesus explained that his life would be sacrificed.

- Through the shedding of his blood, the community of believers would be saved from sin and death.
- Through Jesus there would be a new and everlasting covenant with God.

Jesus' Last Supper was something very different from all other Passover meals that had been celebrated. This is the way part of it is described in Luke's Gospel:

> Then he took the bread, said the blessing, broke it, and gave it to them, saying, "This is my body, which will be given for you; do this in memory of me." And likewise the cup after they had eaten, saying, "This cup is the new covenant in my blood, which will be shed for you."
> Luke 22:19–20

The bread and wine still looked and tasted like bread and wine, but they were now what Jesus said they were: his very Body and Blood. Jesus told his Apostles to repeat in his memory what he had done at the Last Supper. They would do this in the **Eucharist**, the Sacrament of his Body and Blood. Through this sacred meal, they would remember what Jesus did for all of us by his Death and Resurrection. Jesus would be really present to them.

66

Optional Activity

Have a volunteer read John 6:66–69. Discuss what the disciples might have felt when they saw people return to their former way of life rather than continuing to follow Jesus. What reason does Peter give for remaining with Jesus? (Peter believed and was convinced that Jesus was the Holy One of God.)

Why were Jesus and his Apostles gathered at the Last Supper? What happened at the Last Supper?

We celebrate the Eucharist at Mass.

Very shortly after Jesus' Resurrection the small community of believers began to do what Jesus had told them to do in his memory. They worshiped together as one people drawn together by the Holy Spirit and united in the risen Christ. Their celebrations consisted of listening to the Scriptures, reflecting on them, and recognizing Jesus' presence in the Eucharist.

Through history the celebration of the Eucharist has been called by many different names. Some of them are "the Lord's Supper," "the breaking of the bread," "the Holy Sacrifice," and the name *Eucharist* itself, which means, "to give thanks to God." However, the name most often used for the celebration of the Eucharist is **Mass**, the Church's great prayer of praise and thanks to God the Father.

When we gather to celebrate the Eucharist, the Holy Spirit is present. When we take part in our parish's weekly celebration of the Mass, we recall the great deeds of Jesus Christ by which he saved us. We thank God the Father for the gift of his Son, and through the power of the Holy Spirit the saving power of Jesus is made present to us. When we receive Holy Communion we share in God's life and are nourished and strengthened. We commit to living as God calls us to live.

Sunday, the "Lord's Day," is the principal day for celebrating the Eucharist because it is the day of the Lord's Resurrection. That is why we are obliged as faithful believers to participate in the Mass every Sunday or in the vigil Mass on Saturday evening. We are also obligated to participate in the Mass on Holy Days of Obligation.

Why is the Sunday celebration of the Mass the most important action of our week?

Do YOU Know?

Our ancestors in faith used the term *covenant* to describe God's relationship with them. In the Bible a covenant is a solemn agreement between God and his people, frequently confirmed by a sacrifice to God or a solemn ritual. We read in the Old Testament that God made a covenant with Noah and all living beings after the flood. God made a covenant with Abraham and his descendants. God made a covenant with Moses on Mount Sinai. Jews today honor this covenant, keeping God's laws and following rituals established centuries ago.

In Jesus Christ God has established his new and everlasting covenant. Jesus' Death on the cross is the sacrifice of the new covenant—his life and Death restore humanity's relationship with God.

67

Have the group read Section Two silently. Ask them to compare the way the early Christians celebrated the Eucharist with the way we celebrate it today.

If possible, plan to attend a weekend Mass together. Write on the chalkboard or give the group copies of the times for parish weekend and daily Masses.

Explain that in addition to celebrating the Eucharist on Sunday, we are obliged to participate in the Mass on Holy Days of Obligation. Have the young people look at the chart listing the Holy Days of Obligation page 68. Ask them to note these days and to determine which holy day the Church will observe next.

Have the young people write their responses to the question at the end of Section Two on page 67.

If you have time, do the following.

Have the young people work in small groups to brainstorm ideas for a leaflet to encourage young people to attend Mass. Ask the small groups to present their ideas. As a group, choose one leaflet idea to implement and insert into the parish's weekly bulletin. If possible, have volunteers distribute the parish's weekly bulletin with leaflet insert at an upcoming Mass.

Do YOU Know?

Read the "Do You Know?" feature on page 67. Explain that God invited human beings to experience his love and forgiveness in his covenant with Noah and all living beings. In his covenant with Abraham, God promised that Abraham's descendents would become a great nation, in return God asked that Abraham serve and worship God alone. In his covenant with Moses, God asked that the Israelites worship God alone as the one true God, in return God would make them his special people.

Answers for page 67:

Left:

Jesus and his Apostles were celebrating the Passover meal. (See page 66.)

Right:

Accept all reasonable answers.

The Eucharist is both a sacrifice and a meal.

Have the young people read Section Three silently.

Use Section Three to develop an understanding of the Eucharist as both a meal and a sacrifice. Emphasize that, although the bread and wine at Mass still look the same, they are no longer really bread and wine. They have become the Body and Blood of Christ; they are now our spiritual food and drink. Jesus is with us under the appearances of bread and wine. This is called the *Real Presence* of Christ in the Eucharist. (Real Presence receives a full treatment in Chapter 11, "The Mass.")

Call attention to the chart *Holy Days of Obligation* on page 68. Tell the young people that Catholics are obliged to participate in the Mass on those days.

Read the question at the end of Section Three on page 68. Have the young people describe, in their own words, the Eucharist as a meal and a sacrifice.

The Eucharist is both a sacrifice and a meal.

The Eucharist gives our lives purpose, meaning, and hope. But we must be open to Jesus Christ's presence in the Eucharist.

As Catholics we know that the Eucharist, our great prayer of thanksgiving, is both a meal and a sacrifice. Remembering the following points might make it easier to understand why we believe the Eucharist is a meal:

- Jesus gave us the Eucharist at the Passover meal. Jesus said to his disciples, "Take and eat; this is my body" (Matthew 26:26).
- We eat and drink Jesus' Body and Blood each time we receive Holy Communion.
- We are nourished in faith and strengthened for discipleship, just as food and drink provide us physical nourishment.

To better understand the Eucharist as sacrifice, we should look at the meaning of sacrifice in Jesus' time. When the priests of the Old Testament made sacrifices to the one true God, they offered the necessities of life—the meatiest and most pure lamb of their flock, the ripest wheat from their harvest, the finest wine from their grapes. They did not kill animals to be cruel. They surrendered to God the Creator the things they needed to live and flourish. Their sacrifice, then, was both a symbol of their appreciation for the gift of Creation and a giving of their lives to God.

The Mass is the sacrifice of Jesus giving himself totally for us on the cross.

- The Mass is a memorial of the saving work of Jesus' suffering, Death, and Resurrection.
- In the breaking of the bread and the pouring out of the cup, Jesus' sacrificial offering to the Father is made present.
- The Eucharist is also the sacrifice of the Church. Our joys, pain, prayers, and work—those things that make each of us who we are—are united with Christ's sacrifice.
- It is Christ himself acting through the ministry of the priest who offers the Mass.

What do we mean when we say that the Mass is both a meal and a sacrifice?

The Church in the United States observes six Holy Days of Obligation:

1. Solemnity of Mary, Mother of God (Jan 1)
2. Ascension (when celebrated on Thursday during Easter season)*
3. Assumption of Mary (Aug 15)
4. All Saints' Day (Nov 1)
5. Immaculate Conception (Dec 8)
6. Christmas (Dec 25)

*(Most dioceses celebrate the Ascension on the following Sunday.)

68

Optional Activity

Provide quiet time for the young people to reflect on the Eucharist as Jesus' gift of himself. Distribute pieces of paper and pens. Encourage the young people to write a prayer of thanksgiving for the Eucharist.

Answer for page 68:

meal: See bulleted items, left column.
sacrifice: See bulleted items, right column.

GROWING IN FAITH

PRAY

During the Mass we pray together a memorial acclamation to express our faith in the risen Jesus who gave his life for our Salvation. We pray:

✝ When we eat this Bread and drink this Cup,
we proclaim your Death,
O Lord,
until you come again.
Amen.

REMEMBER

The Church teaches...

- The Eucharist, the Sacrament of Christ's Body and Blood, is the third and only repeatable Sacrament of Initiation.
- The Eucharist is a memorial of Jesus' saving Death and Resurrection.
- Jesus Christ is truly and really present in the Eucharist under the appearances of bread and wine.
- The celebration of the Eucharist is called the Mass, which is both a meal and a sacrifice.

Faith Words

Passover (p. 65)
Eucharist (p. 66)
Mass (p. 67)

REFLECT & ACT

The refrain of the Communion song "We Remember" often sung at Mass includes the words "We remember, we celebrate, we believe." Think about what you have learned about the Eucharist.

Name at least one important truth of our faith for each of the three actions below:

We remember...

We celebrate...

We believe...

What blessings will you thank God for the next time you participate in the Mass?

69

Conclusion (__ min.)

Growing in Faith

Have the young people close their books. Ask them what they have learned in this lesson about the Passover event. Draw from them what they know about the Eucharist as a sacrifice of Christ's Body and Blood. Finally, what do they now know about the Eucharist as a memorial of Christ's Death and Resurrection, the Eucharist as a meal, and the Eucharist as a sacrifice? Open the books to page 69. Was everything from the **Remember** and **Faith Words** sections named? If not, point these out and help the group name the remaining concepts.

Invite the young people to read the **Reflect and Act** section and to write out their responses in the spaces provided. If desired, play some soft instrumental music while they do this.

Turn to the **Pray** section on page 69. Have a volunteer read the paragraph. Then, offer the closing prayer together.

CATECHISM FOCUS

"The holy Eucharist completes Christian initiation. Those who have been raised to the dignity of the royal priesthood by Baptism and configured more deeply to Christ by Confirmation participate with the whole community in the Lord's own sacrifice by means of the Eucharist." (*CCC*, 1322)

For additional reference and reflection, see *CCC*, 1324–1327.

Answers for page 69:

Accept all reasonable answers.

CHAPTER 11

GOALS

to understand the Mass, the Eucharistic celebration, as the central act of Catholic worship; to learn about the parts of the Mass

GETTING READY

- *Materials needed:*

photos or images of several types of Catholic churches for optional activity

Prayer table environment: empty bowl, Bible, decorative cloth

Poster board and markers for the Opening Prayer

Pencils/pens and small pieces of paper for the Opening Prayer

Lectionary and missalette or hymnal for Section One

Adult Focus

"Christ is always present in his Church, especially in 'liturgical celebrations.' Communion with Jesus Christ leads to the celebration of his salvific presence in the sacraments, especially the Eucharist. The Church ardently desires that all the Christian faithful be brought to that full, conscious and active participation which is required by the very nature of the liturgy." (*General Directory for Catechesis*, 85)

The worshiping community gathers at the Mass to admit sinfulness, to be reconciled, and to stand together to praise and thank God in whom "'we live and move and have our being'" (Acts of the Apostles 17:28).

How can we help one another and those we serve to experience the Mass as a vital, joyful, and prayerful celebration?

Introduction (__ min.)

Gather the group around the prayer table. Recall that the Mass is the celebration of the Eucharist. It is also the time in which we come together as a community to worship and pray. During the general intercessions at Mass, we offer prayers for the Church, the world, those who suffer and are in need, and the people of our parish. Explain that there is also a time for each individual to offer his or her own prayers either silently or aloud.

Distribute small pieces of paper and pens. Ask each person to write an intercessory prayer, using the following as a simple formula:

For ___ [person/group] ___, that God will ___ [specific request] ___, we pray to the Lord.

Begin by making the Sign of the Cross together. Offer a brief prayer, asking God to hear and respond to the needs for which we pray. Invite the young people

We can be an active presence to one another as we gather for the liturgy by being hospitable.

We can be active listeners to the Word of God by first reflecting on the readings at home and then paying careful attention during the proclamation at the Mass.

We can become actively engaged in the Eucharistic Prayer by remembering what God has done in our lives, summoning a desire to give thanks, gathering the needs of those around us into our prayer, and making our responses with conviction.

Finally, the most effective way to be full and active participants is to live our Amens. By our actions between liturgies we say Amen to justice, Amen to compassion, Amen to the peace of Christ.

Reflection

Think about your participation at Mass. Are there ways that you could participate more fully? How can you help your young people learn to participate more fully in the Mass?

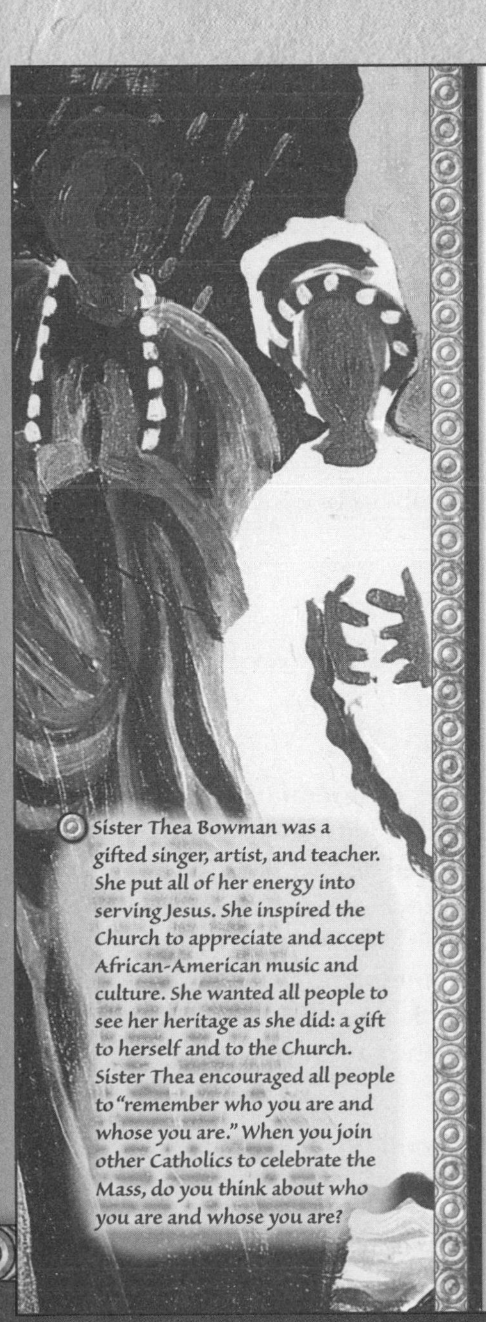

Sister Thea Bowman was a gifted singer, artist, and teacher. She put all of her energy into serving Jesus. She inspired the Church to appreciate and accept African-American music and culture. She wanted all people to see her heritage as she did: a gift to herself and to the Church. Sister Thea encouraged all people to "remember who you are and whose you are." When you join other Catholics to celebrate the Mass, do you think about who you are and whose you are?

In the Liturgy of the Word we listen to the Word of God.

The **liturgy** is the official public prayer of the Church. In the liturgy we proclaim and celebrate the mystery of Christ. The word *liturgy* comes from a Greek word that means "a public work" or "a service in the name of or on behalf of the people." In the liturgy we are brought together by Jesus, in the unity of the Holy Spirit, to bless God our Father and thank him for all of his blessings. We meet Christ in the liturgy, and in it we share in the mystery of his life, Death, and Resurrection. Jesus told us that "where two or three are gathered together in my name, there I am in the midst of them" (Matthew 18:20).

The Mass—the celebration of the Eucharist—is the central and most important act of worship. In every corner of the world, Catholics are called together to participate in the Mass, to raise their voices in praise and thanksgiving to God. We can hear the words of the Mass spoken in every language. But the basic structure of the Mass is always the same, no matter where we are.

The Mass has two principal parts, the *Liturgy of the Word* and the *Liturgy of the Eucharist*. Two additional parts begin and end the Mass. Each part of the Mass draws us into the mystery that we celebrate, strengthens our baptismal grace, and unites us as members of the Church, the Body of Christ.

The beginning of the Mass brings us together as an assembly, the parish community gathered together to worship. We prepare to listen to God's Word and to celebrate the Eucharist by:

- making the Sign of the Cross and responding to the priest's greeting

71

to offer their intercessory prayers, with the others responding: Lord, hear our prayer.

After the prayers have been offered, conclude by praying the Our Father together.

Read the paragraph on page 71 about Thea Bowman. Discuss the question. Share ways in which the young people might apply Sister Thea's reminder, "Remember who you are and whose you are" the next time they are participating in the Mass.

Presentation (__ min.)

In the Liturgy of the Word we listen to the Word of God.

Read together the first two paragraphs in Section One on page 71. Share this quote with the young people: "In Christian tradition [liturgy] means the participation of the People of God 'in the work of God'" (*CCC*, 1069).

Discuss together ways in which we, as Christians, participate in the "work of God." (Possible responses: by praying and reflecting on Scripture; by acting in loving ways towards one another; by promoting just treatment of all people; by protecting the environment; by helping those in need.)

Explain that in the liturgy, especially the Mass, we come together as a believing community to worship God and to be reminded of our commitment to love one another.

Continue reading Section One. Note the parts of the Mass. Explain that the *Introductory Rites* begin the Mass, and the *Concluding Rites* end the Mass.

Have a Lectionary available, as well as a hymnal or missalette. Invite volunteers to find the readings for the upcoming Sunday and read them to the class. Have other volunteers look in the hymnal for songs that might be appropriate for the Mass.

On the chalkboard or poster board, make an outline of the Liturgy of the Word. Have volunteers list the readings under the appropriate heading: *First Reading, Second Reading,* and *Gospel*. Include the songs that were selected in the outline. Then, refer to this outline as the young people plan and design a program for the upcoming Sunday Mass.

Discuss the questions at the end of Section One on page 72. Direct the young people to write their responses in the space provided.

- asking God for mercy
- joining the priest in praying the Glory to God.

During the Liturgy of the Word we hear God's Word proclaimed to us. In each of the readings, we open our hearts and listen as a community to God as he speaks to us and guides us. The book containing all the readings that we use at Mass is called the **Lectionary**. It is not the whole Bible but a collection of parts of the Bible arranged for reading at Mass. The Church has chosen the Bible readings for each Mass to help us celebrate each Sunday and season. The Lectionary also has different readings for Masses during the week.

On Sundays there are usually three readings:

- The first reading is most often taken from the Old Testament. It recalls God's saving actions throughout history. We respond by saying or singing an Old Testament psalm.
- The second reading is taken from the New Testament, often from one of the letters, or Epistles, of Saint Paul. It is never taken from one of the Gospels.
- The third reading is always from one of the four Gospels (Matthew, Mark, Luke, or John). The reading of the Gospel is special. Only a deacon or priest can proclaim the Gospel, and everyone stands for its reading.

After the readings the priest or deacon gives a homily—or explanation of the readings—to help us better understand God's Word and how to live it. We respond to what we have heard in the readings and the homily by saying the Creed together. Then in the general intercessions, or prayer of the faithful, the needs of the Church, of the world, of those who suffer and are in need, and of the local community are remembered and offered to God.

In the Liturgy of the Eucharist we offer and receive the gift of Jesus.

The second principal part of the Mass is the Liturgy of the Eucharist. It begins with the presentation and preparation of the gifts of bread and wine. These are the same simple, basic elements of human nourishment that Jesus used at the Last Supper. Members of the assembly present the gifts of bread and wine to the priest or deacon. He accepts these gifts as well as money or other gifts

What do we hear in the Liturgy of the Word? How do we respond to what we hear?

72

Optional Activity

Compile images of several types of Catholic churches (city, suburban, rural, modern, etc.) and discuss the similarities and differences among them. Ask: In what ways do you think the churches reflect the communities that worship in them? How do you think the Church is enriched by the variety of church buildings?

If possible, have the young people research the history of your parish.

Answers for page 72:

We hear God's Word proclaimed to us. We respond to the readings and the homily by our profession of faith in words, the Creed.

offered for the Church and the poor. The priest then prepares the bread and wine at the altar. These offerings will become for us the Body and Blood of Christ.

The **Eucharistic Prayer** is the heart of the celebration of the Mass. In this prayer the priest leads us in lifting up our hearts in praise and thanksgiving to God through Jesus Christ. All gathered give thanks to God the Father for his blessings.

The priest does and says what Jesus did and said at the Last Supper—what Jesus commanded us to do in memory of him. The priest says over the bread, "FOR THIS IS MY BODY," and over the wine, "FOR THIS IS THE CHALICE OF MY BLOOD." This is called the *Consecration*. Through the actions and words of the priest and by the power of the Holy Spirit, the bread and wine are changed and become the Body and Blood of Christ. The true presence of Jesus Christ in the Eucharist under the appearances of bread and wine is called the **Real Presence**.

The Church, gathered together in the unity of the Holy Spirit and united with Christ, offers the sacrifice of the Mass to God the Father. At Mass we also offer our own lives—our worries and needs as well as our joys—and join them to Christ's self-offering. After praying for our needs and for the members of the Church, both living and dead, we raise our voices in joyful praise and sing "Amen." With this response the Eucharistic Prayer ends.

The Lord's Prayer and the Sign of Peace move us toward receiving Holy Communion. Again following what Jesus himself did, the priest breaks the consecrated Host. Everyone sings or prays the Lamb of God. Those properly prepared receive the Body and Blood of Christ.

The Church teaches that to receive Holy Communion we must be free of serious sin. A person is freed from serious sin by celebrating the Sacrament of Penance and Reconciliation. As a sign of respect and reverence for the Eucharist, we must also have not taken any food or drink for one hour before receiving Holy Communion. This is called the **eucharistic fast**. Water and medicine may be taken during the eucharistic fast.

The Host may be received in the hand or on the tongue. If we receive the Host in the hand, we place it reverently in our mouths ourselves. All join in singing the Communion song, another sign of the unity of those gathered.

The Church encourages us to receive Holy Communion each time we participate in Mass. By receiving Holy Communion we are:

- nourished with the Sacrament of the Eucharist
- forgiven of our venial sins and strengthened to avoid serious sin
- made one with Christ and one another. We are no longer many. We are now one in the love of Christ.

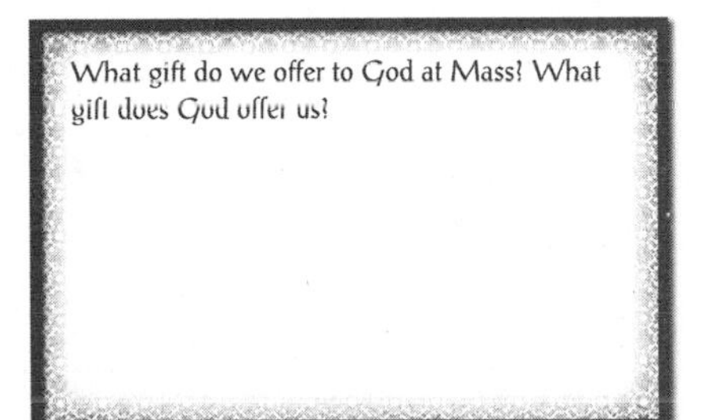
What gift do we offer to God at Mass? What gift does God offer us?

73

In the Liturgy of the Eucharist we offer and receive the gift of Jesus.

Have volunteers read Section Two on pages 72–73. Ask the group why they think Jesus chose bread and wine for the Eucharist. (They are basic elements for human nourishment and were part of the Passover celebration.) Explain that Jesus also called himself the *Bread of Life* and the *True Vine*.

The Eucharistic Prayer includes words of praise and thanksgiving to God. It is also a prayer in which we remember that Jesus instituted the Eucharist at the Last Supper. During the Eucharistic Prayer, the priest says and does what Jesus did and said at the Last Supper. It is during the Consecration that by the power of the Holy Spirit, and through the actions and words of the priest, the bread and wine become the Body and Blood of Christ. The true presence of Jesus Christ in the Eucharist under the appearances of bread and wine is called the *Real Presence*.

Point out that the Eucharistic Prayer ends with the great Amen. Discuss the significance of the Lord's Prayer and the Sign of Peace that we offer to one another. Talk about what the priest does during the Lamb of God: The eucharistic bread is broken so that it may be shared in Holy Communion which is the Body of Christ.

Have the young people underline what takes place during the Liturgy of the Eucharist. Use their findings to make an outline of the Liturgy of the Eucharist on the chalkboard or poster board.

Answers for page 73:

We offer the gifts of bread and wine as well as money or other gifts for the Church and the poor. We also offer our own lives and join them to Christ's self-offering. God gives us the gift of his Son; Jesus' presence in our lives; nourishment in the Sacrament of the Eucharist; unity with Christ and one another.

Refer to this outline as the young people continue working on the program they are designing for the upcoming Sunday Mass.

Read the questions at the end of Section Two on page 73. Have the young people respond to the questions in the space provided.

At the end of Mass we are sent forth to bring God's love to others.

Have the young people read Section Three on page 74 silently.

Point out that the priest or deacon may use alternate words of dismissal such as: "Go and announce the Gospel of the Lord." Go back over the bulleted statements on page 74 together and name specific things young people can do when they "go forth" from the Mass. Write responses on the chalk board or poster board.

Some additional suggestions:

- We can share our time and talent with others by __________.
- We can avoid injustice and prejudice by ______________.
- We can respect our bodies by ______________________.
- We can respect the bodies of others by ______________________________.
- We can care for those who are poor, sick, and lonely by ______________________________.
- We can participate in family, parish, or community by ____________________________.

Encourage the group to put these ideas into action each week. Set aside time in the next lesson for feedback on how they did this.

Answer for page 74:

Many ideas are given on this page. Accept all reasonable answers.

At the end of Mass we are sent forth to bring God's love to others.

Mass is a word taken from the Latin word for "sending forth." At the end of Mass the priest or deacon blesses the assembly and says, "Go in peace." This is the peace that Jesus promised to his friends. It is the peace that the world cannot give: the peace of Christ.

There are many ways we can bring the love of Christ to others:

- We can share our time and talents with others, realizing as we do that God acts in and through them. Others can experience God's love in and through us, by our faith and generosity.
- We can avoid all forms of injustice and prejudice based on race, sex, or nationality. In this way we can bring the peace of Christ to others.
- We can respect our bodies and the bodies of others as Temples of the Holy Spirit. In this we are living as Christ calls us.

By striving daily to grow closer to God and to all of God's people, we are living the Mass.

We should also remember that we are followers of Jesus Christ, who came, not to be served, but to serve. Ways we might serve the Lord include the following:

- caring for the poor, the sick, and the lonely
- respecting life, especially the dignity of human life
- participating in family, parish, and community activities.

How does your participation in the Mass strengthen you to serve others?

Do YOU Know?

The liturgy is the work of the Body of Christ. As members of the Body of Christ, the Church, we are called to active participation at Mass through prayers, songs, gestures, actions, and silence. Just as each part of the Mass has a specific function, each of us gathered—the assembly, priest, deacon, altar servers, readers, extraordinary ministers of Holy Communion, and choir—has a specific role. Each person at Mass has an important role, and each of us helps everyone gathered to participate more fully in the Mass.

74

Do YOU Know?

Read the "Do You Know?" feature on page 74 together. Have the group name people they know who have different roles in the liturgy.

GROWING IN FAITH

PRAY

Jesus' disciples asked him, "Lord, teach us to pray" (Luke 11:1). In response to their plea, Jesus gave them the Our Father. Also known as the Lord's Prayer, the Our Father is the summary of the whole Gospel and therefore the most basic prayer of the Church. In the Our Father we pray for the fulfillment of God's Kingdom. When we pray it together, it is a sign that we are one with the Lord and with one another.

✝ Our Father,
who art in heaven,
hallowed be thy name;
thy kingdom come;
thy will be done on earth
as it is in heaven.
Give us this day our daily bread;
and forgive us our trespasses
as we forgive those
who trespass against us;
and lead us not into temptation,
but deliver us from evil.
Amen.

REFLECT & ACT

Four words sum up the four actions of an active participant in the eucharistic celebration: listen, offer, receive, and serve.

In your private prayer and in communal prayer, in what ways do you listen? What do you offer?

In your personal prayer and in public prayer, what do you receive and how do you serve?

REMEMBER

The Church teaches...

- The liturgy is the official public prayer of the Church. In the liturgy we proclaim and celebrate the mystery of Christ.
- At the Mass we enter into and celebrate Christ's Paschal Mystery—his suffering, Death, Resurrection, and Ascension—as he asked his disciples to do.
- The Mass has two principal parts: the Liturgy of the Word and the Liturgy of the Eucharist.
- Through the words and actions of the priest and by the power of the Holy Spirit, the bread and wine become the Body and Blood of Christ.
- We are sent forth from Mass to love and serve others.

Faith Words

liturgy (p. 71)
Lectionary (p. 72)
Eucharistic Prayer (p. 73)
Real Presence (p. 73)
eucharistic fast (p. 73)

75

Conclusion (__ min.)

Growing in Faith

Have the young people close their books. Ask them what they have learned in this lesson about the Mass—the Liturgy of the Word and the Liturgy of the Eucharist. Draw from them what they know about the liturgy, the Lectionary, the Eucharistic Prayer, and the Real Presence. Open the books to page 75. Was everything from the **Remember** and **Faith Words** sections named? If not, point these out and help the group name the remaining concepts.

Invite the young people to read the **Reflect and Act** section. Help them to name some of the gifts they receive in prayer. (Examples: comfort, guidance, feeling closer to God and the Christian community, being inspired or lifted out of depression, learning more about God's Word) Then, have them write out their responses in the spaces provided.

Read the paragraph under **Pray** on page 75. Then, join hands and pray the Our Father together.

If you have time, do the following.

Invite a priest or deacon to visit the class to explain his participation in the liturgy. You might also ask the director of liturgy, a reader, an extraordinary minister of Holy Communion, or any other liturgical minister to visit the class. These people might also explain what their participation in the celebration of the Mass means to them.

CATECHISM FOCUS

"It is this mystery of Christ that the Church proclaims and celebrates in her liturgy so that the faithful may live from it and bear witness to it in the world." (*CCC*, 1068)

For additional reference and reflection, see *CCC*, 1391–1401.

Answers for page 75:
Accept all reasonable answers.

CHAPTER 12

GOALS:

to understand the Sacrament of Penance and Reconciliation; to learn how to form and examine one's conscience

GETTING READY

- ***Materials needed:***

Prayer table environment: Bible and decorative cloth

Mark the Bible passage for the parable of the Prodigal Son (Luke 15:11–32)

List the four parts of scenario-making for the additional activity in Section Two (see page 79)

Adult Focus

When Jesus raised Lazarus from the dead, he performed a miracle. When he forgave Zacchaeus, the woman caught in adultery, and the sinful woman at the home of the Pharisee, he restored them to complete relationship with God. Forgiveness is a wondrous gift extended freely to us by a loving God.

The Church freely offers us, in the Sacrament of Penance and Reconciliation, an opportunity to encounter Christ and experience the miracle of forgiveness. This sacrament raises us from the death of sin, which alienates us from God, our true selves, and those around us. When we cooperate with God's grace, the Sacrament of Penance and Reconciliation restores us to healthful and harmonious relationships.

By all Gospel accounts, reconciliation is an occasion of great joy—both for the forgiver and the forgiven

Introduction (__ min.)

Gather the group with their books around the prayer table. Offer the Prayer of Saint Francis on page 121 together.

After a moment of silence, read aloud the poem on page 77. Ask the young people to identify who is being addressed in the poem, and the attitude of the poet towards that person.

Continue the discussion by asking what the poet says about:

- mercy
- reconciliation

Ask the young people if they have ever experienced mercy and reconciliation in their lives. In what ways did it affect their relationship with others?

CHAPTER 12

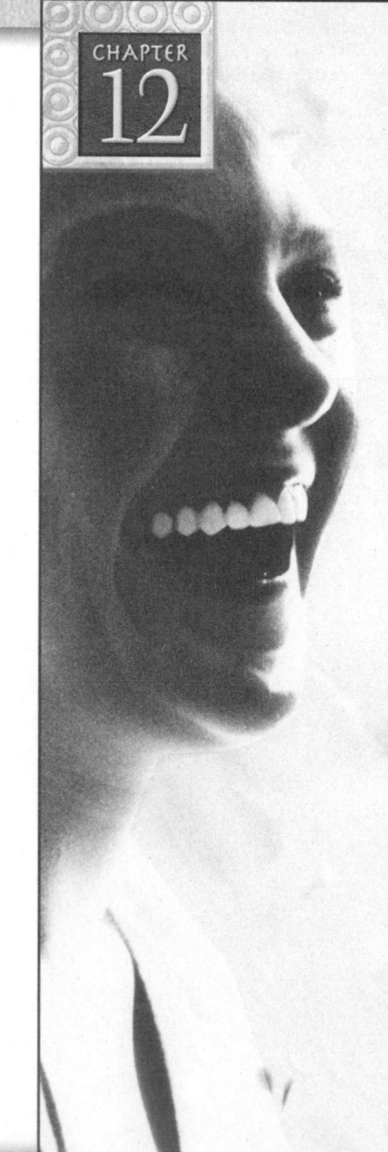

The Sacrament of Penance and Reconciliation

Oh, mercifullest one of all,
Oh, generous as dear,
None lived so lowly, none so small,
Thou couldst withhold thy tear:

How swift, in pure compassion,
How meek in charity,
To offer friendship to the one
Who begged but love of thee!

Oh, gentle word, and sweetest said!
Oh, tender hand, and first
To hold the warm, delicious bread
To lips burned black of thirst.

"After Spanish Proverb"
Dorothy Parker

one. Likewise, in the Church, this sacrament is intended to be a joyful celebration of homecoming. The sacrament is not about judgment, blame, criticism, or punishment. Instead, it is about "restoration of the dignity and blessings of the life of the children of God, of which the most precious is friendship with God" (*CCC*, 1468).

Young people sense the reality of sin, within and without. They need to be reassured that no matter what they have done or failed to do, Jesus is inviting them personally to come to him and unburden their hearts. When they choose to be reconciled, they are allowing Christ to do for them what he did for Zacchaeus, the woman caught in adultery, and the sinful woman he met at the home of the Pharisee. They are opening themselves to the miracle of "Your sins are forgiven. . . . Your faith has saved you; go in peace" (Luke 7:48, 50).

Reflection

How have you experienced reconciliation in your life? How has the Sacrament of Penance brought you joy or peace? How can you best reassure the young people in your care of God's continual love and forgiveness? How might they benefit from your experience of the Sacrament of Penance?

Sin harms our relationship with God.

We know from the Old Testament that God is "a merciful and gracious God, slow to anger and rich in kindness and fidelity, continuing his kindness for a thousand generations, and forgiving wickedness and crime and sin" (Exodus 34:6–7). The greatest Teacher of God's mercy and compassion is Jesus, the Son of God. By the things he did and the way he lived, Jesus showed us God's mercy.

We all need God's forgiveness because we all are inclined to sin. When we freely choose to turn away from God and turn toward something that is not God, we sin. **Sin** is a thought, word, deed, or omission against God's law that harms us and our relationship with God and others. When we sin, our relationship with God is weakened by our unwillingness to live as God calls us to live.

Sin is always a personal choice. The world is a challenging place in which to live, and we are often tempted to do what is wrong. But a temptation is not a sin. It is an attraction to sin. Everyone is tempted. Even Jesus was tempted. In order to overcome temptation and avoid sin, we need God's grace to be strong in making good choices.

There are different types of sin. A **mortal sin** is a very serious sin that turns us completely away from God because it is a choice we freely make to do something that we know is seriously wrong. In order for a sin to be a mortal sin, three conditions are necessary:

- The sinful action or attitude must involve a grave and serious matter.
- We must have clear knowledge that what we are doing is mortally sinful.
- We must freely choose and fully consent to this serious evil.

77

Presentation (__ min.)

Sin harms our relationship with God.

Read Section One on pages 77–78 aloud. This section refers to personal sin.

Ask the group to define sin. (Sin is a thought, word, deed, or omission against God's law that harms us and our relationship with God and others.) Emphasize the difference between temptation and sin, noting that it is not a sin to be tempted.

Ask the group name the difference between mortal sin and venial sin. Have the young people underline the three conditions for mortal sin in their books. (See page 77.)

Discuss questions at the end of Section One on page 78. Have the young people write their responses in the space provided.

We celebrate God's love and forgiveness.

Ask the group to think about what keeps a person from sinning and list these responses on the chalkboard. Their answers might vary from knowing God's laws to having someone influence you to choose to do good.

Have the group read Section Two on pages 78–79 silently. Discuss what a conscience is and draw upon any examples they named earlier that refer to aspects of a "well-formed conscience."

Stress the different ways that our conscience is formed: through learning Church teachings and understanding God's laws, through prayer and reflection, through developing a sense of values, learning about norms and rules of good behavior, and through advice and guidance from others.

Discuss the questions at the end of Section Two on page 79. Have the young people write their responses in the space provided.

All three conditions must be met for any sin to be considered mortal.

Less serious sin that weakens our friendship with God but does not turn us completely away from him is called **venial sin**. Venial sins do harm to others, to ourselves, or to our relationship with God and others.

Jesus taught us that God's mercy far exceeds any wrong or harmful action on our part. By his Death on the cross and his rising to new life, Jesus saves us from sin. We must be willing to admit our weakness, however, and to turn to God for forgiveness and compassion.

What is sin? How does it affect our relationship with God and with others?

We celebrate God's love and forgiveness.

Jesus Christ, the Son of God, forgave the sins of those who truly believed in him. Jesus willed that his Apostles do the same:

> "Peace be with you. As the Father has sent me, so I send you." And when he had said this, he breathed on them and said to them, "Receive the holy Spirit. Whose sins you forgive are forgiven them, and whose sins you retain are retained."
> John 20:21–23

Only bishops (the successors of the Apostles) and priests forgive our sins in the Sacrament of Penance and Reconciliation. They do this in the person of Christ and through the power of the Holy Spirit. The **Sacrament of Penance and Reconciliation** is the sacrament by which our relationship with God and the Church is restored and our sins are forgiven. We celebrate God's love and forgiveness.

When we are baptized, Original Sin and all the sins we have committed are forgiven. We are born into new life with Christ. The grace we receive at Baptism, however, does not keep us from sinning. We are still free to choose and to act, and at times we act without thinking of the consequences. But our conscience helps us to think about the consequences of our actions, and helps us to think before we act.

Conscience is our ability to know the difference between good and evil, right and wrong. Conscience is always to be formed by the teachings of Christ and his Church. We are called upon to continue forming our conscience throughout life and to obey the judgment of our conscience. Our conscience however, must be well-formed or we risk making wrong choices.

78

Optional Activity

Read aloud to the group the parable of the Prodigal Son (Luke 15:11–32). Explain that it is a story about penance and reconciliation. Discuss:

- **What does this parable tell us about forgiveness? penance? reconciliation?**
- **Why does the father hold a celebration for his repentant son?**

Ask the group to think of alternate titles for this parable. What do these titles emphasize about the story?

Answers for page 78:

See Glossary, page 126. Accept all reasonable answers.

Our conscience is formed in many ways:

- by learning all we can about our faith and the teachings of the Church
- by praying to God, asking the Holy Spirit to strengthen and guide us
- by reading and reflecting on Scripture
- by seeking advice from wise people we respect, such as parents, teachers, parish priests, and responsible friends
- by examining our conscience on a regular basis, thinking about how we have treated God, ourselves, and others.

Sometimes we may not take the time to see the impact our choices and actions have. We lose sight of where we are going. We may not realize the positive direction our lives have taken, or that we have strayed from the path that God calls us to take. When we examine our conscience, we honestly ask ourselves about our relationship with God and others.

When we receive the Sacrament of Penance we must confess our serious sins and should even confess our less serious sins.

Have you ever had a disagreement with someone and then reconciled with the person? Think about what happened. What did you do? What did the other person do?

Do YOU Know?

During an examination of conscience, we ask the Holy Spirit to help us judge the direction of our lives. Here are some possible questions you can ask yourself:

- Do I make anyone or anything more important to me than God? Have I found time to read Scripture and listen to God's word? Do I pray?
- Have I treated God's name and the name of Jesus with reverence?
- Do I participate in Mass and keep Sunday holy by what I say and do?
- Have I respected, obeyed, and cared for my parent(s) and guardians? Have I been kind and considerate to my brothers and sisters?
- Am I a person who respects all life? Am I patient with the elderly, aware of the hungry and homeless, and respectful of those different from me?
- Do I treat my own body and the bodies of others respectfully? Have I harmed myself, or encouraged others to harm themselves, by improper use of things like drugs, alcohol, or food?
- Have I been selfish or stolen anything from anyone? Have I shared my belongings?
- Am I a truthful person? Have I been fair and honest with friends, family, teachers, and myself?
- Do I try to do God's will in my relationships with others? Have I been happy for others when they have the things they want or need?
- Have I made God my treasure rather than material possessions?

79

Do YOU Know?

Explain that an examination of conscience is a way to reflect on the choices we have made. Ask: Why do you think reflecting on our choices helps us to do better in the future?

Read the "Do You Know" feature on page 79. Begin with quiet time for reflection, reminding the young people to ask the Holy Spirit to help them as they examine their conscience. Have volunteers take turns reading each question, pausing after each one. Conclude by praying an Act of Contrition (see page 121).

If you have time, do the following.

Form the class into small groups. Instruct them to develop a story about people in conflict and what they did to resolve it. Each story should have four parts (have these written on poster board or chalkboard beforehand):

- **Set the scene** Where does this take place? Who is involved? What are they doing?
- **Create the rift** What happens? Who gets hurt? How does each person react? What needs to be reconciled?
- **Spark some awareness** What does each person's conscience tell him/her to do?
- **Suggest a solution** What happens to bring people together again? Who helps this happen? What does each person need?

As these scenarios are presented to the whole group, open it up for further suggestions for reconciling from the rest of the class. Have them discuss the role of faith and the Church in any of the stories.

Answers for page 79:
Accept all reasonable answers.

We celebrate the Sacrament of Penance.

Read together Section Three on page 80. Review the ways to celebrate the Sacrament of Penance and Reconciliation. Remind the young people that it is through absolution in the Sacrament of Penance that God forgives our sins through the person of the priest or bishop. Have the young people underline the four main parts of the sacrament.

Have the young people memorize the Act of Contrition on page 121 in the text. Help them to understand the meaning of *absolution*, the words of forgiveness spoken by the priest.

Ask:

- What is the most important act of a person receiving the Sacrament of Penance?
- What is perfect contrition?
- What should the penitent do before confessing his or her sins?
- Why is a penance an important part of celebrating the Sacrament of Penance?

We celebrate the Sacrament of Penance.

As we prepare to seek and receive God's forgiveness, we should examine our conscience quietly and prayerfully. We should focus on whatever might separate us from God's life of grace. But we should also confess our venial sins as well. You may want to discuss this with the priest to whom you will confess your sins.

We can celebrate the Sacrament of Penance individually or communally. When we assemble as a community to celebrate the sacrament, each of us meets with the priest individually and privately for confession and absolution. There are four main parts to the Sacraments of Penance:

- *Contrition.* Contrition is sorrow for our sins with a firm purpose not to sin again. When our contrition comes from believing in God and loving him it is called perfect contrition. Contrition is the most important act of the penitent, or person seeking forgiveness and reconciliation. Sadness for the sin and the desire to sin no more must be genuine. Our intention must be to sin no more.
- *Confession of sins.* The penitent speaks with the priest, telling him what sins were committed. In confessing our sins we take responsibility for our actions and can be reconciled with God and the Church. The priest cannot tell anyone what he has heard in confession. We call this the seal of confession.
- *Penance.* Since sin weakens us and our relationship with God and others, we need to do something to show we are sorry for the sin. The priest gives us an act of penance to perform, such as saying a prayer or doing a good deed.
- *Absolution.* The priest, in the person of Christ and through the power of the Holy Spirit, absolves (forgives) the penitent's sins. The priest makes the Sign of the Cross over the penitent and says the prayer of absolution.

The Sacrament of Penance is a wonderful way to praise God and thank him for his mercy and forgiveness. It is also a way to grow in God's life of grace and in the love of one another.

The Church Celebrates the Sacrament of Penance

Rite for Reconciliation of Individual Penitents

The priest greets me.

I make the Sign of the Cross.
The priest asks me to trust in God's mercy.

He or I may read something from the Bible.

I talk with the priest about myself.
I confess my sins.
The priest talks to me about loving God and others.
He gives me a penance.

I make an Act of Contrition.
In the name of God and the Church, the priest gives me absolution. (He may extend or place his hands on my head.)

Together the priest and I give thanks to God for his forgiveness.

Rite for Reconciliation of Several Penitents with Individual Confession and Absolution

We sing an opening hymn and the priest greets us.
The priest prays an opening prayer.

We listen to a reading from the Bible and a homily.

We examine our conscience.
We make an Act of Contrition.
We may say a prayer or sing a song, and then pray the Our Father.

Each of us then meets individually and privately with the priest.

I confess my sins. The priest gives me a penance.

In the name of God and the Church, the priest gives me absolution. (He may extend or place his hands on my head.)

After everyone has met with the priest, we join together to conclude the celebration. The priest blesses us, and we go in the peace and joy of Christ.

80

Optional Activity

Have volunteers research the times for the celebration of the Sacrament of Penance in the parish and to report this information back to the group at the next session.

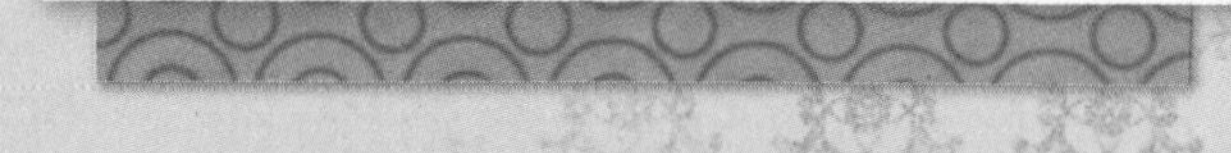

GROWING IN FAITH

PRAY

✝ Lord Jesus,
you chose to be called
the friend of sinners.
By your saving death and resurrection
free me from my sins.
May your peace take root in my heart
and bring forth a harvest
of love, holiness, and truth.
Amen.

REMEMBER

The Church teaches...

- Sin is freely choosing—by thought, word, deed, or omission—to do something that we know is wrong and against God's will.
- Our conscience is our ability to know the difference between good and evil, right and wrong.
- In the Sacrament of Penance, our sins are forgiven. We are reconciled to God, the Church, and one another.
- Priests act in the person of Christ to forgive our sins.
- The sins that we confess to the priest are protected by the seal of confession, which obliges the priest to total secrecy.

Faith Words

sin (p. 77)
mortal sin (p. 77)
venial sin (p. 78)
Sacrament of Penance and Reconciliation (p. 78)
conscience (p. 78)

REFLECT & ACT

Is it difficult for you to ask forgiveness from God, the Church, or someone else? Why or why not?

Why do we call the sign of God's love and forgiveness the Sacrament of Penance?

81

Conclusion (__ min.)

Growing in Faith

Have the young people close their books. Allow several minutes for quiet reflection. Invite the group to pray the Jesus Prayer (see page 121) silently.

Ask them what they have learned in this lesson about sin, mortal sin, venial sin, conscience, and the Sacrament of Penance and Reconciliation.

Reopen the books to page 81. Was everything from the **Remember** and **Faith Words** sections named? If not, point these out and help the group name the remaining concepts.

Invite the young people to read the **Reflect and Act** section and to write out their responses in the spaces provided. If desired, play some soft instrumental music while they do this.

Turn to the **Pray** section on page 81. Offer the prayer together.

CATECHISM FOCUS

"Sin is before all else an offense against God, a rupture of communion with him. At the same time it damages communion with the Church. For this reason conversion entails both God's forgiveness and reconciliation with the Church, which are expressed and accomplished liturgically by the sacrament of Penance and Reconciliation." (*CCC*, 1440)

For additional reference and reflection, see *CCC*, 1468–1470.

Answers for page 81:

Left:
Help the young people to understand that asking for forgiveness is difficult for most people.

Right:
Because in this sacrament we are reconciled to God, the Church, and one another.

Unit 3 Assessment

A. Choose the correct term to complete each statement.

Venial sins	**Holy Communion**	**Passover**
Consecration	**sin**	**Mass**
Lectionary	**Conscience**	**Liturgy of the Word**
Contrition	**Sacrament of Penance and Reconciliation**	**liturgy**
Liturgy of the Eucharist	**Sunday**	**Eucharist**

1. The ___Sacrament of Penance and Reconciliation___ is the sacrament by which our relationship with God and the Church is restored and our sins are forgiven.
2. The ___Mass___ is the celebration of the Eucharist; the Church's great prayer of praise and thanks to God the Father.
3. ___Passover___ is the feast on which Jewish people remember the miraculous way that God saved them from death and slavery in ancient Egypt.
4. ___Holy Communion___ is the Body and Blood of Christ that we receive and by which we are nourished in the Mass.
5. The ___Lectionary___ contains the collection of readings from the Bible that are proclaimed at Mass.
6. The ___Liturgy of the Word___ is part of the Mass during which we hear God's Word proclaimed.
7. Our ___conscience___ is our ability to know the difference between good and evil, right and wrong.
8. The ___Liturgy of the Eucharist___ is the part of the Mass in which we offer and receive the gift of Jesus.
9. The ___Eucharist___ is the Sacrament of the Body and Blood of Christ.
10. The ___Consecration___ is the part of the Eucharistic Prayer when the priest says and does what Jesus did at the Last Supper.
11. ___Sin___ is a thought, word, deed, or omission against God's law that harms us and our relationship with God and others.
12. ___Sunday___, is the Lord's Day, the principal day for celebrating the Eucharist.
13. The ___liturgy___ is the official public prayer of the Church.
14. ___Contrition___ is sorrow for sins with a firm purpose not to sin again.
15. ___Venial sins___ are less serious sins that weaken our relationship with God but do not turn us completely away from him.

B. Circle the response that does *not* belong.

1. On the first Passover the Israelites
   - (a.) refused to listen to Moses, their leader.
   - b. killed a young lamb.
   - c. sprinkled the lamb's blood on their doorposts.
   - d. ate a special meal.

2. On the night before he died, Jesus
   - a. celebrated Passover with his friends.
   - b. explained to his disciples that his life would be sacrificed.
   - (c.) was crucified.
   - d. gave us the Eucharist.

3. When we celebrate Mass we
   - a. share in Christ's Paschal Mystery.
   - b. participate in a meal and a sacrifice.
   - c. commit to living as God calls us to live.
   - (d.) are freed from Original Sin.

4. In the Sacrament of Penance and Reconciliation
   - a. our sins are forgiven.
   - b. we are reconciled to God.
   - c. we experience God's mercy.
   - (d.) our intention is to sin again.

5. The Eucharist is
   - (a.) our first welcoming into the Church.
   - b. a meal because Jesus said, "Take and eat."
   - c. a sacrifice because it is a memorial of Jesus' Death.
   - d. the Church's great prayer of thanksgiving.

C. Share your faith by responding thoughtfully to these questions.

1. How did Jesus want his disciples to remember him? Jesus wanted his disciples to remember what he did for all of us by his Death and Resurrection through the Eucharist.

2. What would help you understand and participate more fully in the Mass?
   Accept all reasonable responses.

3. At the end of Mass we are "sent forth" to love and serve others. What does that mean to you?
   Answers will vary. They may include: I can share my time and talents; I can avoid all forms of injustice and prejudice; I can respect my body and the bodies of others as Temples of the Holy Spirit.

4. What can you do to form your conscience so that you will make right choices?
   Answers will vary. They may include: learn about my faith and the teachings of the Church; pray; read and reflect on Scripture; seek good advice; examine my conscience

5. How can celebrating the Sacrament of Penance help you to be more forgiving of others?
   Accept all reasonable responses.

CHAPTER 13

GOALS

to learn the meaning of each of the Ten Commandments

GETTING READY

■ *Materials needed:*

Prayer table environment: Bible and decorative cloth

Magazines for optional activity in Section Two

Dictionary for the "Do You Know?" feature

Adult Focus

"Do not think I have come to abolish the law or the prophets. I have come not to abolish but to fulfill." (Matthew 5:17)

These words of Jesus are part of the magnificent Sermon on the Mount found in Matthew's Gospel (Matthew 5:1—7:29). In this sermon, Jesus addresses the ways to live a moral life, to honor and trust God, to pray, and to treat others. Through his teachings, Jesus is directing his followers to fulfill the spirit of the Law.

By his teaching and example, Jesus requires his followers to keep the Ten Commandments. He summarizes the spirit of the Ten Commandments this way: "You shall love the Lord, your God, with all your heart, with all your soul, and with

Introduction (__ min.)

Gather the young people around the prayer table. Ask the group to remember a time in which their actions caused suffering for themselves or others. Encourage them to think specifically about whom their actions affected, and how, if any, resolution was brought to the situation.

Offer a prayer thanking God or asking him for peace and healing in these situations.

Discuss the reasons why it is important to have rules in our families, in our Church, in our society. Ask: What are positive aspects of rules?

Recall the Sacrament of Penance and Reconciliation. Ask: What is God offering us in this sacrament? (his forgiveness) How do we know when we have done something wrong and need God's forgiveness? (our conscience)

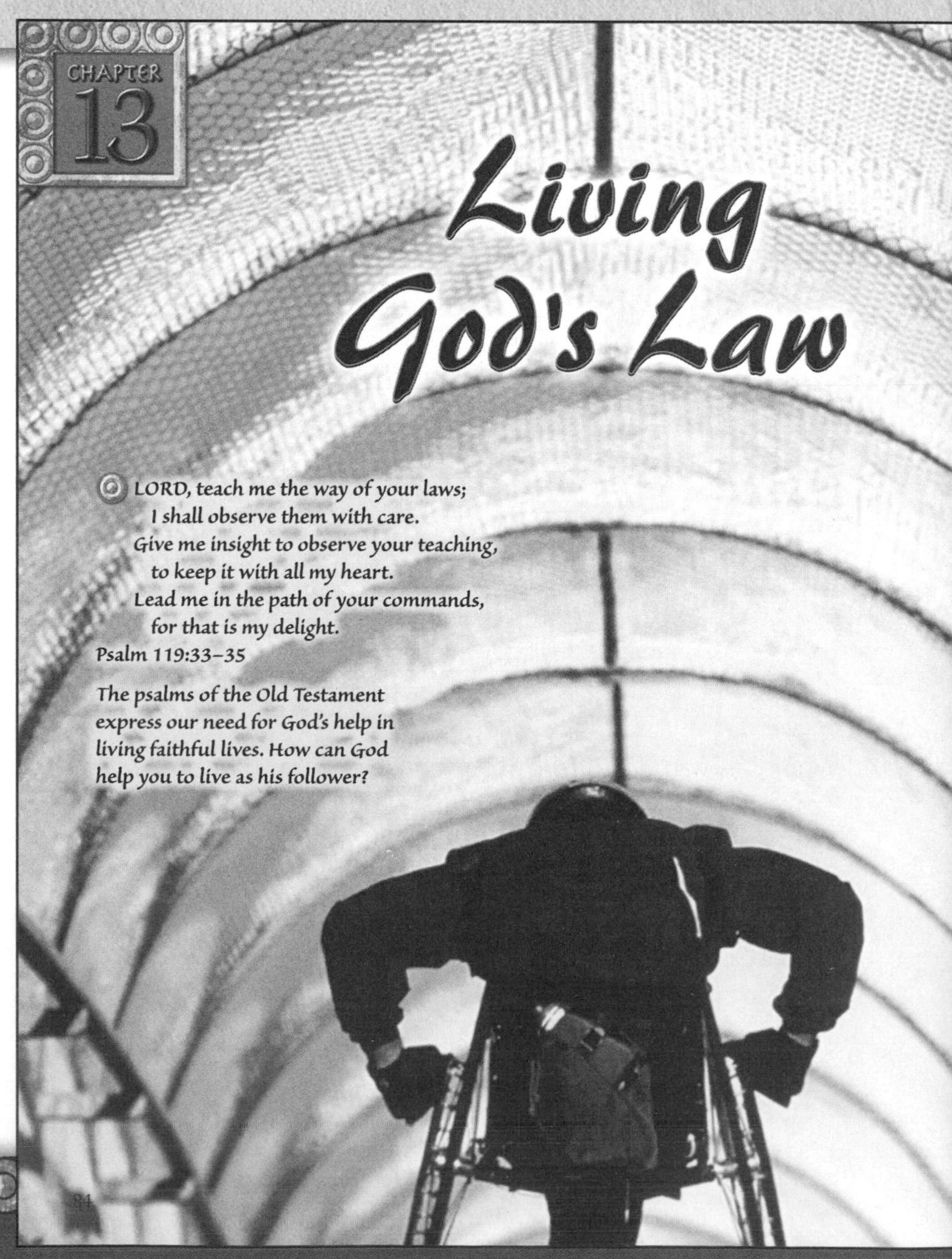

all your mind. This is the greatest and the first commandment. The second is like it: You shall love your neighbor as yourself. The whole law and the prophets depend on these two commandments" (Matthew 22:37–40).

The Sermon on the Mount concludes with a lesson about placing one's home on a solid foundation (Matthew 7:24–27). Keeping the Ten Commandments sets us on firm ground where we are reminded of our need to put God first in our lives, to be reverent, faithful, honest, respectful, nonviolent, and just. Living God's Law points the way to a world in which women and men, children and parents, neighbors and communities live in harmony and happiness.

Reflection

How would you describe the "spirit" of the Ten Commandments? What do you want your young people to understand about Jesus' command to love God and others?

The Ten Commandments teach us how to live as God's people.

Over and over again God reached out with love to the Israelites. From the Old Testament we learn that God wanted to form them into a holy people, a nation that would be set apart. And God did this by entering into a covenant with them.

The Israelites cherished the covenant God made on Mount Sinai with their great leader Moses, who led them out of slavery in Egypt. The reason for this covenant was that God wanted the Israelites to be free, not only from physical and political bondage, but also from the spiritual slavery of sin.

God's covenant requires a response from the people. God revealed to Moses that the Israelites would have certain responsibilities in observing the covenant. We read in the Book of Exodus that "when Moses came to the people and related all the words and ordinances of the LORD, they all answered with one voice, 'We will do everything that the LORD has told us'" (Exodus 24:3). God's commands were summarized in what we now call the Ten Commandments. The **Ten Commandments** are the laws of God's covenant given to Moses on Mount Sinai.

The Catholic Church teaches that the Ten Commandments are God's law for us, too, and that no human law can change them. When we are faithful to God and obey his commandments, we grow closer to him in friendship and love. When we live by the Ten Commandments, we grow in holiness and happiness.

The first three commandments focus on our direct relationship with God. The remaining seven center on our relationship with ourselves and one another.

85

Read the excerpt from Psalm 119 on page 84 and discuss the question that follows. Ask why the author of the psalm describes being on the path of God's commands a "delight." Why do some people have a negative opinion of rules?

Presentation (__ min.)

The Ten Commandments teach us how to live as God's people.

Ask the group how many of the Ten Commandments they can name. What do they know about these commandments?

Have volunteers read aloud Section One on pages 85–86. Discuss the following questions:

- What is the difference between a covenant and any other agreement? (A covenant is a solemn agreement between God and his people to be faithful to each other.)

What did the people promise God? (They promised to worship God alone and to obey all of his commandments.)

What did God promise the people? (God promised that they would be his special people who would live in freedom to worship him.)

Review the first three commandments with the group. Help them to see that each of these commandments deals with an individual's relationship with God.

Discuss the questions at the end of Section One on page 86. Have the young people write their responses in the space provided.

Using the list on page 86, encourage the young people to memorize the Ten Commandments.

The First Commandment reminds us that we worship and serve the one true God. God alone is our Salvation. False gods, such as the exaggerated desire for power, wealth, or popularity, do not give us what God does. Denying God's existence, atheism, is a sin against the First Commandment.

When we live by the spirit of this commandment, we place our trust in the one true God, not in superstitious or occult practices. We adore God when we acknowledge that he is the Creator and Savior and that we are totally dependent upon him for our life and happiness. We pray and give witness to God and to our belief in him. The First Commandment calls us to believe in God, to hope in him, and to love him above all else.

The Second Commandment directs us to honor God's name. Respecting God's name is a sign of the respect that God, in all of his mystery and sacredness, deserves. The followers of Jesus show respect for his name and for the names of Mary and the saints. The Second Commandment also helps us to appreciate the gifts of speech and communication and to use them with care and respect.

THE TEN COMMANDMENTS

1. I am the LORD your God: you shall not have strange gods before me.
2. You shall not take the name of the LORD your God in vain.
3. Remember to keep holy the LORD's Day.
4. Honor your father and your mother.
5. You shall not kill.
6. You shall not commit adultery.
7. You shall not steal.
8. You shall not bear false witness against your neighbor.
9. You shall not covet your neighbor's wife.
10. You shall not covet your neighbor's goods.

Annual March for Life in Washington, D.C.

As Catholics we observe the Third Commandment by participating in the celebration of Mass on Sunday, the Lord's Day, and by keeping that day holy. We celebrate the Resurrection and the new life Christ has given us. The Church teaches that we are obligated to participate in Mass on Sundays and that we can keep Sunday holy in several ways:

- by participating in prayer
- by refraining from unnecessary work
- by serving the sick, elderly, and needy
- by spending time with our families.

Observing the Third Commandment helps us to develop family, social, and spiritual lives. We must be mindful of those who cannot rest on Sundays, and we should not place any unnecessary demands on others, so that they, too, can keep the Lord's Day.

How is our relationship with God strengthened by living out the first three commandments?

86

Optional Activity

Have the young people work with a partner to compile a slideshow of images that illustrate the first three commandments. Encourage them to be creative, for example: perhaps they will use captions or music in their slideshows. As the young people learn about the remaining seven commandments, have them compile images for these commandments, too. Allow time for the young people to present their completed slideshows.

Answer for page 86:

Possible answers include: The First Commandment reminds us that we worship and serve the one true God. The Second Commandment directs us to honor God's name. The Third Commandment teaches us to participate in Mass on Sundays and to keep Sunday holy.

 The Ten Commandments call us to live with respect for others.

The Fourth Commandment requires us that after honoring God, we should honor, respect, obey, and care for our parents and guardians. We should show honor, affection, and gratitude toward our extended families and the elderly. This respect also extends to all of those in authority, such as responsible government leaders, those in law enforcement, and teachers. In fulfilling the Fourth Commandment, we can imitate the way that Jesus showed love and respect toward Mary and Joseph.

The Fifth Commandment requires us to respect the sacredness of life and the dignity of the person. Murder, abortion, suicide, and euthanasia deny the gift of life. We believe that every human being—from conception to natural death—has the God-given right to life. Abortion is not a matter of choice.

In a world torn apart by violence, war, and ethnic and religious strife, the Church opposes armed conflict as a solution to political and social problems. In recent years the pope and the bishops of the United States have spoken out strongly against the use of nuclear and chemical weapons. God's law calls us to work untiringly for peace on earth.

Respect for the human person extends beyond direct killing of others or oneself. We are to respect human life and the human body by:

- avoiding anything that could injure or endanger life, such as uncontrolled anger, the use of narcotics, or excessive eating and drinking
- taking proper care of our own health
- caring for the environment in which all life flourishes.

The Sixth Commandment upholds the sacredness of the gift of the human person—body and soul—as made in the image and likeness of God. The gift of human sexuality helps us to express our partnership in God's created love. The Sacrament of Matrimony unites a man and woman in a sacred union. Anything or anyone who violates this vowed commitment through adultery, unfaithfulness, or abuse is harming God's gift of human sexuality. All sexual activity outside of marriage is wrong.

Every baptized person is called to the virtue of **chastity**, a gift from God that calls us to use our human sexuality in a responsible and faithful way. Our bodies are Temples of the Holy Spirit, and as such must be respected by ourselves and others. Our model of chastity is Jesus Christ.

The Sixth Commandment also reminds us to treasure our human sexuality, because it is something truly beautiful. Any action that violates or harms the dignity and sacredness of our bodies is wrong. Our understanding and appreciation of our human sexuality deepens as we learn to love and be loved by others.

How can we live out the Fourth, Fifth, and Sixth Commandments?

87

 The Ten Commandments call us to live with respect for others.

Read Section Two on page 87 aloud.

Point out the emphasis on respect in these three commandments:

- respect for our parents and guardians (Fourth Commandment)
- respect for the sacredness of life and the dignity of persons (Fifth Commandment)
- respect for the human person (Sixth Commandment).

With the group, review each commandment. Ask for specific ways in which each one can be kept by young people. Explain to the young people that certain actions such as masturbation, fornication, pornography, and homosexual acts violate or harm the dignity and sacredness of their bodies. These actions are wrong. (For more information on Church teaching, consult *CCC*, 2351–2359.)

Discuss the question at the end of Section Two on page 87. Have the young people write their responses in the space provided.

Optional Activity

Have the group think of ways in which people encourage respect for each other. Some suggestions could be through individual actions, music, art, movies, books, etc. Have young people share with the group specific examples in each category. Encourage them to explain why they chose each example.

Answer for page 87:

Possible answers include: The Fourth Commandment teaches us to honor our parents and guardians. The Fifth Commandment teaches us to respect life and the dignity of each person. The Sixth Commandment upholds the sacredness of the human person and reminds us to treasure our sexuality.

The Ten Commandments call us to live responsibly.

Have the young people read Section Three on page 88 silently. Discuss the ways the Seventh, Eighth, Ninth, and Tenth Commandments help us to live our lives in a responsible way. Encourage the group to name ways that are specific to their ages and circumstances.

Discuss the following questions:

- Why are stealing and cheating sins of injustice? (They are offenses against the Seventh Commandment, which protects people's rights to share God's gifts and have equal respect.)
- Why do you think the Eighth Commandment forbids destructive gossip? (This commandment requires us to honor others' good names.)
- Why is pornography sinful? (It is a form of visual violence that disrespects human sexuality and demeans those who produce or consume it.)
- How does the media challenge young people today in living out the Tenth Commandment?

Discuss the question at the end of Section Three on page 88. Have the young people write their responses in the space provided.

Answer for page 88:

Possible answers include: When we are faithful to God and obey his commandments, we grow closer to him in friendship and love—we grow in holiness and happiness. (See page 85.)

Do YOU Know?

A **virtue** is a good habit that helps us to act according to God's love for us. There are four virtues known as the Cardinal Virtues: *prudence* helps us to make sound judgments and directs us to what is good; *justice* consists in the firm and constant will to give God and neighbor their due; *fortitude* ensures firmness in difficulties and constancy in the pursuit of the good; *temperance* helps us to keep our desires under control.

The Ten Commandments call us to live responsibly.

The Seventh Commandment upholds justice in all its forms. This commandment protects the right of all people to share in God's gifts and to have equal respect. Stealing, cheating, and dishonesty in any form are against this commandment.

We are also reminded that jealousy and prejudice harm our relationship with God and others. Preoccupation with material goods will not bring the happiness that following God will. We are to use the resources we have to help poor and needy people. We should also use wisely and preserve the earth's resources.

Respect for truth is necessary in a society of openness and honesty. The Eighth Commandment holds us responsible for the truth. It teaches us to honor the good name of all people and to avoid anything that would injure another's reputation:

- We are to tell the truth in all situations.
- We are to respect the privacy of others, and keep a trust or confidence someone has shared with us, unless someone will be harmed by our silence.
- We are to treat all people with equal respect no matter their race, gender, religion, or age. This equality is the truth that comes from being made in God's image.
- We are to give witness to the truth of Jesus Christ through our words and deeds.

The Ninth Commandment calls for a single-mindedness and control with regard to sexual matters. It calls us to a positive attitude toward our sexuality, which is only one dimension of our humanity. Purity of mind and heart requires modesty which is part of the virtue of temperance. **Modesty** is the virtue by which we dress, act, speak, and think in ways that show respect for ourselves and others. Pornography is visual violence. It harms the dignity and sacredness of our bodies.

The Tenth Commandment warns against envy, or any willful desire to possess property that belongs to others. Envy, which includes sadness at the sight of another's goods, has no place in our lives and cannot lead us to true happiness. This commandment also forbids greed and the desire to obtain earthly goods without limit. We are called to act and share with justice.

How do the Ten Commandments keep us in a right relationship with God and others?

Do YOU Know?

Read the "Do You Know?" feature on page 88 together. Have a volunteer use a dictionary to find the definition of the word *cardinal*. Ask: Why do you think the virtues of prudence, justice, fortitude, and temperance are called the *cardinal virtues*? Discuss different situations in which young people have the opportunity to practice these virtues. Invite volunteers to role-play some of these situations.

GROWING IN FAITH

PRAY

Living by the commandments gives us an inner peace and joy that no one can take away from us. But we need God's help in order to walk firmly in his way. And so we pray:

✝ Teach me, LORD, your way
that I may walk in your truth,
single-hearted and
revering your name.
Psalm 86:11

REMEMBER

The Church teaches...

- The Ten Commandments guide us in our relationship with God and with one another. No human law can change them.
- The Ten Commandments are not mere rules; they are laws directing us to live the covenant we have with God.
- The first three commandments guide our relationship with God. The remaining seven commandments deal with our relationships to self and to others.
- Living according to the commandments is a serious responsibility. It is the only way to true happiness and peace.

Faith Words

Ten Commandments (p. 85)
chastity (p. 87)
modesty (p. 88)
virtue (p. 88)

REFLECT & ACT

God gave us the Ten Commandments out of love. They are a clear path away from the unhappiness of sin to happiness with God.

Why do you think God's commandments direct us in the way to live and use our freedom?

What can you tell others about the commandments as a help to living a happier life?

89

Conclusion (__ min.)

Growing in Faith

Have the young people close their books. Ask them what they have learned in this lesson about the Ten Commandments and the virtues of chasity and modesty. Reopen the books to page 89. Was everything from the **Remember** and **Faith Words** sections named? If not, point these out and help the group name the remaining concepts.

Invite the young people to read the **Reflect and Act** section. Encourage them to reflect on the Ten Commandments. Then, have the young people respond to the questions in the spaces provided. If desired, play some soft instrumental music while they do this.

Read the paragraph under **Pray** on page 89 and offer the prayer together.

CATECHISM FOCUS

"What God commands he makes possible by his grace." (*CCC*, 2082)

For additional reference and reflection, see *CCC*, 2052–2063.

Answers for page 89:

Left:
Accept all reasonable answers.

Right:
Accept all reasonable answers.

CHAPTER 14

GOALS

to learn the meaning of the Great Commandment, the New Commandment, and the Beatitudes; to understand the Christian virtues of faith, hope, and charity

GETTING READY

- ***Materials needed:***

Prayer table environment: Bible and decorative cloth

Notebook paper and pens for Section Two and the optional activity in Section Three

Bible for the "Do You Know?" feature

Adult Focus

Most of us would be tempted to buy a book called *Eight Ways to Be Happy*. But what if the author promoted a message of self-love and material success at any price? Would we realize that true happiness could not be found this way?

Jesus has given us eight ways to be happy. They are called the Beatitudes. We find them in Matthew's Gospel (5:3–10). When Jesus proclaimed the Beatitudes from the mountaintop, he spoke to the crowds in a formula that would have been familiar to them. Many listeners would have known by heart the psalmist's lesson, "Happy those concerned for the lowly and poor" (Psalm 41:2), as well as Proverbs' "Happy those who keep my ways" (Proverbs 8:33). They would have recognized that the Beatitudes called them to a high ethical

Introduction (__ min.)

Gather the group with their books around the prayer table.

Invite the group to sit quietly for a few minutes and reflect on how God loves them.

Read the Reflection on page 90 together and discuss the questions that follow.

Explain that today's lesson is going to focus on Jesus' way of loving.

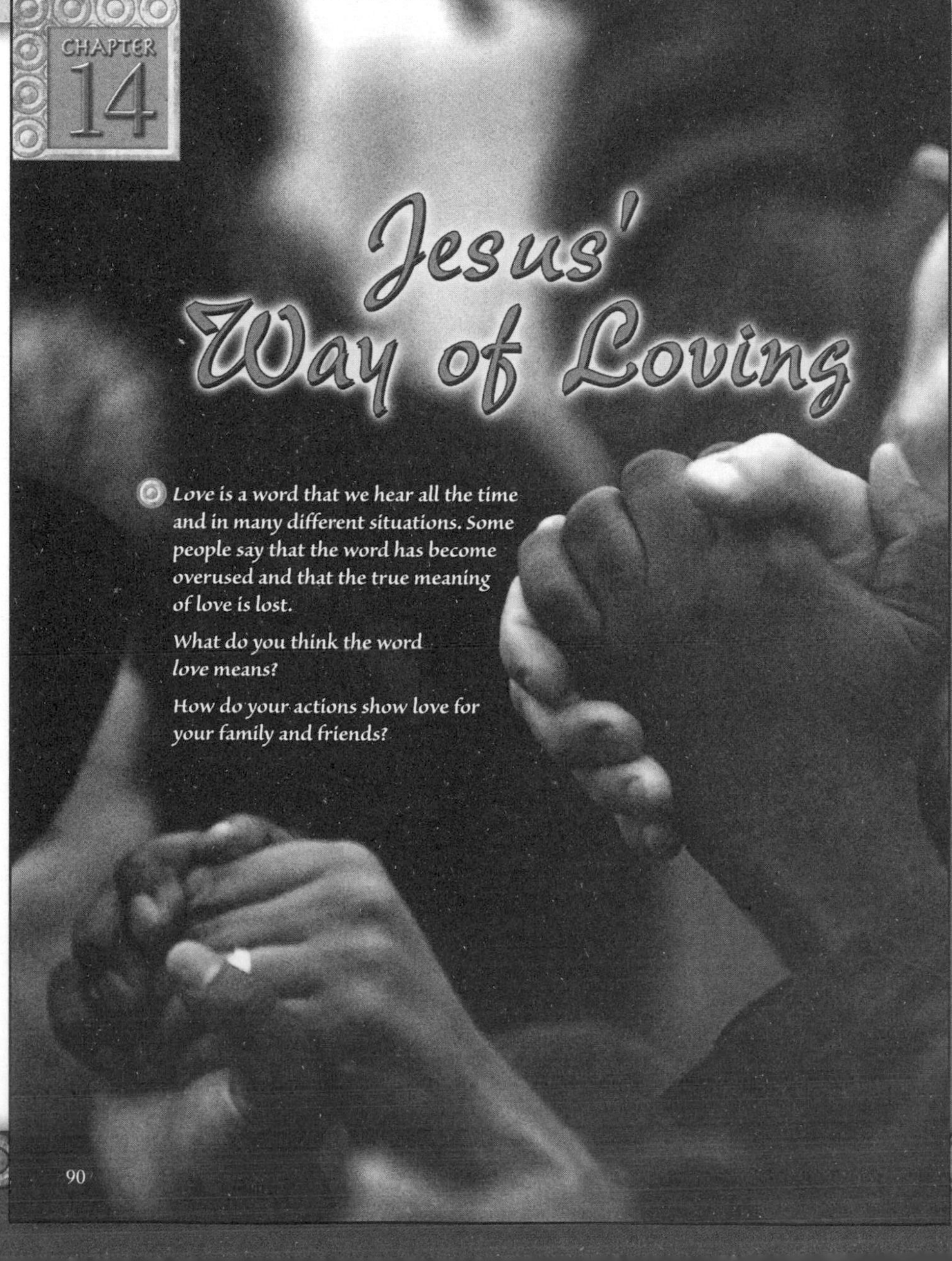

standard. They would have been amazed at the authority of the Teacher who affirmed their potential for spiritual maturity.

The Beatitudes instruct us on how we are to fulfill the spirit of Jesus' New Commandment to love others as he has loved us. They imply that we are all, by God's grace, capable of heroic virtue. They challenge us to live simply, place our hope in God, and identify with those who are struggling simply to live.

They remind us to obey the will of God, treat others with kindness, and behave humbly. They lead us to be repentant, merciful, and just. They call us to be peaceable and to be makers of peace. We are to have undivided hearts and to be undaunted by whatever we suffer for Jesus' sake.

Reflection

The Beatitudes are a trumpet blast from the Lord, rousing us to strive for the sanctity for which we were created. Like the Magnificat (Luke 1:46–55), they challenge us to change the world and to "lift up the lowly." In teaching the Beatitudes to young people, we prepare them to become strong witnesses to the life of Jesus. What is your favorite beatitude? Why? Think of how you might share this with your group.

 Jesus asks us to love.

God's laws guided his people in the right way to live. At times, however, the people forgot or turned away from the way of God. In making the covenant and in giving the Ten Commandments, God wanted the people to observe the commandments out of love for him and for one another. The great prayer of the Old Testament summed up the commandments:

> Hear, O Israel! The LORD is our God, the LORD alone! Therefore, you shall love the LORD, your God, with all your heart, and with all your soul, and with all your strength.
> Deuteronomy 6:4–5

The people were also told, "You shall love your neighbor as yourself" (Leviticus 19:18). The Ten Commandments were concrete laws that showed them how to love God and neighbor.

Jesus observed and respected the laws of the covenant. He told his disciples, "Do not think that I have come to abolish the law or the prophets. I have come not to abolish but to fulfill" (Matthew 5:17).

Once a scholar asked Jesus which commandment in the law was the greatest. Jesus replied by bringing together the teachings of the Old Testament into the *Great Commandment:*

> You shall love the Lord, your God, with all your heart, with all your soul, and with all your mind. This is the greatest and the first commandment. The second is like it: You shall love your neighbor as yourself. The whole law and the prophets depend on these two commandments.
> Matthew 22:37–40

91

Presentation (__ min.)

 Jesus asks us to love.

Have various volunteers read each paragraph under Section One on pages 91 and 92.

Ask if it is possible to keep the commandments without loving God and others. Stress that Jesus built his teachings upon God's Law. Explain that Jesus grew impatient with people who held to the letter of the law while ignoring the spirit of the law. Give an example of how this might work today, such as someone going to church out of habit, not out of love for God. Encourage the young people to think of other examples.

Stress that the New Commandment of Jesus requires his disciples to love one another as Jesus has loved them. Encourage the young people to learn the New Commandment by heart.

Talk about the meaning of love of enemies. How do you think Jesus' disciples reacted to the New Commandment? What does our society and our media seem to value more: power over enemies or love of enemies?

Have the young people respond, in writing, to the question at the end of Section One on page 92.

The Beatitudes are guidelines for true happiness.

Have the young people read Section Two on pages 92 and 93 silently.

Ask the group:

- Why were the people in need of someone to show them the path to true freedom?
- What did Jesus challenge the people to do?

Read the Beatitudes on page 93 slowly and reverently. Ask volunteers to define the Beatitudes. (teachings that describe how to live as Jesus' disciples)

Explain the message of each of the Beatitudes to the group:

(Matthew 5:3) This beatitude tells us about our attitude toward the things we have; we should not be overly attached to possessions. Our confidence should be in God. We are called to share whatever we have with others.

(Matthew 5:4) We are to be signs of hope despite the sadness, evil, and injustice we see in the world. As Jesus' disciples, we are to comfort those who suffer injustice and loss.

When the disciples of Jesus reflected on his life and teaching, they realized how important love was to Jesus. By word and example Jesus had urged them to love as he did.

He taught them to love God our Father totally. Everything that Jesus did was directed to his Father. We read that Jesus went off to the desert or to the mountains frequently to be alone with God and to pray. In fact, Jesus' whole life could be summed up as always doing the will of his Father.

So, it is not surprising that on the night before he died, Jesus told his disciples:

> I give you a new commandment: love one another. As I have loved you, so you also should love one another. This is how all will know that you are my disciples, if you have love for one another.
> John 13:34–35

This command from Jesus to his disciples is known as the **New Commandment**. Jesus wanted his disciples to love as he loved and to act as they knew he would act so that everyone they met would know him through them.

Later on, Jesus stressed that he himself had come as a perfect example of love for all of us. Jesus said to his disciples, "Love one another as I love you. No one has greater love than this, to lay down one's life for one's friends" (John 15:12–13). Jesus did lay down his life for us. And in doing so, Jesus showed how great his love for us was.

What can you do to love others as Jesus has loved you?

Do YOU Know?

The Blessed Virgin Mary is our most perfect model of faith, hope, and love. She entrusted herself entirely to God when she said, "May it be done to me according to your word" (Luke 1:38). Mary remained strong in hope despite the many difficulties and sorrows she faced as Jesus' mother. She expressed her deep faith in God in her Magnificat, or song. Throughout her life, Mary glorified God and loved Jesus and his disciples.

The Beatitudes are guidelines for true happiness.

In the time of Jesus, God's people were again in need of someone to lead them to true freedom. As a nation they had suffered through many wars and domination by foreign rulers. They were looking for the Messiah to free them from this oppression and to show them the path to true freedom.

God had given the Israelites the gift of the Law of Moses as their way of life. Jesus wanted to teach again its lesson: love God and love neighbor. He told the people that his Father is the God of love, not of fear.

When Jesus spoke to the people, he sensed that their spirits were low. They had lost their way. Jesus challenged the people to take a giant step toward freedom, no matter how painful it seemed. Jesus promised that those who suffer for the sake of the Kingdom of God would be rewarded. In Matthew's Gospel, Jesus' Sermon on the Mount gives the way to true happiness called the Beatitudes.

92

Do YOU Know?

Read the "Do You Know?" feature on page 92 together. Have a volunteer look up and read the Magnificat, Mary's prayer of praise (Luke 1:46–55).

Answer for page 92:

Help the young people to see that the answers can be found in their day-to-day living. Accept all reasonable answers.

The Beatitudes

Blessed are the poor in spirit,
for theirs is the kingdom of heaven.

Blessed are they who mourn,
for they will be comforted.

Blessed are the meek,
for they will inherit the land.

Blessed are they who hunger and thirst
for righteousness,
for they will be satisfied.

Blessed are the merciful,
for they will be shown mercy.

Blessed are the clean of heart,
for they will see God.

Blessed are the peacemakers,
for they will be called children of God.

Blessed are they who are persecuted for
the sake of righteousness,
for theirs is the kingdom of heaven.

Matthew 5:3–10

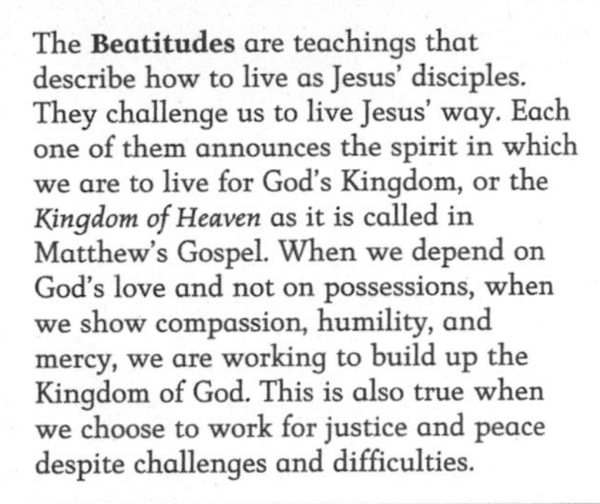
The **Beatitudes** are teachings that describe how to live as Jesus' disciples. They challenge us to live Jesus' way. Each one of them announces the spirit in which we are to live for God's Kingdom, or the *Kingdom of Heaven* as it is called in Matthew's Gospel. When we depend on God's love and not on possessions, when we show compassion, humility, and mercy, we are working to build up the Kingdom of God. This is also true when we choose to work for justice and peace despite challenges and difficulties.

In what ways can you live the spirit of the Beatitudes in your family, school, or neighborhood?

The Solitude of Christ, Maurice Denis, 1918

93

(Matthew 5:5) The meek are the humble—that is, those who realize that their talents and abilities come from God. We are to use our God-given talents and abilities to do what is good, showing love for God and others.

(Matthew 5:6) The greatest desire of those who hunger and thirst for righteousness is for God's power and presence to be at work in the world. As Jesus' disciples we try to do God's will. We put our trust in God and carry out Christ's work of justice.

(Matthew 5:7) Those who show love and forgive others will themselves receive love and forgiveness in God's Kingdom. We are to show compassion to all people.

(Matthew 5:8) The clean of heart are those who are open to God and God's Law. They are sincere in everything they do. We are to be faithful Christians and find Christ in others.

(Matthew 5:9) God wants all people to love one another and to have the peace that comes from loving him and trusting in his will. We are called to be reconcilers in our homes, communities, and world. We are to bring people together.

(Matthew 5:10) Prophets were often persecuted when they brought people God's message. We are to live out our Christian faith even when others do not understand our beliefs.

Invite volunteers to describe one way to live out each of the Beatitudes.

Have the young people write their responses to the question at the end of Section Two on page 93.

Optional Activity

Imagine that Mary was going to visit the group to talk about her experiences. Have the group brainstorm questions they would want to ask her about her life. What sort of things would they want to know about her? What would they want to ask her about their own lives?

Answers for page 93:

Accept all reasonable answers.

Jesus calls us to follow him in faith, hope, and love.

Have the group read Section Three on page 94 silently.

Discuss the theological virtues with these young people striving to grow in the spiritual life. Help them to see that a virtuous life, far from being a boring one, is a life filled with challenge and commitment. Ask the young people to explain in their own words the virtues of faith, hope, and charity. Stress that these three virtues are gifts from God.

Persons of faith, hope, and charity are people who are willing to take risks and sacrifice, and not to compromise Christian values. Have the young people complete these statements by describing persons who practice the theological virtues:

- A person of faith ________.
- A person of hope ________.
- A person of charity ________.

How do we grow in a life of virtue? (We grow through reflecting on Scripture and participating in the sacraments, through prayer, through an active life in the Church community, and through works of justice and charity.)

Have the young people write their responses to the question at the end of Section Three on page 94. Invite volunteers to share their responses.

Jesus calls us to follow him in faith, hope, and love.

Christians of all times and places have tried to follow Jesus' New Commandment and live the Beatitudes. The early Christians discovered very quickly that to do this they would need a change of heart. They would have to live a life of virtue.

A virtue is a good habit that helps a person live according to God's love for us. Three virtues stand out as the most important of all: faith, hope, and charity. These are known as **theological virtues** because they have God as their source, motive, and object. They are gifts from God and mark the Christian way of life.

Faith is the gift from God by which we believe in God and all that he has revealed, and all that the Church proposes for our belief. Through the gift of faith we have a deep and abiding relationship with God, who loves us completely. Faith allows us to place our trust in God and to act as God wants us to. All disciples of Christ must not only keep the faith, but also profess it, witness to it by our words and actions, and pass it on to others.

Hope is the gift from God by which we desire eternal life, place our trust in Christ's promises, and rely on the help of the Holy Spirit. People of hope never give up on God, themselves, or on the relationship they have with God. They know that, even when things look bad, evil will not finally overcome good, and hatred will never extinguish love. This is the promise that Jesus made to us.

The challenge of hope is to act as God wants us to and to seek ways to work for justice and peace in the world. Hope helps us to remember that our true destiny is to be happy forever with God.

Saint Paul tells us that "faith, hope, love remain, these three; but the greatest of these is love" (1 Corinthians 13:13). The love we are speaking about, however, is the virtue of charity. **Charity** is the gift from God that enables us to love him above all things and to love our neighbor as ourselves.

With the help of this virtue, we follow the Great Commandment: We love God above all other things and our neighbors as ourselves. This love we have for God can become a powerful force in our lives and in our world. It can help us to appreciate our gifts and talents and to love ourselves as God loves us. It helps us to love even those who are known as our enemies.

To love others can be a joy, easy and immediately fulfilling. To love others can also require sacrifice, and the ability to forgive others and to welcome forgiveness in our own lives.

The gift of love is all around us. Jesus has shown us how to recognize it and how to use this gift in the world. This is the meaning of being a disciple of Christ.

What or who helps you to be a loving, faithful, and hopeful person?

94

Optional Activity

Invite the young people to write a story about someone who is faithful, hopeful, and/or loving. The story should include the following elements:

- **what challenges that person faces**
- **how he or she shows faith, hope, or charity through that challenge**
- **how this life/action touches someone else.**

Answers for page 94:

Accept all reasonable answers. Allow each person to give a reason for his or her choice.

GROWING IN FAITH

PRAY

Silently reflect on these words of Saint Paul:

✝ Love is patient, love is kind. It is not jealous, [love] is not pompous, it is not inflated, it is not rude, it does not seek its own interests, it is not quick-tempered, it does not brood over injury, it does not rejoice over wrongdoing but rejoices with the truth. It bears all things, believes all things, hopes all things, endures all things. Love never fails.

1 Corinthians 13:4–8

REMEMBER

The Church teaches...

- Jesus taught the Great Commandment, to love God above all others and to love others as ourselves.
- Jesus offered us a New Commandment to love one another as Jesus has loved us.
- The Beatitudes are teachings that describe how to live as Jesus' disciples.
- Faith, hope, and charity are the theological virtues because they are gifts from God that have God as their source, motive, and object.

Faith Words

New Commandment (p. 92)
Beatitudes (p. 93)
theological virtues (p. 94)
faith (p. 94)
hope (p. 94)
charity (p. 94)

REFLECT & ACT

Remember a happy time in your life. What brought you that happiness? How was it like or unlike the happiness of living the way Jesus wants us to?

Saint Paul teaches us that love is much more than a feeling. What can you do to show love to the people in your life?

95

CATECHISM FOCUS

"The Beatitudes depict the countenance of Jesus Christ and portray his charity. . . . they shed light on the actions and attitudes characteristic of the Christian life; they are the paradoxical promises that sustain hope in the midst of tribulations; they proclaim the blessings and rewards already secured, however dimly, for Christ's disciples." (*CCC*, 1717)

For additional reference and reflection, see *CCC*, 1716–1729.

Conclusion (__ min.)

Growing in Faith

Have the group close their books. Ask them what they have learned in this lesson about the Great Commandment, the New Commandment, the Beatitudes, and the theological virtues. Reopen the books to page 95. Was everything from the **Remember** and **Faith Words** sections named? If not, point these out and help the group name the remaining concepts.

Invite the young people to read the **Reflect and Act** section. Encourage them to think of ways of showing love to the people in our lives. Then, have them write their responses in the spaces provided. If desired, play some soft instrumental music while they do this.

Point out the **Pray** section on page 95. Explain that Saint Paul wrote a beautiful description of love to the Christians in Corinth (1 Corinthians 13:4–7). Read and pray together the passage.

Answer page 95:

Left:
Accept all reasonable answers.

Right:
Have the young people reflect on the prayer from Saint Paul. Help them to see that being patient, kind, etc. are among the ways to show love.

CHAPTER 15

GOALS

to understand the Christian mission of prayerful service; to learn about the Church's social teachings, including the Works of Mercy

GETTING READY

- ***Materials needed:***

Prayer table environment: Bible and decorative cloth

Bibles—preferably one for each young person

Adult Focus

Jesus' parable of the Good Samaritan (Luke 10:30–37) intends to lead us beyond the inclination to draw a line between those people who "deserve" our care and those who do not. By his extravagant ministry to the Jewish victim, the Samaritan shows us what God's loving mercy looks like.

Mercy does not discriminate. It does not set limits or count the cost. It is filled with kindness. The merciful Samaritan is a model of what Christ himself does for those who lie broken, bleeding, and neglected. He stops to help and to heal. Christ can also be found in the injured man lying by the roadside, awaiting the kindness and mercy of a passing stranger.

Introduction (__ min.)

Gather the group with their books around the prayer table. Give a Bible to each young person. Have volunteers take turns and read aloud Luke 10:25–29. Focus on the question: "Who is my neighbor?" Invite the young people to share their answers. Ask the group to think about certain situations in which it might be difficult to love their neighbor. Encourage them to call upon the Holy Spirit for the courage to love. Offer the Prayer to the Holy Spirit on page 120.

After the prayer, read the paragraph on page 97. Ask: What is does it mean to love God? to love our neighbor? Discuss the question together. Point out the art on pages 96-97. Ask: How does this art reflect the question? What challenges or concerns does it pose for us?

Read the parable of the Good Samaritan in Luke 10:30–37. Explain that this parable was

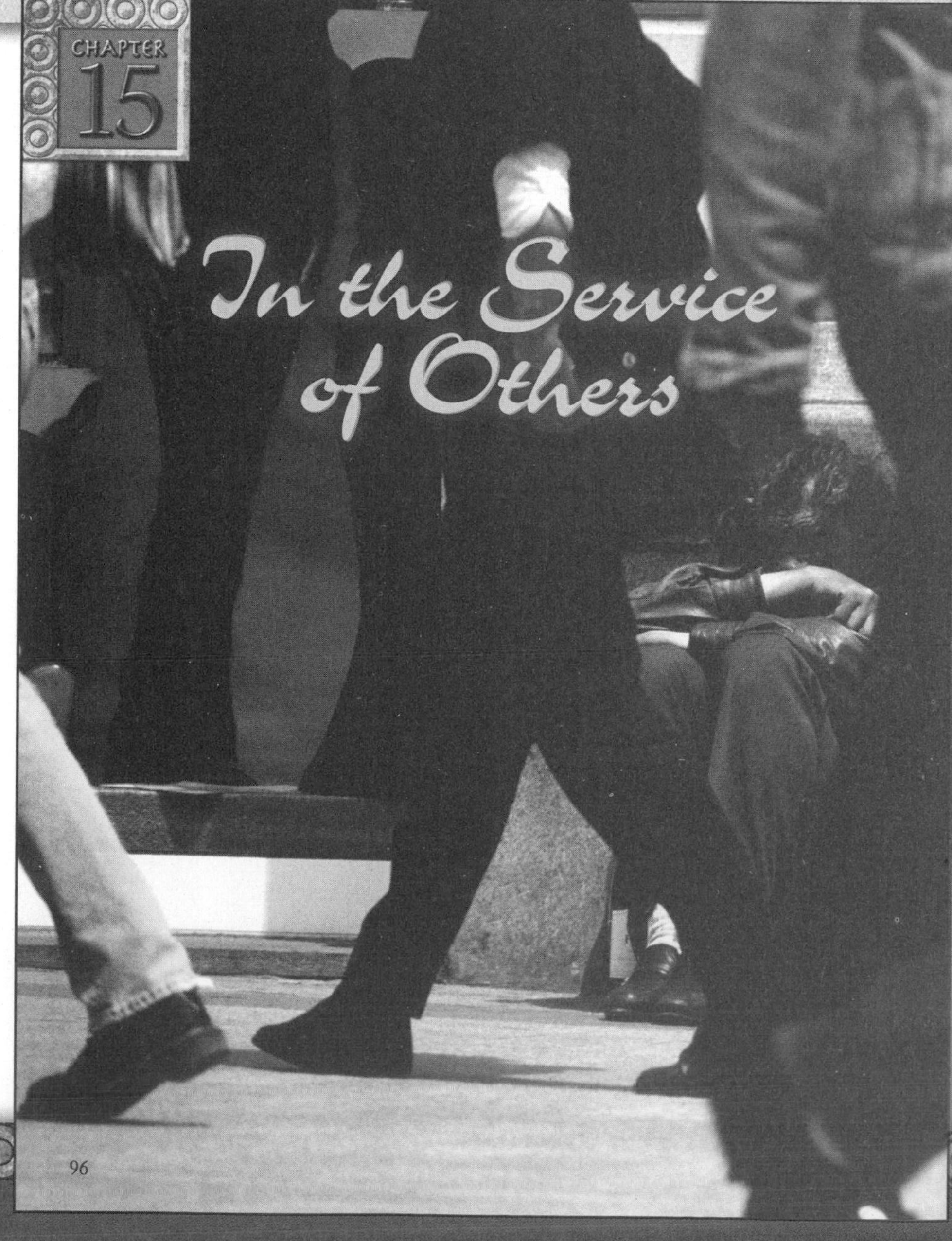

As a Catholic community we care for those who are sick, provide for those who are poor, feed those who are hungry, and come to the aid of those who are in need physically and spiritually. We are called to take up Works of Mercy. When we perform these Works of Mercy with love, we can identify ourselves with Christ who is in need, Christ who ministers, and Christ who is the bond of compassion.

The Church calls us to ensure that all people are treated with dignity and respect. Catholic social teaching commits us to the welfare of every person. These social doctrines require us to respect the life, dignity, and rights of every human person. We are called to strengthen the family, practice solidarity with all people, value labor, and commit ourselves to serving the poor.

Reflection

Reflect upon the Spiritual and Corporal Works of Mercy, listed on page 98. What sort of needs do you see around you, even among your young people, and how will you respond?

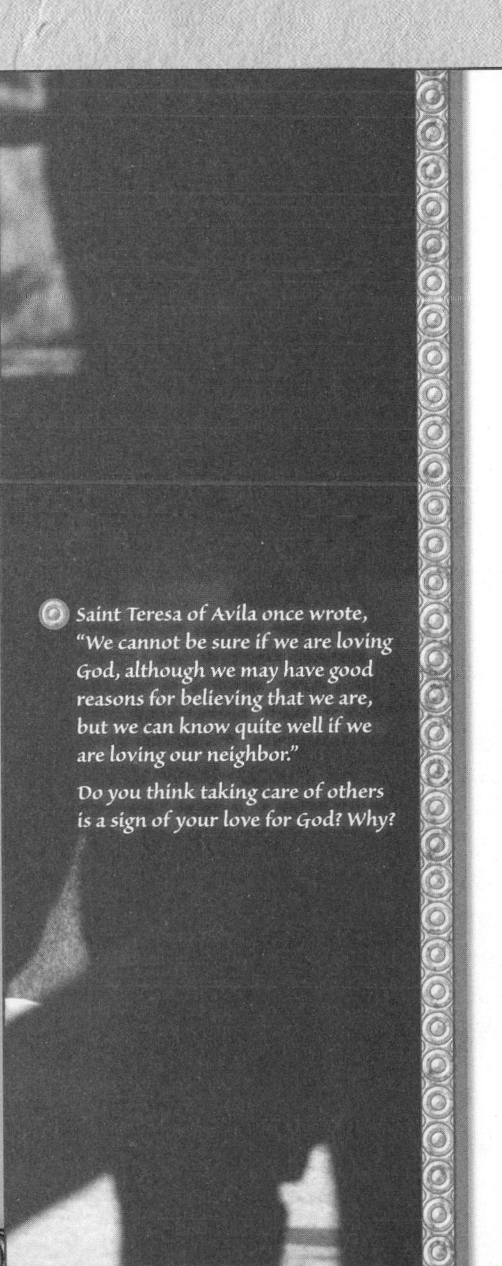

Saint Teresa of Avila once wrote, "We cannot be sure if we are loving God, although we may have good reasons for believing that we are, but we can know quite well if we are loving our neighbor."

Do you think taking care of others is a sign of your love for God? Why?

 We will be judged by our love.

Jesus' whole life was a shining example of service to others. He told his disciples, "I am among you as the one who serves" (Luke 22:27). When we help others, we are following in Jesus' footsteps.

When Jesus gave the Great Commandment to love God and our neighbors as ourselves, a scholar questioned him, asking, "And who is my neighbor?" (Luke 10:29) Jesus answered by telling the parable of the Good Samaritan.

According to the story a man who was on a journey was robbed, beaten, and left on the road to suffer. As he lay there, three people came along; but the first two passed by the suffering man. The third was a man from the country of Samaria, a hated enemy of the victim's country. The Samaritan stopped and took care of the man's wounds, brought him to an inn, and even paid for his care.

After telling the story Jesus asked who of the three men was a neighbor to the man attacked by robbers. The answer came, "The one who treated him with mercy"; and Jesus said, "Go and do likewise" (Luke 10:37).

At the end of our lives, how will we be judged for carrying out our Christian responsibilities? Jesus described the Last Judgment to help us understand the importance of our actions today. The **Last Judgment** is Jesus Christ's coming at the end of time to judge all people. We read in the New Testament that Jesus explained that some people will share in the joys of Heaven and the others will not. To those who performed deeds of mercy, Jesus will say:

> For I was hungry and you gave me food, I was thirsty and you gave me drink, a stranger and you welcomed me, naked and you clothed me, ill and you cared for me, in prison and you visited me.
> Matthew 25:35–36

Jesus' answer to the question "Who is my neighbor?" Encourage the group to keep the story in mind as they read the chapter.

Presentation (__ min.)

 We will be judged by our love.

Have volunteers read aloud Section One on pages 97–98. Ask the young people to recall the parable of the Good Samaritan. Discuss the following:

- Every person is created by God and therefore is worth our attention, care, and respect; everyone is our "neighbor."
- When we show love and compassion to others, we are showing love for God.

After reading the list of the Corporal and Spiritual Works of Mercy, ask volunteers to suggest ways that young people can live them out.

Discuss the question at the end of Section One on page 98. Have the young people write their responses in the space provided.

Catholic social teaching helps us to live Jesus' command to love others.

Introduce Section Two by explaining that the Church holds strongly to the dignity and worth of each person. Read aloud the first paragraph under Section Two on page 98.

Have different volunteers read aloud each of the themes of Catholic social teaching based on the U.S. Bishops' document, *Sharing Catholic Social Teaching: Challenges and Directions*. Stop after each theme to highlight key points and to encourage young people to describe, in their own words, what the theme is about.

Those being judged will ask him when they did all of these things for him, and Jesus will reply, "Amen, I say to you, whatever you did for one of these least brothers of mine, you did for me" (Matthew 25:40).

In his story of the Good Samaritan and his teaching on the Last Judgment, Jesus was talking about mercy. When we show mercy to someone who is suffering, we show love and compassion. Jesus taught that what we do for others, we are doing for him. The **Works of Mercy** are acts of love by which we care for the bodily and spiritual needs of others. They call us to live as Christ wants us to. The Works of Mercy are divided into two categories:

- The Corporal Works of Mercy focus on the physical and material needs of others.
- The Spiritual Works of Mercy focus on the needs of the heart, mind, and soul.

How could the world be different if we all lived out the Works of Mercy?

98

Do YOU Know?

Many parishes have programs to help their members practice the Works of Mercy. What programs in your parish can help you treat others as Jesus did?

Corporal Works of Mercy
Feed the hungry.
Give drink to the thirsty.
Clothe the naked.
Visit the imprisoned.
Shelter the homeless.
Visit the sick.
Bury the dead.

Spiritual Works of Mercy
Admonish the sinner.
Instruct the ignorant.
Counsel the doubtful.
Comfort the sorrowful.
Bear wrongs patiently.
Forgive all injuries.
Pray for the living and the dead.

Catholic social teaching helps us to live Jesus' command to love others.

The Catholic Church teaches us that responding to the needs of others is a central part of our faith. **Catholic social teaching** is the teaching of the Church that calls all members to work for justice and peace as Jesus did. It commits us to the welfare of every person. It helps us see that each and every person shares the same human dignity. Catholic social teaching helps us follow Jesus' command to love others as he has loved us.

There are seven themes that are very important to the social teaching of the Church.

Life and Dignity of the Human Person
Human life is sacred because it is a gift from God. We are all God's children and share the

Read the "Do You Know?" feature on page 98 together. Stress the difference between the Corporal and Spiritual Works of Mercy as described at the end of Section One.

Answer for page 98:

Possible answers include: If we all focused on each other's needs, everyone would be taken care of.

Students, teachers, and community members participate in a peace march and rally in Dorchester, Mass. on Sept. 11, 2006.

same human dignity from the moment of conception to natural death. Our dignity—our worth and value—comes from being made in the image and likeness of God. This dignity makes us equal. As Christians we respect all people, even those we do not know.

Call to Family, Community, and Participation
As Christians we are involved in our family life and community. We are called to promote the common good and to care for those most in need by participating in social, economic, and political life, using the values of our faith to shape our decisions and actions.

Rights and Responsibilities of the Human Person
Every person has a fundamental right to life. This includes the things we need to have a decent life: faith and family, work and education, health care and housing. We also have a responsibility to others and to society. We work to make sure the rights of all people are being protected.

Option for the Poor and Vulnerable
We have a special obligation to help those who are poor and in need. This includes those who cannot protect themselves because of their age or their health. At different times in our lives we are all poor in some way and in need of assistance.

Dignity of Work and the Rights of Workers
Our work is a sign of our participation in God's work. People have the right to decent work, just wages, and safe working conditions, and to participate in decisions about their work. There is value in all work. Our work in school and at home is a way to participate in God's work of Creation. It is a way to use our talents and abilities to thank God for his gifts.

Solidarity of the Human Family
Solidarity affirms that we are all brothers and sisters, each responsible for the good of all. Each of us is a member of the one human family, equal by our common human dignity. The human family includes people of all racial, cultural, and religious backgrounds.

Name one way your parish can respond to Catholic social teaching, (see pages 98–100).

99

Read the question at the end of Section Two on page 99. Have the young people write their responses in the space provided.

If you have time, do the following.

You might also want to plan a project to do together that will help young people live out a Corporal or Spiritual Work of Mercy. This might be connected with a parish program, community service organization, or initiated by the young people themselves. For example:

- Make sack lunches for a soup kitchen or homeless shelter.
- Make cards or gifts for residents of a nursing home or hospital.
- Pray for those who are mourning the death of a loved one.
- Help present a religious education lesson to a pre-school or kindergarten class.

Optional Activity

Read the parable of the Good Samaritan again (see page 97). Distribute paper and pencils to the group. Encourage the young people to think of ways to retell the parable in a modern setting. If time permits, encourage volunteers to share their modern parables with the group.

Answers for page 99:
Accept all reasonable answers.

Catholics have special laws to help live the Christian life.

Have volunteers read aloud Section Three on page 100. Review the Precepts of the Church with the group. Help the group to understand that by following these precepts helps us to live as faithful and responsible members of the Church. Direct the young people's attention to the fifth Precept of the Church. Discuss what this precept means. Emphasize that while those who are able should contribute monetarily, this is not necessarily possible for young people. Brainstorm ways in which young people can "Contribute to the support of the Church." (Suggestions: offering some kind of service to their parish, praying for the work of Holy Father, etc.)

Help the group to see that we can accomplish a great deal in our own individual parish communities. Remind them that the parish is the local point of our Christian life and thus our outreach to the rest of society. It is important for each of us to be active in parish life and activities.

Have young people write their responses to the question at the end of Section Three on page 100.

We all suffer when one part of the human family suffers, and are each called to love our neighbor as ourself.

Care for God's Creation

God created us to be stewards, or caretakers, of his Creation. We must care for and respect the environment. We have to protect it for the future generations. When we care for Creation, we show respect for God the Creator.

The awareness of the richness of Catholic social teaching is growing. We have a serious responsibility to promote the common good of all people. Failure to fulfill this responsibility can lead to unjust situations and conditions that negatively impact society and its institutions. We call this social sin.

Catholics have special laws to help live the Christian life.

Catholics have a special set of laws that are called **Precepts of the Church**, laws of the Church that help us to see that loving God and others is connected to a life of prayer, worship, and service. They guide our behavior and teach us how we should act as members of the Church. We also share in the Church's mission of **Evangelization**—the sharing of the Good News of Jesus Christ and the love of God with all people, in every circumstance of life.

The Precepts of the Church are usually summarized as follows:

1. You shall attend Mass on Sundays and Holy Days of Obligation and rest from servile labor.
2. You shall confess your sins at least once a year.
3. You shall receive the Sacrament of the Eucharist at least during the Easter season.
4. You shall observe the days of fasting and abstinence by the Church.
5. You shall help to provide for the needs of the Church.

The Precepts of the Church call us to a life of prayer and service. These laws remind us that our Catholic life is one of balance—a balance between our prayer and sacramental life and the missionary efforts of the Church throughout the world. The fundamental way we accomplish all of this is in our individual parish community.

How can following the Precepts of the Church help you to share the Good News of Jesus Christ?

Answers for page 100:

Possible answers may include: People will see that I am happy, and want to know why. People all over the world will be helped by my contributions. My peers will see in me someone who is trying to live out the Good News of Jesus Christ.

GROWING IN FAITH

PRAY

One of the ways to fulfill the Spiritual Works of Mercy is to pray for peace and live peacefully with others. Many popes have encouraged us to pray for peace. Pray together the following prayer:

✝ Mary, Queen of Peace,
We entrust our lives to you.
Shelter us from war, hatred,
and oppression.
Teach us
to live in peace,
to educate ourselves for peace.
Root peace firmly in our hearts
and in our world.
Amen.

A Prayer for Justice and Peace
Blessed Pope John Paul II

REMEMBER

The Church teaches...

- The Works of Mercy help us to live as Jesus Christ wants us to live.
- The Corporal Works of Mercy address the physical and material needs of others; the Spiritual Works of Mercy address the needs of the heart, mind, and soul.
- Responding to the needs of others is a central part of our faith. Catholic social teaching is founded on the life and work of Jesus and based on the human dignity of the person.
- The Precepts of the Church express some of the most important obligations we have as Catholics, to grow in holiness and to share in the Church's work of Evangelization and service.

Faith Words

Last Judgment (p. 97)
Works of Mercy (p. 98)
Catholic social teaching (p. 98)
Precepts of the Church (p. 100)
Evangelization (p. 100)

REFLECT & ACT

How does Catholic social teaching call us to follow the example of Jesus?

Which of the Works of Mercy do you most practice in your family? in your parish? in your school?

101

Conclusion (__ min.)

Growing in Faith

Have the young people close their books. Ask them what they have learned in this lesson about the Last Judgment, the Works of Mercy, Catholic social teaching, the Precepts of the Church, and evangelization. Reopen the books to page 101. Was everything from the **Remember** and **Faith Words** sections named? If not, point these out and help the group name the remaining concepts.

Invite the young people to read the **Reflect and Act** section.

Then, have them write their responses to the questions in the spaces provided. If desired, play some soft instrumental music while they do this.

Encourage the young people to name one Work of Mercy they will do this week. (Suggestions: visit an elderly parishioner; collect clothing for the poor; practice patience with parents and siblings; compose a family prayer for relatives who have died.)

Have a volunteer read aloud the paragraph in the **Pray** section on page 101. Then, have the group pray together Blessed Pope John Paul II's prayer for justice and peace.

CATECHISM FOCUS

"Of all visible creatures only man. . . . is called to share, by knowledge and love, in God's own life. It was for this end that he was created, and this is the fundamental reason for his dignity." (*CCC*, 356)

For additional reference and reflection, see *CCC*, 1928–1948.

Answers for page 101:

Left:
Possible answers include: Catholic social teaching helps us to follow Jesus' command to love others as he has loved us. (See page 98.)

Right:
Accept all reasonable answers.

CHAPTER 16

GOALS

to understand the Church's belief in life after death; to appreciate Mary as the greatest of the saints

GETTING READY

■ *Materials needed:*

Prayer table environment: Bible and decorative cloth

Refreshments for a closing celebration

Bibles—preferable one for each young person

Paper strips, markers, glue or staples for the activity in Section Two

One Faith, One Lord *program survey (see pages XII and XIV) for each young person*

Adult Focus

Christ shows us the way to the Father. He is our Resurrection and life. We express this central belief and our promised future with words such as *Heaven*. It signifies our desire to be with God in a new life that is everlasting. When we attempt to describe what Heaven will be like, our limited words fail us. Saint Paul tells us,

> "What eye has not seen, and ear has not heard,
> and what has not entered the human heart,
> what God has prepared for those who love him"
> (1 Corinthians 2:9).

The "last things"—judgment, Purgatory, Heaven, and Hell—are actually the first things in a Christian's life. At Baptism, each of us is called out of the darkness into a new life in Christ. This fundamental relationship with the triune God destines us to everlasting union with Father, Son,

Introduction (__ min.)

Gather around the prayer table. Explain that this is the final lesson of the program. Ask the young people to reflect on all that they have learned. Lead the group in the following prayer:

Lord God,
your Spirit of wisdom fills the earth
and teaches us your ways.

Look upon these young people.
Thank you for the ways they have
learned, grown, and taken
delight in new discoveries.
Help them to persevere in their
studies
and give them the desire to learn
all things well.

Grant that they may follow Jesus
Christ,
the way, the truth, and the life,
for ever and ever.

Amen.

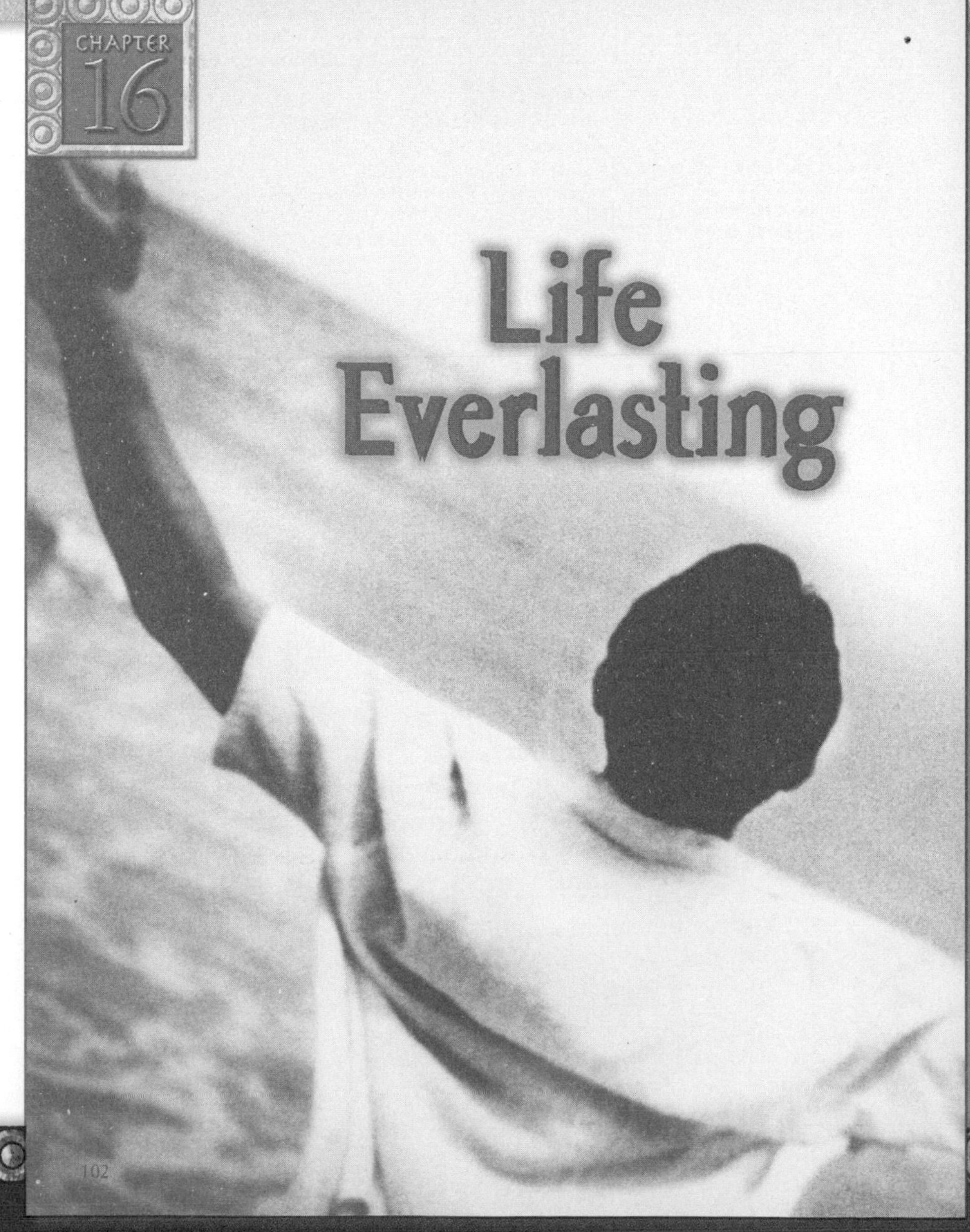

and, Holy Spirit. By God's grace and our cooperation with it, we are able to show in our love for God and one another our desire to be with God in Heaven. The choice, certainly, is ours. God invites us to turn to him, a lifelong conversion until we return to him.

Think about your earthly pilgrimage now. This faith journey is made in the company of other Christians who have hope in the Resurrection of the body and life everlasting. Following Christ's example, we can open ourselves to God's transforming love by trusting in his promise of eternal life to those who do his will. Meditate on Matthew 25:31–46. Begin to realize "whatever you did for one of these least brothers of mine, you did it for me" (Matthew 25:40) means that God's compassion and mercy embraces us now and at the hour of our death.

Reflection

How can you help your group explore the mystery of life and death so that they will come to understand the words used in the *Rite of Christian Burial:* "Life is changed, not ended"?

In this last chapter of *One Faith, One Lord,* spend some time going back over the experiences of the past year/program. What has enriched you throughout the year/program?

When Cardinal Joseph Bernardin, Archbishop of Chicago from 1982–1996, was dying, people asked him about Heaven and the afterlife. He told them about his first trip to Italy, his parents' homeland. Upon arrival, he was sure he had been there before. "Somehow I think crossing from this life into life eternal will be similar," he said. "I will be home."

What questions do you have about death and the afterlife?

1 The mystery of death is answered in the Resurrection of Jesus Christ.

Throughout the ages death has haunted and puzzled men and women everywhere. Death is a great mystery of life.

In early Old Testament times, people were not sure about life after death. They considered the possibility that men and women might live on through their children. That is why the aged and childless Abraham and Sarah were so overjoyed when they heard that they would have a son, Isaac. They believed that parents, by passing on their heritage, would continue to live in their offspring.

In later Old Testament times the ancient Jews considered life after death as some kind of vague existence. For this reason they believed that the greatest gift they could receive from God was to live a long life.

In the time of Jesus two opposite opinions were held about life after death. Some Jews believed there was no life after death; others had a growing understanding of an afterlife and believed in life after death.

Jesus himself left no doubt as to his own teaching on life after death. He told his followers that God promised life, not death, and explained that life after death is different from our human experience.

Most Christians in the early Church believed in resurrection. It was so central to the faith of early Christians that Saint Paul wrote, "If there is no resurrection of the dead, then neither has Christ been raised. And if Christ has not been raised, then empty [too] is our preaching; empty, too, your faith" (1 Corinthians 15:13–14).

Recall that the last words of the prayer are *for ever and ever.* Direct attention to the title of chapter 16, *Life Everlasting.* Ask: How does our belief in God give us hope of life everlasting? (God created us with a soul, the invisible spiritual reality that makes each of us human and that will never die.)

Read the story about Cardinal Bernardin on page 103. Encourage the young people to share their answers to the question.

Presentation (__ min.)

The mystery of death is answered in the Resurrection of Jesus Christ.

Have volunteers read aloud Section One on pages 103–104. Emphasize that Christians have hope in life after death because of our belief in the Resurrection of Jesus.

Discuss the quote from Saint Paul on page 103. Ask:

◎ What did Saint Paul mean when he said that the faith is "empty" if we do not believe in Christ's Resurrection? (Christ's Resurrection gave us new life, and restored our relationship with God.)

◎ What gave the early Christians the courage to die for their faith? (the hope and faith of Christ's Resurrection)

Discuss the question at the end of Section One on page 104. Have the young people write their responses in the space provided.

We look forward to life everlasting.

Have volunteers read aloud Section Two on pages 104–105.

Ask the young people to describe what they associate with Heaven, Purgatory, and Hell. How is each different? What role does our free will have for eternal life?

Emphasize the importance of the choices that we make to help the young people recognize that all choices have consequences—good or bad. Explain that Hell is the result of life of sinful and selfish choices.

Discuss the role of hope in our understanding of Heaven, Purgatory, and Hell. Explain that Heaven is the fulfillment of our hope because it is union with God. Purgatory carries with it the certainty of life in Heaven, so it is the continuation of our hope. Emphasize that Hell is the absence of hope because it is a state of eternal separation from God. Ask: How can we strengthen our hope in eternal life?

With this hope and faith in Christ's Resurrection, the Christian community was able to endure persecution and suffering. Their faith was not shaken by rejection and ridicule. Even though Christians loved and cherished the gift of life as Jesus did, they also knew that dying for their faith was a sharing in the redemptive Death of Christ. Christ had conquered death. They would rise to new life in the risen Lord.

Jesus was unique and extraordinary in his life and Death. He died on the cross, but he was raised to new life by God his Father. We believe Christ's Resurrection gives us the hope of rising to new life after death. For the Christian, death is not the final chapter in life.

What does it mean for you to share in Christ's Resurrection?

We look forward to life everlasing.

Creeds are statements of faith. Each week at the Sunday Mass, the Church professes its belief in the Resurrection of the body with these words from the Nicene Creed: "I look forward to the resurrection of the dead and the life of the world to come." This belief is expressed again in the Apostles' Creed: "I believe in the . . . resurrection of the body, and life everlasting."

When a person dies, life is not ended but changed. When we die our souls are separated from our bodies. When Jesus comes in glory at the end of time our bodies will be resurrected and united with our souls.

In the important moments of Christian life—from birth to death—the Church community supports and guides its members.

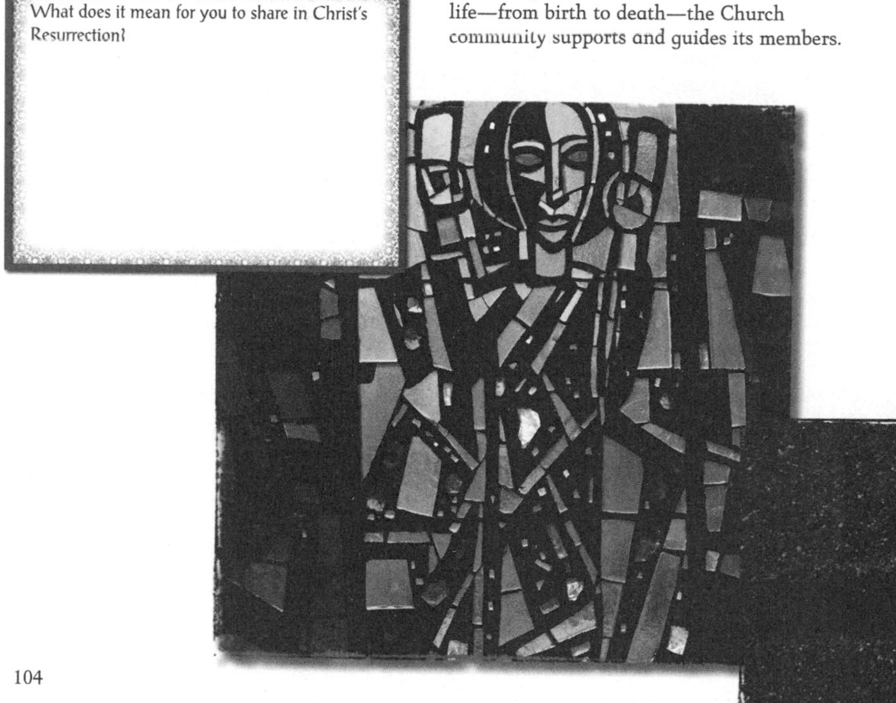

104

Optional Activity

Read aloud stories from the Gospels about Jesus raising people from the dead. Some suggestions are the daughter of Jairus (Mark 5:21–24, 35–43), the widow's son (Luke 7:11–17), and Lazarus (John 11:1–44). Discuss the stories and compare what each says about our hope in eternal life.

Answer for page 104:

Sharing in Christ's Resurrection gives us the hope of rising to new life after death.

The Last Judgment at the end of the world will affirm before the entire world whether we chose to love or not to love. However, at the moment of our death we face our particular judgment, at which we are judged in relation to how well we loved and served God and one another.

For those who have followed God's way and have served Christ, death will be the beginning of endless peace and happiness. This is **Heaven**—the ultimate happiness of living with God forever. But many people need to go through a process of purification from sinfulness. This process is called **Purgatory**. Yet, those experiencing Purgatory are certain of Heaven. The Church reminds us not to forget those who have died but always to remember them in our prayers, especially at Mass.

A very different beginning awaits those who freely chose a life of sin and selfishness. They were not sorry for their sins and had no intention of changing their ways. They will have nothing but eternal misery in Hell. **Hell** is the state of everlasting separation from God.

No one is condemned to Hell without freely deciding to reject God and his love. When we sin, we turn away from God, but he never turns away from us. God wills that every person born should be saved and share eternal life.

There are people who have not even heard of Christ or his Church. If they seek God sincerely and try to do what is right, they, too, can be saved. The Church calls all of these beliefs about death, judgment, Purgatory, Heaven, and Hell the *last things*.

What do you think about this statement: "We do not judge others. God alone is the just and merciful judge"?

Do YOU Know?

All those who have gone before us, who are now with God, continue to pray for us and for our good. We believe that they are joined to those of us still living as Christ's disciples on earth. This is what we call the **Communion of Saints**: the union of all the baptized members of the Church on earth, in Heaven, and in Purgatory. This unity is most clearly expressed in the Mass when the priest prays the Eucharistic Prayer.

105

If you have time, do the following.

Make a paper chain representing the Communion of Saints. Have each young person write on individual paper strips the names of people, such as:

- saints whose names the young people share
- family members or ancestors
- people from the parish or community who have died
- patron saints of the parish, school, and diocese
- friends
- other ideas.

Display the chain in the prayer space when complete. Encourage the young people to remember these members of the Communion of Saints in their prayers.

Do YOU Know?

Read the "Do You Know?" feature together. Stress the beautiful connection we have through the Communion of Saints with those believers who have gone before us.

Answer for page 105:

Accept all reasonable answers.

Mary is the greatest of the saints.

Have volunteers read Section Three on page 106. Encourage the young people to think of reasons why this chapter, which talks about life everlasting, concludes with a chapter on Mary and her role in our life of faith. What can we learn about our faith in Christ and life everlasting from the life of Mary?

Mary was the perfect follower of Jesus, and the mother of all who follow her Son. Stress that we are not alone on our journey of faith. We are part of a faithful, hopeful, loving Communion of Saints on Heaven and on earth.

Read the questions at the end of Section Three on page 106. Talk about any special ways your parish honors Mary throughout the year. Discuss the specific reasons for each celebration in Mary's honor.

Encourage the young people to talk about any saints that they honor. How do they honor these saints? Why do they honor these particular saints?

Have the young people write their responses to the questions in the space provided.

Mary is the greatest of the saints.

For over 2000 years the Church has been blessed with the holy lives of men and women who have accepted the challenge to live the message of Christ. They are our heroes and heroines in faith and have come from all walks of life. Some have been kings and queens. Some have been poor and needy. Most have lived their lives just as we do. But all have responded to God's love and shared that love with others. They have lived according to God's way. These are the saints, and we are brothers and sisters with them, especially when we follow the path to holiness. The word *saint* means "one who is made holy."

Mary is the greatest saint. God chose Mary to be the Mother of the Savior. She did not hesitate to say yes to God's call to be the Mother of Jesus, the Son of God and our brother.

As a faithful daughter of Israel, Mary reflected on God's word and carried it out in her life. She gave birth to Jesus, dedicated her life to him, and was present at his Crucifixion. On the day of Pentecost Mary was also there, praying with the other disciples as they waited for the coming of the Holy Spirit. She really could be considered Christ's first disciple, the one who heard the Good News of God's love in the world and who acted on it. She is a true model, or example, of holiness.

The Church teaches us several things about Mary. One of them is that Mary is our mother, too. We learn in John's Gospel something more about Mary and her relationship to us. According to this Gospel, as Jesus was hanging on the cross he saw his mother and the disciple John. Jesus said to Mary, "Woman, behold, your son," and to John he said, "Behold, your mother" (John 19:26–27). Not only is Mary the Mother of God, she is the mother of all who follow her Son.

Because Mary was to be the Mother of the Son of God, who was sinless, God privileged her from the moment she was conceived in her mother's womb. The **Immaculate Conception** is the truth that God preserved Mary from Original Sin and from all sin from the very moment she was conceived. We also believe in the truth that at the end of her earthly life, God brought Mary body and soul to Heaven to live forever with the risen Jesus. We call this truth the **Assumption**.

During the Church year we celebrate many feasts to honor Mary, including the Immaculate Conception on December 8 and the Assumption of Mary on August 15. It seems that every culture has a special title for her. In Mexico, Mary has the title Our Lady of Guadalupe. She has also been proclaimed the Patroness of the Americas. Yet she is more to us than a devotional figure, distant and seemingly removed from our everyday experiences. Mary was blessed by God to be full of grace, but she was also a real human being who faced life's struggles and joys.

Does your parish honor Mary in any special way? What saints does your family honor?

106

Optional Activity

Invite the young people to learn more about a particular saint. Working individually or in pairs, have the young people research the life of that saint, and share how he or she courageously followed the path to holiness. Encourage the young people to visit *The Lives of the Saints* featured on www.weliveourfaith.com.

Answers for page 106:

Accept all reasonable answers.

GROWING IN FAITH

PRAY

Mary is the Mother of Christ and our mother, too. We can ask her to pray with and for us.

✝ Hail Mary, full of grace,
the Lord is with you!
Blessed are you among women,
and blessed is the fruit of your womb, Jesus.
Holy Mary, Mother of God,
pray for us sinners,
now and at the hour of our death.
Amen.

REMEMBER

The Church teaches...

- The "last things" is a term that refers to death, judgment, Purgatory, Heaven, and Hell.
- God wishes for all people to be saved and to live forever with him in Heaven.
- Those who are not saved have freely chosen to separate themselves from God.
- Mary is the greatest of the saints. God preserved Mary from Original Sin and from all sin from the very moment she was conceived. This truth is called the Immaculate Conception.
- We believe that at the end of her life, God brought Mary body and soul to Heaven to live forever with the risen Jesus. This truth is called the Assumption.

Faith Words

Heaven (p. 105)
Purgatory (p. 105)
Hell (p. 105)
Communion of Saints (p. 105)
Immaculate Conception (p. 106)
Assumption (p. 106)

REFLECT & ACT

How does our belief in the Resurrection of Jesus encourage us to live holy lives?

Were you named after a saint? Do you have a patron saint? Does your parish or school? What can you do to learn more about the life of these saints?

107

Conclusion (__ min.)

Growing in Faith

Have the young people close their books. Ask them what they have learned in this lesson about the "last things," the Communion of Saints, Mary, the Immaculate Conception, and Assumption. Reopen the books to page 107. Was everything from the **Remember** and **Faith Words** sections named? If not, point these out and help the group name the remaining concepts.

Invite the young people to read the **Reflect and Act** section and to write their responses in the space provided.

Read the paragraph under **Pray** on page 107. Pray the Hail Mary together.

Distribute the *One Faith, One Lord* program surveys. (See pages XII and XIV.) Allow some time for reflection. Encourage the young people to answer the questions completely. After they have finished, have the young people compare their recent answers with their earlier answers. What has changed during the year/program? Invite the young people to share their observations with the group.

If possible, close the year/program with refreshments to celebrate the time spent learning about the Catholic faith together.

CATECHISM FOCUS

"At the end of time, the Kingdom of God will come in its fullness. Then the just will reign with Christ for ever, glorified in body and soul, and the material universe itself will be transformed." (*CCC*, 1060)

For additional reference and reflection, see *CCC*, 1042–1060.

Answers for page 107:

Left:
We believe that we will rise to new life after death.

Right:
Guide the young people to any resources the parish might have. Diocesan offices have lending libraries of books and videos, DVDs, etc. and there are many Internet sites that might be utilized.

Unit 4 Assessment

A. Choose the correct term to complete each statement.

Beatitudes	**Precepts of the Church**	**Ten Commandments**
Resurrection	**New Commandment**	**Corporal Works of Mercy**
Communion of Saints	**Virtue**	**Evangelization**
Faith	**Moses**	**Heaven**
Hope	**Charity**	**Spiritual Works of Mercy**

1. The ___Corporal Works of Mercy___ are acts Christians are called to do to relieve the physical and material needs of others.
2. The ___Precepts of the Church___ are laws of the Church that help us to see that loving God and others is connected to a life of prayer, worship, and service.
3. ___Evangelization___ means sharing the Good News of Jesus Christ and the love of God with all people, in every circumstance of life.
4. The ___Beatitudes___ are teachings that describe how to live as Jesus' disciples.
5. ___Moses___ was the leader of the Israelites to whom God gave the Ten Commandments.
6. The ___Communion of Saints___ is the union of all the baptized members of the Church on earth, in Heaven, and in Purgatory.
7. The ___Ten Commandments___ are the laws of God's covenant given to Moses on Mount Sinai.
8. Christ's ___Resurrection___ gives us the hope of rising to new life after death.
9. The ___New Commandment___ calls us to love God and others as Jesus has loved us.
10. The ___Spiritual Works of Mercy___ are acts Christians are called to do to relieve the spiritual, mental, and emotional needs of others.
11. A ___virtue___ is a good habit that helps us to act according to God's love for us.
12. ___Heaven___ is the ultimate happiness of living with God forever.
13. ___Charity___ is the gift from God that enables us to love him above all things and our neighbor as ourselves.
14. ___Hope___ is the gift from God by which we desire eternal life, place our trust in Christ's promises, and rely on the help of the Holy Spirit.
15. ___Faith___ is the gift from God by which we believe in God and all that he has revealed, and all that the Church proposes for our belief.

B. Circle the response that does *not* belong.

1. God made a covenant with the Israelites so that they could
   (a.) have plenty to eat.
   b. be free from slavery in Egypt.
   c. be free from the slavery of sin.
   d. live as faithful people.

2. The theological virtues are
   a. hope.
   b. charity.
   (c.) courage.
   d. faith.

3. Catholic social teaching
   a. is founded on the life and work of Jesus.
   b. helps us to respect the dignity of all people.
   c. influences our work and our society.
   (d.) is a new teaching of the Church.

4. Jesus taught that at the end of life we will be judged on
   (a.) our power.
   b. our love.
   c. our service for others.
   d. our willingness to see him in others.

5. Catholics believe that when we die,
   a. life is changed, not ended.
   (b.) we live on only in our children.
   c. we are judged on how we loved God and others.
   d. death will be the beginning of endless happiness.

C. Share your faith by responding thoughtfully to these questions.

1. How do the Ten Commandments help us to be free?
   (Accept all reasonable responses.)

2. Jesus' New Commandment might sound simple, but it demands strength and courage. Explain.
   Jesus loved us to the point of giving his life for us. It is very difficult to love others this way.

3. Recall the story of the Good Samaritan. What important lesson was Jesus teaching in this story?
   He taught that every person, regardless of race, religion, or nationality, is our neighbor.

4. Describe two Works of Mercy that you are able to perform in your life right now.
   (Accept all reasonable responses.)

5. Why do you think Mary is considered the greatest saint?
   (See the "Do You Know?" feature on page 92.)

Semester 2 Assessment

A. Choose the correct term to complete each statement.

Eucharist	**Human dignity**	**liturgy**
Last Supper	**Sacrament of Penance and Reconciliation**	**Mass**
Sin	**Conscience**	**Absolution**
Venial sin	**Confession**	**Immaculate Conception**
Assumption	**Real Presence**	**Church**

1. The ___Assumption___ is the truth that Mary was taken body and soul into Heaven.

2. The ___Church___ is the community of people who believe in Jesus Christ, have been baptized in him, and follow his teachings.

3. The ___Last Supper___ was the Passover meal at which Jesus gave us the Eucharist.

4. ___Conscience___ is our ability to know the difference between good and evil, right and wrong.

5. The ___Sacrament of Penance and Reconciliation___ is the sacrament by which our relationship with God and the Church is restored and our sins are forgiven.

6. ___Sin___ is a thought, word, deed, or omission against God's law that harms us and our relationship with God and others.

7. ___Human dignity___ is the value and worth we share because God created us in his image and likeness.

8. ___Venial sin___ is a less serious sin that weakens our friendship with God but does not turn us completely away from him.

9. The ___Immaculate Conception___ is the truth that God preserved Mary from Original Sin and all sin from the very moment she was conceived.

10. ___Absolution___ is God's forgiveness of our sins through the words and actions of the priest in the Sacrament of Penance and Reconciliation.

11. The ___Eucharist___ is the Sacrament of the Body and Blood of Christ.

12. The ___liturgy___ is the official public prayer of the Church.

13. ___Confession___ is the telling of one's sins to a priest in the Sacrament of Penance and Reconciliation.

14. The ___Mass___ is the celebration of the Eucharist.

15. The true presence of Jesus Christ in the Eucharist under the appearance of bread and wine is known as the ___Real Presence___.

B. Circle the letter beside the correct response.

1. The commandment that teaches us to respect the sacredness of life is
   a. the Eighth Commandment.
   (b.) the Fifth Commandment.
   c. the Fourth Commandment.
   d. the First Commandment.

2. The commandment that teaches us to respect the good name of others and to be honest is
   a. the First Commandment.
   b. the Ninth Commandment.
   c. the Sixth Commandment.
   (d.) the Eighth Commandment.

3. The commandment that teaches us to honor God's name and to show special reverence for the name of Jesus Christ is
   (a.) the Second Commandment.
   b. the Fourth Commandment.
   c. the Tenth Commandment.
   d. the Third Commandment.

4. "You shall confess your sins at least once a year" is one of the
   a. Ten Commandments.
   b. Beatitudes.
   (c.) Precepts of the Church.
   d. Marks of the Church.

5. The Church tells us that Mary
   a. was divine, not human.
   (b.) is the Mother of God and our mother, too.
   c. was kept by God from life's struggles.
   d. was not present at the Crucifixion.

C. Answer as completely and thoughtfully as you can.

1. As Christians we believe that we share in Christ's Resurrection. What does that mean to you?
   That we too will rise from death to new life.

2. As followers of Jesus Christ we are called to serve others in his name. How can someone your age do this? (Accept all reasonable responses.)

3. Mortal sin is the most serious sin against God. What three conditions make a sin mortal?
   1. the sinful action or attitude must involve a grave or serious matter 2. we must have clear knowledge that what we are doing is mortally sinful 3. we must freely choose and fully consent to this serious evil

4. As Catholics we are to respond to the needs of others in our world. Tell about one of these needs that you would like to do something about, and why.
   (Accept all reasonable responses.)

5. You have finished this book, *One Faith, One Lord*. Explain one thing you have learned that will help you to be a better follower of Jesus Christ.
   (Accept all reasonable responses.)

GOAL

to understand the meaning of a vocation

GETTING READY

The material on these pages can be used to supplement a chapter in the book or as a lesson for enrichment.

Adult Focus

For many of your group, the concept of a "vocation" may be a new one. They may be prone, like many people, to seeing one's vocation as synonymous with one's job. While the calling to a certain way of life may bring newer and deeper meanings to one's work, it goes beyond it and into every aspect of a person's life. Our vocation, our "special mission in life," is the particular way in which we love and serve God. Whether in a monastery, a home, a foreign mission, a hospital, a parish, a business, or the community at large, Christ's light is needed everywhere. It is up to each and every one of us, by virtue of our Baptism, to respond. It's our *calling*.

To what have you been called in your life?

What questions are your young people likely to have about vocations? How can you prepare yourself to answer them?

Vocation: Called to Serve

"Each of you has a special mission in life, and you each are called to be a disciple of Christ. Many of you will serve God in the vocation of Christian married life; some of you will serve him as dedicated single persons; some as priests and religious. But all of you must be the light of the world. To those of you who think that Christ may be inviting you to follow him in the priesthood or the consecrated life I make this personal appeal: I ask you to open your hearts generously to him; do not delay your response. The Lord will help you to know his will; he will help you to follow your vocation courageously."

Pope John Paul II
Youth Gathering in St. Louis, Missouri
January 26, 1999

What does the pope mean by "special mission" and "vocation"? Through the Sacrament of Baptism, we all share a mission or common vocation "to be the light of the world." We are called to show others Christ's love by our words and actions, to bring Christ to those who do not know him, and to grow in holiness. But God calls each of us to serve him in a personal and special way, too. This calling is our vocation. A vocation is more than a job we may have or a career we may pursue. A vocation is a calling to a particular way of life through which we can best love and serve God and others.

A vocation is a state of life—a way of living. For most of us discovering our vocation is a gradual process of prayer and questioning in which we are guided by the Holy Spirit and helped by others. This process is called discernment because we are trying to recognize, or discern, God's will for us. When we respond to God and fulfill our particular vocation, we become the person God wants us to be. We use our gifts and talents in ways that make us happy and bring happiness to others. God calls each one of us to serve him in one of the following particular vocations: laity, ordained ministry, or consecrated life.

The laity, or the Christian faithful, are members of the Church who share in the mission to bring the Good News of Christ to the world. All Catholics begin their lives as members of the laity. Many remain members of the laity for their entire lives, following God's call either in marriage or the single life. Marriage provides women and men the opportunity to share God's love with a spouse and to express that love by having children and bringing them up in a loving family. Each family is called to be a domestic Church, "a church in the home." Those called to the single life have the opportunity to share God's message and love through service to the community and the Church. Whether called to the single life or to marriage, women and men can respond to God's call by being active members of their families, parishes, and larger communities.

God calls some baptized men to serve him in the ordained ministry. Through the Sacrament of Holy Orders they are consecrated to the ministerial priesthood as priests and bishops, or to the permanent diaconate. Priests and bishops are ordained to serve the community through teaching, worship, and leadership.

There are two different types of priests: diocesan priests and religious priests. Diocesan

112

CATECHISM FOCUS

"In virtue of their rebirth in Christ there exists among all the Christian faithful a true equality with regard to the dignity and the activity whereby all cooperate in the building up of the Body of Christ in accord with each one's own condition and function." (*CCC*, 872)

For additional reference and reflection, see *CCC*, 871–993.

priests are called to serve in a particular diocese. They help the bishop of that diocese by ministering in parishes. They also may assist in schools, hospitals, and prisons depending upon the local needs. Diocesan priests promise to lead a celibate life, not to marry. They also promise to respect and obey their bishop.

Religious priests are called to a specific religious order or congregation, such as the Franciscans, Dominicans, or Jesuits. These priests follow a religious rule, or plan of life, adopted by their founder.

Religious priests and some women and men who are not ordained are also called to the religious, or consecrated, life. Women religious are known as sisters, or nuns, and male religious who are not ordained as priests are known as brothers. They are involved in a variety of ministries of service to the Church.

Religious priests and religious women and men usually live in community and serve anywhere in the world that they are needed. They take the vows of poverty, chastity, and obedience. By these vows they pledge to own nothing of their own, to live a celibate life, and to be faithful and obedient to their superiors and the Church.

O Lord, help me know your will for me.
Let your light shine in the depths of my heart
that I may know what you want me to do with my life.
Help me believe that you have a special plan for me.
Lord, I know I pass through this life only once;
help me decide how you want me to make a difference.
Like our Blessed Mother, give me the wisdom to hear your voice
and the courage to answer your call.
Above all give me peace of mind and heart.
I offer this prayer in the name of Jesus Christ our Lord.
Amen.

What is a Permanent Deacon?

A deacon is an ordained male minister of the Church who can preach, baptize, witness marriages, and preside at burials. Deacons assist the priest at Mass in ways such as reading the Gospel, preparing the altar, and distributing Holy Communion. Permanent deacons are often married and have an occupation or career to support themselves. A deacon is a sign of the service to which all Christians are called. Deacons do receive the Sacrament of Holy Orders, but they are ordained to assist the bishops and priests and to serve the whole Church. Deacons are not ministers of the Sacraments of Confirmation, Eucharist, Penance, Anointing of the Sick, and Holy Orders.

VOCATION

113

Vocation: Called to Serve

Read the first three paragraphs on page 112. Stress that, because of our Baptism, we all have a special mission to grow in our faith and to share that faith.

Disuss the difference between having a job and living out a vocation. Point out that different *occupations* can be carried out by people with different *vocations*. For example: an artist who is also a priest; a firefighter who is also a married woman, a web site designer who is also a religious sister; a photographer who is also single man. In each case, a vocation is larger and more encompassing than a job. Point out that faith in God is lived out through the promises people make to their communities or spouses. It is their way of life.

Continue reading pages 112 and 113. Talk about the particular vocations recognized by the Church: the laity, ordained ministry, and consecrated life. Ask the group to suggest ways young people can live out their vocations as members of the laity.

Invite volunteers to explain the difference between religious and diocesan priests.

Have the group underline the vows (see page 113) that religious priests and religious men and women follow as they live out their vocations in the consecrated life. Explain that by following the vows of poverty, chastity, and obedience (also known as the *evangelical counsels*), religious men and women are making an effort to focus on the life of service that they have chosen.

Recall the words of Blessed Pope John Paul II on page 112. Offer the prayer for vocations on page 113 together. Encourage the group to pray for those who have chosen their vocation as well as for those who are discerning a vocation at this time.

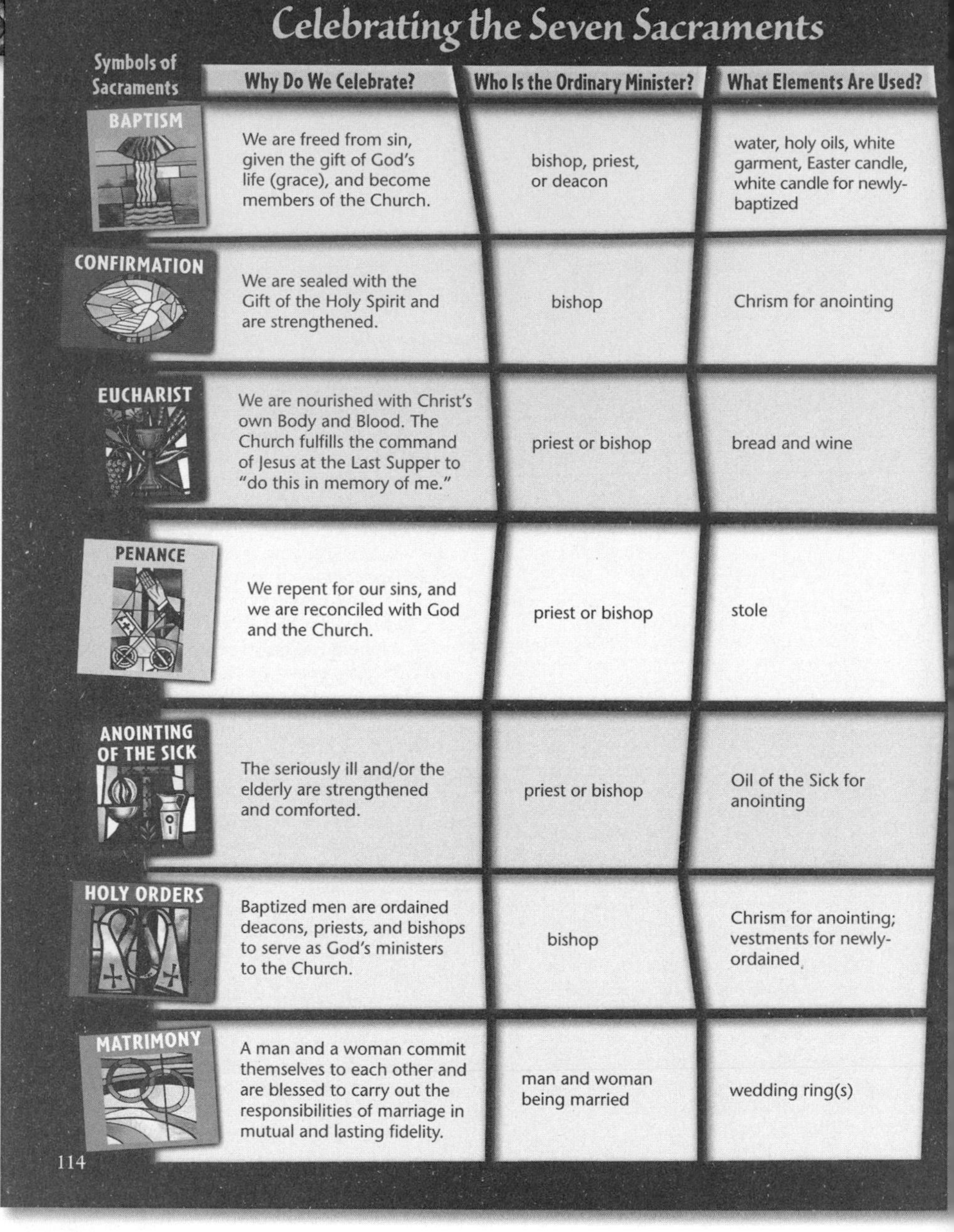

Celebrating the Seven Sacraments

Symbols of Sacraments	Why Do We Celebrate?	Who Is the Ordinary Minister?	What Elements Are Used?
BAPTISM	We are freed from sin, given the gift of God's life (grace), and become members of the Church.	bishop, priest, or deacon	water, holy oils, white garment, Easter candle, white candle for newly-baptized
CONFIRMATION	We are sealed with the Gift of the Holy Spirit and are strengthened.	bishop	Chrism for anointing
EUCHARIST	We are nourished with Christ's own Body and Blood. The Church fulfills the command of Jesus at the Last Supper to "do this in memory of me."	priest or bishop	bread and wine
PENANCE	We repent for our sins, and we are reconciled with God and the Church.	priest or bishop	stole
ANOINTING OF THE SICK	The seriously ill and/or the elderly are strengthened and comforted.	priest or bishop	Oil of the Sick for anointing
HOLY ORDERS	Baptized men are ordained deacons, priests, and bishops to serve as God's ministers to the Church.	bishop	Chrism for anointing; vestments for newly-ordained
MATRIMONY	A man and a woman commit themselves to each other and are blessed to carry out the responsibilities of marriage in mutual and lasting fidelity.	man and woman being married	wedding ring(s)

114

GOALS

to understand the meaning of each of the sacraments; to learn the significance and purpose of sacramental actions

GETTING READY

You may wish to use this chart as an extension of the Chapter 8 lesson, or as a lesson for enrichment.

Adult Focus

The young people in your group are only at a beginning point in their Christian life of faith. For some, learning about the Seven Sacraments is a brand new experience. It is important to help them understand sacramental actions and symbols as ways in which God is present to us and in which we, in turn, respond to God's love.

The chart on pages 114–115 offers a concise look at each of the Seven Sacraments and at the elements, ritual words and actions, and purpose of each one. Take time to review the first column, "Why Do We Celebrate?" Reflect upon the meaning behind the sacraments. How does each one touch a stage or moment in the Christian life of faith? What sacraments have you celebrated? How have you felt God's presence in your life as a result?

CATECHISM FOCUS

"The seven sacraments touch all the stages and all the important moments of Christian life: they give birth and increase, healing and mission to the Christian's life of faith. There is thus a certain resemblance between the stages of natural life and the stages of the spiritual life." (*CCC*, 1210)

For additional reference and reflection, see *CCC*, 1113–1134.

Celebrating the Seven Sacraments

Use the chart on pages 114–115 to teach and review the purpose, ordinary minister, elements, actions, ritual words, and role of the community in each sacrament. Refer to Chapter 8 as needed.

If you have time, do the following.

In Chapter 8, attention was focused on the symbolic elements of the sacraments—water, holy oil, bread and wine, etc. Recall these elements with your young people, using the chart as a reference point. Emphasize the importance of each element in conveying the "actions of the Holy Spirit at work in his Body, the Church" (*CCC*, 1116).

What Do We See?	What Do We Hear?	What Does the Community Do?
Pouring of water over forehead or immersion in baptismal pool; the putting on of the baptismal garment; presentation of candle lit from Easter Candle.	"(Name), I baptize you in the name of the Father, and of the Son, and of the Holy Spirit."	Renew baptismal promises; pray for and welcome new members.
Laying on of hand simultaneously with anointing on forehead; sponsor or godparent places right hand on candidate's shoulder.	"(Name), be sealed with the Gift of the Holy Spirit."	Renew baptismal promises; pray for newly-confirmed and give witness to their faith.
Celebrant or extraordinary minister of Holy Communion offers each communicant the Body and Blood of Christ.	"The Body of Christ." "Amen." "The Blood of Christ." "Amen."	Listen to the Word of God and respond, "Thanks be to God." Sing, pray, share the Sign of Peace. Receive Holy Communion. Go forth to love and serve the Lord.
Sign of the Cross by penitent at beginning of celebration and at absolution; priest extends right hand or both hands over head of penitent in absolution.	"...and I absolve you from your sins in the name of the Father, and of the Son, and of the Holy Spirit."	Experience and proclaim the mercy of God in their own lives; celebrate the Church's ongoing mission of reconciliation.
Anointing of the sick on their foreheads and hands; laying on of hands on heads of those who are ill.	"Through this holy anointing may the Lord in his love and mercy help you with the grace of the Holy Spirit. May the Lord who frees you from sin save you and raise you up."	Celebrate the sacrament with those who are sick; do all they can to help the sick return to health.
Laying on of hands; anointing of the hands of newly-ordained priests.	(For priests): "Almighty Father, grant this servant of yours the dignity of the priesthood. Renew within him the spirit of holiness...."	Pray that the gifts of Heaven will be poured out on the candidate; support him in his ministry.
Joining of right hands by the man and woman; exchange of rings; blessing of bride and groom.	"I, (name), take you, [name], to be my wife [husband]. I promise to be true to you in good times and in bad, in sickness and in health. I will love you and honor you all the days of my life."	Celebrate with the bride and groom; support them in prayer and witness.

THE SEVEN SACRAMENTS

115

Explain that other important aspects of the Seven Sacraments include actions that are filled with symbolic meaning. Draw attention to the fourth column, "What Do We See?" Instruct the young people to read this column and to note each place they find the word *hands*. Some of the terms may be confusing or puzzling to the group. The following paragraphs offer some ways to help them better understand these actions and their meanings.

◎ Discuss what it means to "lay hands" on somebody. Explain that, in the Sacraments of Confirmation and Holy Orders, the bishop and priests, who represent Christ, perform the laying on of hands. This gesture symbolizes the passing on of the Gift of the Holy Spirit to the newly confirmed or ordained person. With the laying on of hands in the celebration of Holy Orders, the charism of authority is given to the new deacon, priest, or bishop to serve the Church in this special way.

◎ Ask the group to name ways in which human touch is healing to another person. Encourage the young people to think of ways this happens within families as well as in healthcare facilities. Refer to the "laying on of hands" that occurs within the Anointing of the Sick. It symbolizes and brings about the healing touch of Christ.

Read together the prayer of blessing for the Anointing of the Sick. Explain that this involves much more than a healing of the body. When someone is gravely ill, such a physical healing may not be possible. The grace of this sacrament is one that brings strength, peace, and courage to those who are seriously ill or facing death. Be especially sensitive to questions or anxieties the young people may have about death, dying, or chronic illness. Continue to emphasize the strengthening and peace-giving grace this sacrament confers.

◎ Talk about experiences the young people have had in attending a Catholic wedding. What did they notice about it? Were they aware of the blessing and bonding symbols of the ritual? Point out the sacramental action of the woman and man joining their right hands. Talk about what this signifies.

Note that the couple confers this sacrament on each other. Jesus acts through them and through their promise to always love and be true to each other. A priest or deacon witnesses their marriage as a representative of the Church. The promises made to each other join the couple in a marriage bond that is perpetual and exclusive. Discuss what such a vow means. What are ways married couples live out such a promise? What challenges might they face in doing so?

GOALS

to learn the cycle of feasts and seasons that make up the liturgical year; to understand the liturgical year as the way in which the Church celebrates the Paschal Mystery of Christ

GETTING READY

Materials needed: large sheets of paper or poster board, markers

Adult Focus

Unlike the calendars we use for home or work, the Church visually depicts the passing of a year in a cyclic form. The Church's liturgical year celebrates the Paschal Mystery—the suffering, Death, Resurrection, and Ascension of Jesus—through a continuous cycle of seasons and feasts. Like the passing of time within the life of any family, the year has its "high" seasons and its ordinary ones. Such a cycle provides the rhythm and backdrop for the Christian life of prayer and worship.

The passing of time provides an opportunity to hear the story of Jesus and to recognize the witness of Mary and the saints in new and ever expanding ways. Christian believers around the world and throughout time use cherished rituals, symbols, and stories over and over again, making each and every year one of grace.

CATECHISM FOCUS

"The liturgy is the work of the whole Christ, head and body. Our high priest celebrates it unceasingly in the heavenly liturgy, with the holy Mother of God, the apostles, all the saints, and the multitude of those who have already entered the kingdom." (*CCC*, 1187)

For additional reference and reflection, see *CCC*, 1163–1173.

The Church's Liturgical Year

The liturgical year is the name we give to the Church's year. It is our way of celebrating the mystery of Christ as we move from day to day and season to season. Throughout the liturgical year we proclaim and celebrate the different aspects of the mystery of Christ.

The major parts of the Church's year are the seasons: Advent, Christmas, Lent, the Easter Triduum, Easter, and Ordinary Time. Centered around the great feast of the Easter Triduum, the seasons enable us to walk with Jesus once again through his birth, his life on earth, his suffering, Death, Resurrection, and Ascension.

In the Mass and in the Liturgy of the Hours, we rejoice daily in God's presence and power in the world. Priests pray the Liturgy of the Hours as part of their ministry. Some parishes celebrate part of the Liturgy of the Hours called Evening Prayer so that all can join in marking the hour as blessed by God. In monasteries, religious men and women traditionally pray the Liturgy of the Hours at seven different times during the day and night.

Sundays are the heart of our weekly liturgical cycle. Each Sunday we celebrate that Jesus rose from the dead on the first day of the week. Also known as the Lord's Day, Sunday is a time to rest from work, to enjoy God's gift of Creation and family, and to serve those in need.

Feast days mark the liturgical year with celebrations of special events in the lives of Jesus, Mary, and the saints. These celebrations help us to remember that we belong to the Communion of Saints who intercede for us in Heaven.

Advent

Advent is the beginning of our liturgical year. It is the time of preparation for both the celebration of the Lord's first coming at his birth and his second coming at the end of time. The Advent season begins four Sundays before December 25 and ends at the Christmas Eve Vigil Mass.

The traditional color of the vestments and decorations for the days of Advent is purple. It signifies that this is a time of expectation.

Christmas

This season celebrates Jesus' birth and the joyous events associated with it. It is the period from Jesus' birth to the beginning of his public ministry. The Christmas season begins at the Christmas Eve Vigil Mass and ends on the Feast of the Baptism of the Lord.

The primary color of the vestments for this season is white. Gold is also used. These colors signify our joy at the presence of Christ with us.

Lent

The season of Lent begins on Ash Wednesday. During Lent we remember that Jesus suffered, died, and rose to new life to save us from sin and to give us new life in the Kingdom of God. During Lent we work to grow closer to Jesus and to one another through prayer, fasting, and almsgiving. We pray for and support all who are preparing for the Sacraments of Christian Initiation. We prepare for the Easter Triduum. The color for Lent is purple, for penance.

The Easter Triduum

The Easter Triduum is the Church's greatest and most important celebration. The word *triduum* means "three days." During the three days of the Easter Triduum—from Holy Thursday evening, through Good Friday and Holy Saturday, until Easter Sunday evening—we remember and celebrate in the liturgy, with many special traditions and rituals, the suffering, Death, and Resurrection of Jesus Christ. The color for Good Friday is red, for Jesus' suffering. The color for the other days of the Triduum is white.

Easter

The season of Easter begins on Easter Sunday evening and continues until Pentecost Sunday, 50 days later. During this season we rejoice in Jesus' Resurrection and in the new life we have in Jesus Christ. We also celebrate Christ's Ascension into Heaven. The color for the Easter season is white, while Pentecost's color is red and signifies the descent of the Holy Spirit upon the Apostles.

Ordinary Time

During this season we remember and celebrate the teaching, stories, and events of Jesus' life. The emphasis on these Sundays is on the celebration of and instruction in our Christian faith and morals.

The periods of this season occur between the Christmas and Lenten seasons and after the Easter season until Advent. The liturgical color of this season is green, a sign of life and hope.

The Church's Liturgical Year

Have each young person create a calendar depicting the significant events, holidays, and celebrations that will be part of their family's life during the next twelve months. Compare the calendars with the Church's liturgical year. Note any instances when the two calendars intersect, such as a family's celebration of Christmas or Easter. Emphasize that the entire liturgical year is focused on the Paschal Mystery. Review the meaning of this term, and point out how the feasts and seasons of the year are all tied to our faith in Jesus.

Advent and Christmas

Ask the group to share what they know about the season of Advent, including the symbols and rituals that are used both in homes and in parishes.

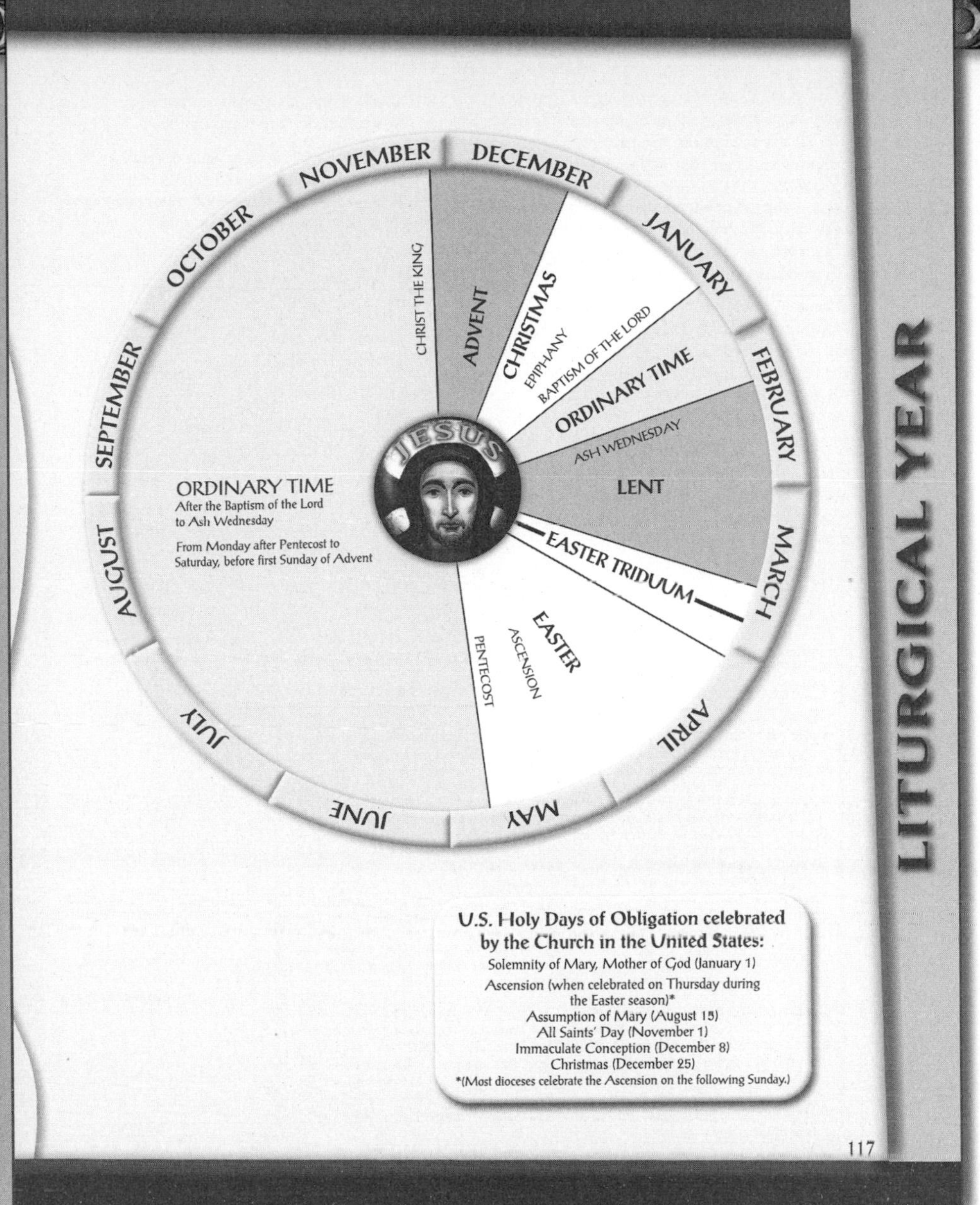

◎ Holy Thursday: Read the account of the washing of the feet (John 13:3–11). Explain that a foot-washing ritual is part of the Holy Thursday celebration, symbolizing the way we should be of service to one another.

◎ Good Friday: Explain that the Passion is the story of the agony in the garden, arrest, trial, Crucifixion, Death, and burial of Jesus. It is read with great feeling on Good Friday. A wooden cross is present in the church and everyone is invited forward during the service to *venerate,* or honor it by kissing or touching it. This is a sign of our faith in Jesus.

◎ Holy Saturday: At dusk a fire is built outside of the church to begin the Easter Vigil, the most solemn ceremony of the Church year. It is a great celebration as we listen to stories from the Old Testament about Salvation and from the New Testament about the joyous news of Jesus' Resurrection. Adults and young people are received into the Church through the Sacraments of Christian Initiation during the Easter Vigil.

◎ Easter Sunday: We celebrate Jesus' Death, burial, and Resurrection at morning Mass with great joy. Songs, customs, and food shared within families remind us of the new life of Christ. Point out that Easter, too, is a season, not just a singular holiday. Refer to the chart and note that it extends from Easter Sunday to the Feast of Pentecost, a period of fifty days.

Emphasize that Christmas is both a *season* and a single holiday. Advent is a time of preparation for this season and has no meaning without the recognition that Christmas celebrates the Incarnation, the truth that the Son of God, the second Person of the Blessed Trinity, became man and lived among us in order to accomplish our Salvation.

Lent and the Easter Season

Ask the group to share what they know about the observance of Lent, including the practices of prayer and penitential acts. Stress that the forty-day season of Lent is meant to help us prepare for Easter, the highest point of the liturgical year. Explain the special nature of the rituals that occur during the Easter Triduum. The following paragraphs refer to aspects of each day's celebration.

Ordinary Time

Read the final paragraph about Ordinary Time and refer to the chart to find the two periods in which this occurs. The young people may want to research the many feasts and saints celebrated throughout the liturgical year.

GOAL

to help young people become familiar with the structure and use of the Bible for catechesis, guidance, and prayer

GETTING READY

You may wish to use this lesson as an extension of page 8 in Chapter 1, or as a lesson for enrichment.

Adult Focus

"Ignorance of Scripture is ignorance of Christ." (Saint Jerome) One of the most exciting tasks of a catechist is to help familiarize young people with Scripture, an ancient and treasured part of our faith.

Using the Bible

Page 118 will help to introduce the young people to the structure of the Bible, as well as how to find a particular passage within it. Refer to it throughout the year as a review about using the Bible within a group setting or for individual reflection and study. If possible, provide every young person with a copy of the Bible for his or her personal use throughout the year.

USING THE BIBLE

Using the Bible

The Bible is a collection of seventy-three books written under the inspiration of the Holy Spirit. The Bible is divided into two parts, The Old Testament and the New Testament. In the forty-six books of the Old Testament, we learn about the story of God's relationship with the people of Israel. In the twenty-seven books of the New Testament, we learn about the story of Jesus Christ, the Son of God, and of his followers.

Because God inspired the human authors of the individual books of the Bible, he is the author of the Bible. That is why in the Liturgy of the Word at Mass the reader concludes a reading by saying, "The Word of the Lord" to which we respond, "Thanks be to God." We are grateful that we have received the Word of God and it is at work in us.

When we read the Bible with attention and respect, we are praying. The Word of God, written down by human authors under the inspiration of the Holy Spirit, enters our hearts and minds. The Holy Spirit enables us to be attentive to what God has revealed through these authors.

The Word of God moves us to become more loving, truthful, forgiving, and compassionate. It strengthens our faith, increases our understanding, and guides us in making good decisions.

One way to use the Bible in prayer is to follow these simple steps:

- Pray for the help of the Holy Spirit.
- Choose one story or teaching of Jesus and read it slowly to yourself.
- Read it again aloud.
- Focus on one or two verses that are especially meaningful to you.
- Ask the Holy Spirit to guide you in living by your chosen verses.
- Thank God for the Word that is living and active in you.

How to Find Your Way in the Bible

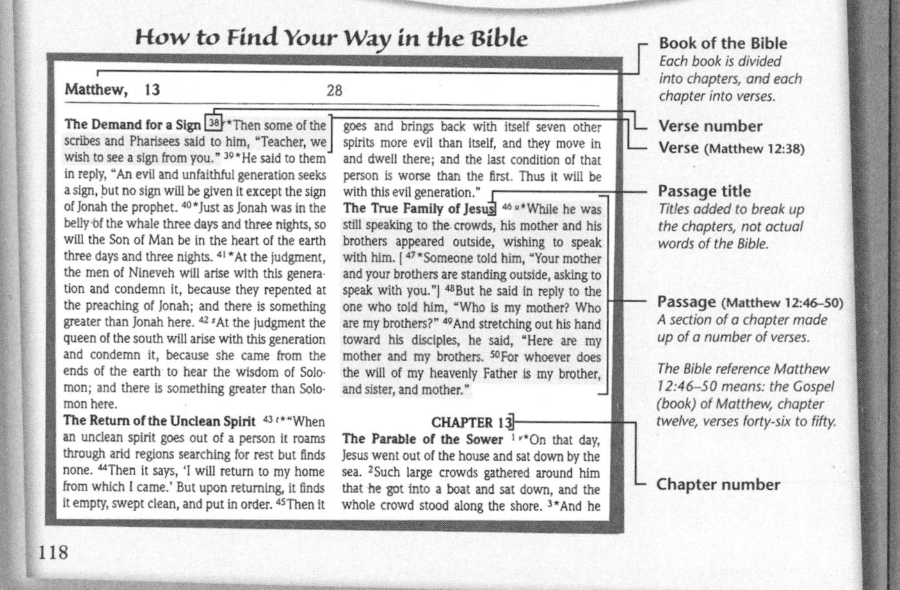

118

Whenever Scripture is cited in the text, have individuals or the group look them up. Use the instructions on page 118 as a starting point.

Introduce young people to the usefulness of a concordance and/or a commentary. Have one available during each lesson and use it whenever a question arises about a particular biblical story, theme, or reference. Computer software programs and Web sites are great tools for locating specific Bible passages and meanings.

Use the Bible for prayer. The psalms are a primary source for prayer. Other possibilities are blessings that are used at the beginning or end of the Epistles and the prayers of Jesus, particularly those included in the Gospel of John.

Have young people illustrate parables and stories, using various forms of art, such as drawing, painting, clay, murals, collages, etc.

Act out stories and parables. Give each young person a role to play, even if it's simply being a bystander, a tree, or a "voice in the crowd."

Have young people retell biblical accounts in their own words. This can be done orally or in some type of written assignment.

Use the Bible to help young people develop stronger consciences and moral convictions. The Beatitudes, the Commandments, and Sermon the Mount are all helpful for this purpose.

SIGN OF THE CROSS

In the name of the Father,
and of the Son,
and of the Holy Spirit.
Amen.

GLORY TO THE FATHER

Glory to the Father,
and to the Son,
and to the Holy Spirit:
as it was in the beginning,
is now, and will be for ever.
Amen.

OUR FATHER

Our Father, who art in heaven,
hallowed be thy name;
thy kingdom come;
thy will be done on earth
as it is in heaven.
Give us this day our daily bread;
and forgive us our trespasses
as we forgive those
who trespass against us;
and lead us not into temptation,
but deliver us from evil.
Amen.

APOSTLES' CREED

I believe in God,
the Father almighty,
Creator of heaven and earth,
and in Jesus Christ, his only Son, our Lord,
who was conceived by the Holy Spirit,
born of the Virgin Mary,
suffered under Pontius Pilate,
was crucified, died and was buried;
he descended into hell;
on the third day he rose again from the dead;
he ascended into heaven,
and is seated at the right hand of God the
Father almighty;
from there he will come to judge
the living and the dead.

I believe in the Holy Spirit,
the holy catholic Church,
the communion of saints,
the forgiveness of sins,
the resurrection of the body,
and life everlasting.
Amen.

HAIL MARY

Hail Mary, full of grace,
the Lord is with you!
Blessed are you among women,
and blessed is the fruit
of your womb, Jesus.
Holy Mary, Mother of God,
pray for us sinners,
now and at the hour of our death.
Amen.

Traditional Prayers

Note to the Catechist

Some of the most familiar traditional prayers are contained on these pages. Notes accompany them, offering ideas for explaining a prayer style or for adding an expanded activity. Use these pages throughout the year in conjunction with any of the chapter lessons.

Trinitarian Prayers

Point out that Christian prayer and worship begins with the Sign of the Cross as a way to dedicate ourselves to God. Note how this prayer and the Glory to the Father are addressed to the Father, Son, and Holy Spirit. Praying to the Blessed Trinity is another identifying aspect of Christian prayer.

Our Father

The Our Father is one of our most important prayers. It comes to us from Jesus who, recorded in the Gospels of Matthew and Luke, taught to his disciples. Have the young people look up these two passages (Matthew 6:9–13 and Luke 11:2–4). Explain that the version from Matthew is the one used at Mass and for communal prayer. Note that a large section in the *Catechism of the Catholic Church* (Part IV) is devoted to the Our Father.

Hail Mary

The Hail Mary, like most Marian prayers, contains two parts. The first praises God for the gifts given to Mary. It is derived in part from the greeting she received from the angel Gabriel (Luke 1:26–38). The second part asks her to pray for us. This is a form of *intercessory* prayer. Explain to the young people that we do not pray *to* Mary as we do to God. Rather, we ask her to pray on our behalf, to "intercede" for us. See another Marian prayer, the Hail, Holy Queen on page 121.

What is a Creed?

As you help your young people learn both the Apostles' Creed and the Nicene Creed (page 120), take time to discuss these particular prayer forms. A *creed* is a statement of Christian beliefs. The Apostles' Creed is a summary of the faith of the Apostles. The Nicene Creed expands upon the Apostles' Creed and was drawn up at the two first Ecumenical Councils in the fourth century. It is the creed professed each Sunday at Mass.

Prayer to the Holy Spirit

We learn from John's Gospel that Jesus told his disciples that he would send the Holy Spirit to them after he was gone. "When he comes, the Spirit of truth, he will guide you to all truth." (John 16:13) Encourage your young people to pray often to the Holy Spirit, particularly during times of difficulty, confusion, or challenge.

Notice the use of the words *heart*, *fire*, and *love* in this prayer. When we pray, we can bring all of our deepest and most heartfelt needs to God. Use this prayer as a journal exercise. Instruct the young people to pick out a single line or phrase that speaks to their hearts. Have them write a prayer of their own, using that phrase as inspiration.

Morning and Evening Prayers

"Prayer is the life of the new heart. It ought to animate us at every moment." (*CCC*, 2697) Too many of us get caught up in schedules that are rushed and hectic. It makes prayer "at every moment" seem impossible. That is why the Church has long advocated the use of time set aside for prayer at particular hours of the day. It is part of the "rhythm" that accompanies a strong spiritual life.

Ask your young people to name the times they most often pray. What makes it hard to maintain a prayer routine? Have them develop a schedule for prayer. What "hours" fill their days? When and how can they pause for prayer throughout the day? Encourage them to use these two prayers, morning and evening, as a starting point.

Nicene Creed

I believe in one God,
the Father almighty,
maker of heaven and earth,
of all things visible and invisible.

I believe in one Lord Jesus Christ,
the Only Begotten Son of God,
born of the Father before all ages.
God from God, Light from Light,
true God from true God,
begotten, not made, consubstantial with the Father;
through him all things were made.
For us men and for our salvation
he came down from heaven,
and by the Holy Spirit was incarnate of the Virgin Mary,
and became man.

For our sake he was crucified under Pontius Pilate,
he suffered death and was buried,
and rose again on the third day
in accordance with the Scriptures.
He ascended into heaven
and is seated at the right hand of the Father.
He will come again in glory
to judge the living and the dead
and his kingdom will have no end.

I believe in the Holy Spirit, the Lord, the giver of life,
who proceeds from the Father and the Son,
who with the Father and the Son is adored and glorified,
who has spoken through the prophets.

I believe in one, holy, catholic and apostolic Church.
I confess one Baptism for the forgiveness of sins
and I look forward to the resurrection of the dead
and the life of the world to come.
Amen.

120

Prayer to the Holy Spirit

Come, Holy Spirit,
fill the hearts of your faithful.
And kindle in them the fire of your love.
Send forth your Spirit and they shall be created.
And you will renew the face of the earth.
Amen.

A Morning Prayer

God our Father,
work is your gift to us,
a call to reach new heights
by using our talents for the good of all.
Guide us as we work and teach us to live
in the spirit that has made us your sons and daughters,
in the love that has made us brothers and sisters.
Grant this through Christ our Lord.
Amen.

An Evening Prayer

Lord God,
send peaceful sleep
to refresh our tired bodies.
May your help always renew us
and keep us strong in your service.
We ask this through Christ our Lord.
Amen.

Grace Before Meals

Bless us, O Lord,
and these your gifts
which we are about to receive
from your goodness.
Through Christ our Lord.
Amen.

Grace After Meals

We give you thanks for all your gifts,
almighty God,
living and reigning now and for ever.
Amen.

Act of Contrition

My God,
I am sorry for my sins
with all my heart.
In choosing to do wrong
and failing to do good,
I have sinned against you
whom I should love above all things.
I firmly intend, with your help,
to do penance,
to sin no more,
and to avoid whatever leads me to sin.
Our Savior Jesus Christ
suffered and died for us.
In his name, my God, have mercy.
Amen.

Hail, Holy Queen

Hail, Holy Queen, mother of mercy,
hail, our life, our sweetness,
and our hope.
To you we cry, the children of Eve;
to you we send up our sighs,
mourning and weeping in this land of exile.
Turn, then, most gracious advocate,
your eyes of mercy toward us;
lead us home at last
and show us the blessed fruit
of your womb, Jesus:
O clement, O loving, O sweet Virgin Mary!
Amen.

The Jesus Prayer

Lord Jesus Christ, Son of God, have mercy
on me, a sinner.
Amen.

Prayer of Saint Francis

Lord, make me an instrument of
your peace:
where there is hatred, let me sow love;
where there is injury, pardon;
where there is doubt, faith;
where there is despair, hope;
where there is darkness, light;
where there is sadness, joy.

O Divine Master, grant that I may not
so much seek
to be consoled as to console,
to be understood as to understand,
to be loved as to love.

For it is in giving that we receive,
it is in pardoning that we are pardoned,
it is in dying that we are born to
eternal life.
Amen.

TRADITIONAL PRAYERS

121

Table Prayer

Grace before meals may very well be the most commonly used prayer of households around the world. The ones contained on this page utilize two other common forms of prayer, *blessing* and *thanksgiving*. Ask your young people about the ways prayer is used around the table in their homes.

Act of Contrition

The Act of Contrition is a prayer offered as part of the Sacrament of Penance. The words may vary, but a prayer of contrition contains two elements:

1. an expression of sorrow and regret for the sin committed
2. a resolution not to sin again.

Explain this to the young people and have them find and underline the words and phrases that express these sentiments. Encourage them to learn this prayer by heart.

The Jesus Prayer

"Christian Tradition has retained three major expressions of prayer: vocal, meditative, and contemplative." (*CCC*, 2699) The use of the simple Jesus Prayer is like a doorway into this tradition. Said once it gives voice to our longing for the love and mercy of Christ. This gives rise to meditation on the presence of Jesus in our lives. Offered repeatedly, it becomes a kind of mantra—a simple way to move into a quiet resting-place with God.

Hail, Holy Queen

The Hail, Holy Queen (*Salve Regina*) is attributed to Blessed Herman the Cripple, an 11th century Benedictine monk, mathematician, and poet. The Hail, Holy Queen is prayed at the end of the rosary.

Prayer of Saint Francis

This lovely prayer is probably one your young people already know. Invite them to make it even more relevant to their lives by having them expand upon it. How would they fill in the lines—"Where there is ___________, let me ________________"?

Catholic Practices

Note to the Catechist

Some of the most familiar Catholic practices are contained on these pages. Notes accompany them, offering ideas for explanation or activities. Use these pages throughout the year in conjunction with any of the chapter lessons.

Sacramentals

Catholicism is a very active and visual religion. Symbols, rituals, and gestures give expression to our most deeply held beliefs. Accessibility to these is not limited to our churches, but extends into everyday life.

In collaboration with their parents, invite the young people to bring from home a rosary or other religious object. Allow them to tell the "story" behind the object: to whom it belongs, where it came from, and what it means to various family members.

The Rosary

The rosary is a devotional prayer in which we remember the events in the lives of Jesus and Mary.

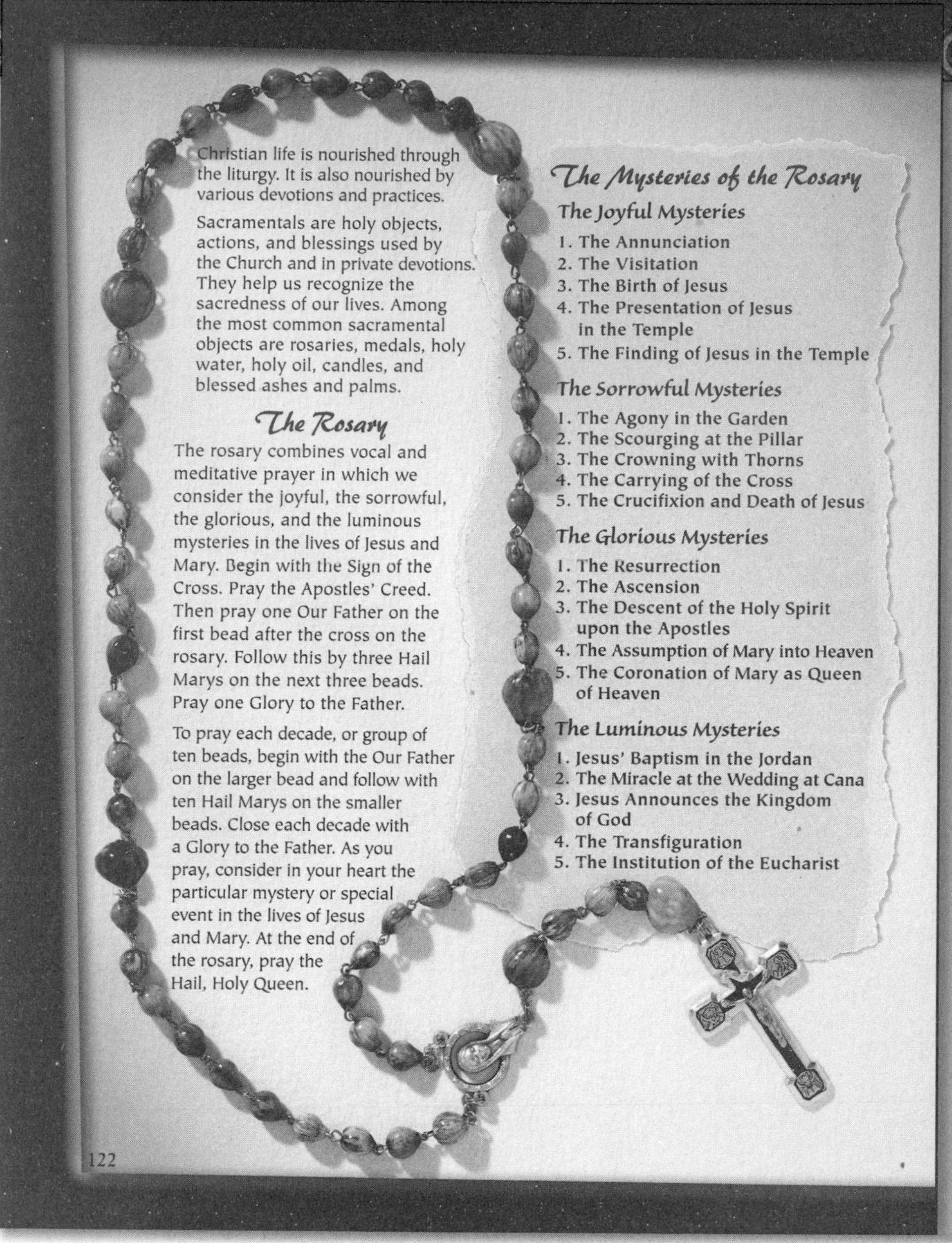

Christian life is nourished through the liturgy. It is also nourished by various devotions and practices.

Sacramentals are holy objects, actions, and blessings used by the Church and in private devotions. They help us recognize the sacredness of our lives. Among the most common sacramental objects are rosaries, medals, holy water, holy oil, candles, and blessed ashes and palms.

The Rosary

The rosary combines vocal and meditative prayer in which we consider the joyful, the sorrowful, the glorious, and the luminous mysteries in the lives of Jesus and Mary. Begin with the Sign of the Cross. Pray the Apostles' Creed. Then pray one Our Father on the first bead after the cross on the rosary. Follow this by three Hail Marys on the next three beads. Pray one Glory to the Father.

To pray each decade, or group of ten beads, begin with the Our Father on the larger bead and follow with ten Hail Marys on the smaller beads. Close each decade with a Glory to the Father. As you pray, consider in your heart the particular mystery or special event in the lives of Jesus and Mary. At the end of the rosary, pray the Hail, Holy Queen.

The Mysteries of the Rosary

The Joyful Mysteries

1. The Annunciation
2. The Visitation
3. The Birth of Jesus
4. The Presentation of Jesus in the Temple
5. The Finding of Jesus in the Temple

The Sorrowful Mysteries

1. The Agony in the Garden
2. The Scourging at the Pillar
3. The Crowning with Thorns
4. The Carrying of the Cross
5. The Crucifixion and Death of Jesus

The Glorious Mysteries

1. The Resurrection
2. The Ascension
3. The Descent of the Holy Spirit upon the Apostles
4. The Assumption of Mary into Heaven
5. The Coronation of Mary as Queen of Heaven

The Luminous Mysteries

1. Jesus' Baptism in the Jordan
2. The Miracle at the Wedding at Cana
3. Jesus Announces the Kingdom of God
4. The Transfiguration
5. The Institution of the Eucharist

122

If possible, provide each young person with a rosary. (You may want to contact an organization in the parish that will sponsor or donate a rosary for each young person in your group.) Encourage the young people to use the rosary as you go over the prayer instructions on page 122.

The mysteries of the rosary (The Joyful Mysteries, the Sorrowful Mysteries, the Glorious Mysteries, and the Luminous Mysteries) are special events in the lives of Jesus and Mary. By custom the Joyful Mysteries are prayed on Monday and Saturday, the Sorrowful Mysteries are prayed on Tuesday and Friday, the Glorious Mysteries are prayed on Wednesday and Sunday, and the Luminous Mysteries are prayed on Thursday.

The Stations of the Cross

From the earliest of days of the Church, Christians remembered Jesus' life and Death by visiting and praying at the places where Jesus lived, suffered, died, and rose from the dead.

As the Church spread to other countries, not everyone could travel to the Holy Land. So local churches began inviting people to "follow in the footsteps of Jesus" without leaving home. "Stations," or places to stop and pray, were made so that stay-at-home pilgrims could "walk the way of the cross" in their own parish churches. We do the same today, especially during Lent.

There are fourteen "stations," or stops. At each one, we pause and think about what is happening at the station. Then we pray:

We adore you, O Christ,
and we bless you,
Because by your holy cross,
you have redeemed the world.

Jesus is condemned to die.

Jesus takes up his cross.

Jesus falls the first time.

Jesus meets his mother.

Simon helps Jesus carry his cross.

Veronica wipes the face of Jesus.

Jesus falls the second time.

Jesus meets the women of Jerusalem.

Jesus falls the third time.

Jesus is stripped of his garments.

Jesus is nailed to the cross.

Jesus dies on the cross.

Jesus is taken down from the cross.

Jesus is laid in the tomb.

123

CATHOLIC PRACTICES

Stations of the Cross

"Apart from the cross there is no other ladder by which we may get to heaven." (Saint Rose of Lima)

From the earliest days of the Church, Christians remembered Jesus' life and Death by visiting and praying at the places in the Holy Land where Jesus lived, suffered, died, and rose from the dead.

As the Church spread to other countries, not everyone could travel to the Holy Land. So local churches began inviting people to "follow in the footsteps of Jesus" without leaving home. "Stations," or places to stop and pray, were made so that stay-at-home pilgrims could "walk the way of the cross" in their own parish churches. We do the same today, especially during Lent. In following Christ along the path to Calvary, we are offered the opportunity to reflect more deeply on what it means to take up our own crosses as his disciples.

Most parishes have multiple copies of the prayers for the Stations of the Cross. If possible, borrow one for each person in your group. Go through the reflections together, noting the response offered after each one. If desired, have the young people write their own prayer for each station, noting any special ways in which they want Jesus to help them on their way.

Prayer Before Reading Scripture

Read the prayer together and discuss what the images of "lamp for my feet" and "light for my path" convey. Why is this a good prayer to use before reading the Bible? Ask the group to name other ways they might offer this prayer. What other times do they need a "lamp for their feet" and a "light for their path"?

Ashes and Palms

Lent is a time of spiritual preparation for those who will be receiving the Sacraments of Initiation at the Easter Vigil. The season of Lent has strong ties to Baptism. This is made evident in two important Lenten rituals.

Invite the group to look carefully at the girl in the picture on page 124. She is taking part in an Ash Wednesday service. Ashes are being placed on her forehead in the form of a cross, marking her again with the sign of Baptism.

Toward the end of Lent we celebrate Passion (Palm) Sunday. Palm branches are blessed and sprinkled with holy water, once again reminding us of our baptismal call to follow Jesus.

Talk to your group about their own Baptism and what they are being invited to do during the seasons of Lent and Easter to grow stronger in their faith.

Most Blessed Sacrament

Where is the tabernacle in your parish church? If possible, take the group to see it and discuss the environmental elements that make it a sacred space. These might include its placement in a quiet part of the church or in a separate chapel; the presence of a candle or lamp that is perpetually lit; or a veiled covering. These alert us to the Real Presence of Jesus in the Most Blessed Sacrament. Encourage the young people to visit the church on their own for quiet prayer and reflection.

CATHOLIC PRACTICES

Prayer before reading Scripture

"Your word is a lamp for my feet,
a light for my path." (Psalm 119:105)

Blessing and Giving of Ashes

On Ash Wednesday, the first day of Lent, we are marked with ashes on our foreheads in the Sign of the Cross. Ashes are a sign of sorrow for sin and a reminder of death.

"Remember that you are dust,
and unto dust you shall return."
(See Genesis 3:19)

Blessing and Giving of Palms

On Passion, or Palm, Sunday at the beginning of Holy Week, the Church distributes blessed palm branches to everyone at Mass. We hold the palms during the Gospel reading in honor of Jesus who was greeted by a crowd bearing palm branches when he entered Jerusalem in triumph on the Sabbath before his suffering and Death.

"Hosanna to the Son of David;
blessed is he who comes
in the name of the Lord;
hosanna in the highest." (Matthew 21:9)

Visit to the Most Blessed Sacrament

Catholics believe that Jesus is truly present in our churches in the Most Blessed Sacrament. The Eucharist is kept in a tabernacle as Holy Communion for the sick and for adoration. The Church encourages us to visit the Most Blessed Sacrament out of gratitude and as an expression of our love and adoration for Jesus Christ. We genuflect or bow to the tabernacle, enter a nearby pew or row, and take a few minutes to share our love, our hopes, our needs, and our thanks with Jesus.

Making a Pilgrimage

Pilgrimages provide special occasions for growth and renewal in prayer. Christians join together to journey to shrines or other holy places for prayer, reconciliation, and the celebration of Eucharist. Often all or part of the journey is made on foot.

"Happy are those who find refuge in you,
whose hearts are set on pilgrim roads."
(Psalm 84:6)

"Pray without ceasing."
(1 Thessalonians 5:17)

124

Pilgrimages

Making a pilgrimage is an act of piety and devotion. For some it is the fulfillment of a promise to visit a particular holy site as part of one's growth in committed faith. These sites include Saint Peter's Basilica in Rome, the Holy Land, shrines, and places where miracles or apparitions have taken place.

Pilgrimages can also occur closer to home. Every diocese has a cathedral where the local bishop presides. Have the group do some research into your diocese.

If possible, make arrangements for them to make a pilgrimage to your diocesan cathedral.

Glossary

Advocate a title of the Holy Spirit, the third Person of the Blessed Trinity

Annunciation the announcement to Mary that she would be the mother of the Son of God

Apostles the twelve men chosen by Jesus to share in his mission in a special way

apostolic succession the name given to describe the Apostles' authority and call to service that has been handed down to their successors, the pope and bishops

Assumption the truth that at the end of her earthly life, God brought Mary body and soul to Heaven to live forever with the risen Jesus

Baptism the first and foundational sacrament by which we become sharers in God's divine life, are freed from Original Sin and all personal sins, become children of God, and are welcomed into the Church

Beatitudes teachings that describe how to live as Jesus' disciples

Bible the written account of God's Revelation and his relationship with his people

Blessed Trinity the three Divine Persons in one God: God the Father, God the Son, and God the Holy Spirit

Catholic social teaching the teaching of the Church that calls all members to work for justice and peace as Jesus did

charity the gift from God that enables us to love him above all things and to love our neighbor as ourselves

chastity the virtue that is a gift from God which calls us to use our human sexuality in a responsible and faithful way

Church the community of people who believe in Jesus Christ, have been baptized in him, and follow his teachings

Communion of Saints the union of all the baptized members of the Church on earth, in Heaven, and in Purgatory

Confirmation the sacrament in which we receive the Gift of the Holy Spirit in a special way

conscience our ability to know the difference between good and evil, right and wrong

diocese a local area of the Church led by a bishop

disciple one who says yes to Jesus' call to follow him

Divine Inspiration the special guidance that the Holy Spirit gave to the human authors of the Bible

Divine Revelation God's making himself known to us

Ecumenical Councils meetings of the pope and bishops to discuss and make decisions on issues of faith, morals, and life of the Church

Eucharist the Sacrament of the Body and Blood of Christ, who is truly present under the appearance of bread and wine

eucharistic fast abstaining from food or drink (other than water and medicine) for one hour before receiving Holy Communion

Eucharistic Prayer the center of the celebration of the Mass and the heart of the Catholic faith; the great prayer of thanksgiving and Consecration

evangelization the sharing of the Good News of Jesus Christ and the love of God with all people, in every circumstance of life

faith the gift from God by which we believe in God and all that he has revealed, and all that the Church proposes for our belief

Gifts of the Holy Spirit seven special gifts that help us to live as faithful followers and true witnesses of Jesus Christ: wisdom, understanding, counsel, fortitude, knowledge, piety, and fear of the Lord

Gospels the accounts found in the New Testament of God's Revelation through Jesus Christ

grace a participation, or sharing, in God's life and friendship

Heaven the ultimate happiness of living with God forever

Hell the state of everlasting separation from God because of lack of contrition for and absolution from mortal sin

hope the gift from God by which we desire eternal life, place our trust in Christ's promises, and rely on the help of the Holy Spirit

human dignity the value and worth we share because God created us in his image and likeness

Immaculate Conception the truth that God preserved Mary from Original Sin and all sin from the very moment she was conceived

Incarnation the truth that the Son of God, the second Person of the Blessed Trinity, became man and lived among us in order to accomplish our Salvation

Glossary

Kingdom of God the power of God's love active in our lives and in our world. It is present now and will come in its fullness at the end of time.

Last Judgment Jesus Christ's coming at the end of time to judge all people

Lectionary the book containing all the readings that we use during the Liturgy of the Word at Mass; it is not the whole Bible but a collection of parts of the Bible arranged for reading at Mass

liturgy the official public prayer of the Church

Marks of the Church the four characteristics of the Church: one, holy, catholic, and apostolic

Mass the Church's great prayer of praise and thanks to God the Father; the celebration of the Eucharist

Messiah the person God planned to send to save people from their sins. Jesus Christ is the Messiah because as Savior he fulfilled God's promise.

modesty the virtue by which we dress, act, speak, and think in ways that show respect for ourselves and others

mortal sin very serious sin that turns us completely away from God because it is a choice we freely make to do something that we know is seriously wrong

New Commandment Jesus' summary of all of his teachings on love: "Love one another. As I have loved you, so you also should love one another. This is how all will know that you are my disciples, if you have love for one another" (John 13: 34–35).

New Testament the second part of the Bible consisting of twenty-seven books about Jesus Christ, the Son of God, his message and mission, and his first followers

Old Testament the first part of the Bible consisting of forty-six books. In them we read about the faith relationship between God and the Israelites, later called the Jews.

Original Sin the first sin committed by the first human beings

parish the community of believers who worship and work together

Paschal Mystery the suffering, Death, Resurrection, and Ascension of Jesus Christ

Passover the feast on which Jewish people remember the miraculous way that God saved them from death and slavery in ancient Egypt

pastor the priest who leads the parish in worship, prayer, and teaching

Pentecost the day on which the Holy Spirit came to Jesus' first disciples as Jesus promised

prayer the raising of our minds and hearts to God

Precepts of the Church laws of the Church that help us to see that loving God and others is connected to a life of prayer, worship, and service

Purgatory a process of purification after death for a person who has sinned; those experiencing Purgatory are certain of Heaven

Real Presence the true presence of Jesus Christ in the Eucharist under the appearance of bread and wine

Resurrection the mystery of Jesus' rising from Death to new life

Sacrament of Penance and Reconciliation sacrament by which our relationship with God and the Church is restored and our sins are forgiven

sacraments effective signs given to us by Jesus Christ through which we share in God's life

sin a thought, word, deed, or omission against God's law that harms us and our relationship with God and others

soul the invisible spiritual reality that makes each of us human and that will never die

stewards of Creation those who take care of everything that God has given them

Ten Commandments laws of God's covenant given to Moses on Mount Sinai

theological virtues the virtues of faith, hope, and charity, which have God as their source, motive, and object

Tradition the living transmission of the Word of God as entrusted to the Apostles and their successors by Jesus Christ and the Holy Spirit

venial sin less serious sin that weakens our friendship with God but does not turn us completely away from him

virtue a good habit that helps a person to act according to reason and faith

witnesses people who speak and act based upon what they know and believe about Jesus Christ

Works of Mercy acts of love by which we care for the bodily and spiritual needs of others

Index

Italicized numbers refer to definitions. **Bold-faced** numbers refer to chapters.

Index

Italicized numbers refer to definitions. **Bold-faced** numbers refer to chapters.